The Politics of Romanticism

Edinburgh Critical Studies in Romanticism

Series Editors: Ian Duncan and Penny Fielding

Available Titles
A Feminine Enlightenment: British Women Writers and the Philosophy of Progress, 1759–1820
JoEllen DeLucia

Reinventing Liberty: Nation, Commerce and the Historical Novel from Walpole to Scott
Fiona Price

The Politics of Romanticism: The Social Contract and Literature
Zoe Beenstock

Forthcoming Titles
Ornamental Gentlemen: Literary Antiquarianism and Queerness in British Literature and Culture, 1760–1890
Michael Robinson

Literature and Medicine in the Nineteenth-Century Periodical Press: Blackwood's Edinburgh Magazine, *1817–1858*
Megan Coyer

Radical Romantics: Prophets, Pirates, and the Space beyond Nation
Talissa J. Ford

Following the Footsteps of Deep Time: Geological Travel Writing in Scotland, 1750–1820
Tom Furniss

The Politics of Romanticism

The Social Contract and Literature

Zoe Beenstock

EDINBURGH
University Press

Edinburgh University Press is one of the leading university presses in the UK. We publish academic books and journals in our selected subject areas across the humanities and social sciences, combining cutting-edge scholarship with high editorial and production values to produce academic works of lasting importance. For more information visit our website: www.edinburghuniversitypress.com

© Zoe Beenstock, 2016, 2017

Edinburgh University Press Ltd
The Tun – Holyrood Road
12(2f) Jackson's Entry
Edinburgh EH8 8PJ

First published in hardback by Edinburgh University Press 2016

Typeset in 10.5/13 Sabon by
Servis Filmsetting Ltd, Stockport, Cheshire,
and printed and bound in Great Britain by
CPI Group (UK) Ltd, Croydon CR0 4YY

A CIP record for this book is available from the
British Library

ISBN 978 1 4744 0103 6 (hardback)
ISBN 978 1 4744 2606 0 (paperback)
ISBN 978 1 4744 0104 3 (webready PDF)
ISBN 978 1 4744 1023 6 (epub)

The right of Zoe Beenstock to be identified as the author of this work has been asserted in accordance with the Copyright, Designs and Patents Act 1988, and the Copyright and Related Rights Regulations 2003 (SI No. 2498).

Contents

Acknowledgements

This project began with doctoral research at McGill University supervised by Monique Morgan; I am extremely grateful for her guidance and happy combination of thoroughness and adventure. I also wish to thank Tom Mole for his assistance with this project and advice at the crucial stage of development into a book. The Fonds québéquois de la recherche sur la société et la culture made this stage of the research possible.

I have been fortunate to work on chapters during a Lady Davis Postdoctoral fellowship at the Hebrew University of Jerusalem, where I benefited from Leona Toker's acute judgment and mentorship, from the guidance of Tzachi Zamir in articulating the book's intellectual odyssey, and from the support of Shuli Barzilai. A timely Kreitman Postdoctoral fellowship at Ben-Gurion University gave me the much-needed uninterrupted freedom to finish writing; I am immensely grateful to the support and nurturance of Efraim Sicher who reminded me to always think towards future projects, and to Barbara Hochman.

I want to express my thanks to Ian Duncan, an insightful, contentious and thoughtful editor to whom I hold an immense debt for many clarifications and for sharpening my understanding of my work. I am extremely grateful to Joshua Wilner for his meticulously attentive, generous comments and fine attention to rhetoric in reading the entire manuscript at the crucial stage of completion. I have been extremely lucky to have both perspectives on this project. Warm thanks are due to Rosie Canaan and Jeffrey Champlin for extracting me from solipsistic crises while writing. My thanks also to Penny Fielding and to Jackie Jones, Adela Rauchova, Barbara Eastman and James Dale of Edinburgh University Press for their support, and to Janet Zimmermann for her work on the index

I am grateful to my new home at the University of Haifa and to the Faculty of Humanities, which provided assistance with indexing and reproductions. 'Destruction of the French Collosus' is printed courtesy of the Lewis Walpole Library, Yale University. The frontispiece of Hobbes's *Leviathan* and of Gillray's 'A Family of Sans-Cullots Refreshing after the Fatigues of the Day' are reproduced courtesy of the National Portrait Gallery, London. Parts of Chapter 6 are forthcoming in *Philosophy and Literature*, 39.2 (October 2016); I am grateful to Taylor Francis for allowing me to reproduce an early and much shorter version of Chapter 4, which was published in *European Romantic Review*, 23.2 (March 2012).

My parents Rachel and Michael Beenstock were an ongoing source of support and wisdom as this book matured. The love and persistence of Ofer Rivlin made it possible. My sons Max and Sasha grew up while I was writing and I dedicate this book to them.

Introduction:
Romanticism and the Social Contract

> One who thinks he is capable of forming a People should feel that he can, so to speak, change human nature. He must transform each individual, who by himself is a perfect and solitary whole, into a part of a larger whole from which this individual receives, in a sense, his life and his being . . . He must, in short, take away all man's own, innate forces in order to give him forces that are foreign to him and that he cannot make use of without the help of others. (Rousseau 1994a: 101)

This book argues that Romanticism develops as a critique of radical changes in political theory of the mid-seventeenth to late eighteenth centuries and of the new theory of a social contract. In the seventeenth century, natural law philosophy devised a modern concept of a self that is independent of society, turning sharply away from the former idea of the individual as dependent on the community. Aristotle's assertion that 'the whole is necessary to the part' had held sway on classical, medieval and early modern cultures, which all variously defined the individual as the subsidiary of a greater social body (Aristotle 1995: 11).[1] However, in the seventeenth century Thomas Hobbes began exploring the new possibility that 'man is made fit for society not by nature, but by training' (Hobbes 1998: 24). By the Enlightenment, the full implications of this change had come into view. The former assumption that the social collective takes priority over individuals had broken down, as part of the Enlightenment's broader unbinding of 'the most usual conjunctions of cause and effect' (Hume 1978: 267).[2] Jean-Luc Nancy elegises the individual who emerges from this change as 'merely the residue of the experience of the dissolution of community. By its nature – as its name indicates, it is the atom, the indivisible – the individual reveals that it is the abstract result of a decomposition' (Nancy 1991: 3). Nancy's quintessentially modern formulation of individualism parts ways with Aristotle, whose legacy now recedes into the past, becoming difficult to distinguish in its somewhat faint and vestigial state. Instead, a new post-Aristotelian formulation of community takes its place and becomes the central model for sociability.[3] Jean-Jacques Rousseau is the most dominant voice of this change. He defines good social institutions as 'those that best know how to denature man', operating counter to human nature, which is now understood in newly asocial terms (Rousseau 2010: 164).

What does British Romanticism have to do with this change? Although this swerve began in the seventeenth century, Charles Taylor argues that it only really percolated the popular imagination at the turn of the nineteenth century (Taylor 2004: 156). Romantic writers belonged to a new generation that was preoccupied with tensions in political theory that had fermented in the century following the British Civil War.[4] What can Romanticism's relationship to social contract theory tell us about the relationship between literature and philosophy? Studies of long nineteenth-century literature and social contract theory sometimes develop a top-down structure, with social contract philosophy as a primary discourse dictating the concerns of literature. Hence, Kevin Cope argues that the realist novel mimics the social contract by 'assembl[ing] jarring private opinions into a generically stable "history"' and arranging individual characters into a unified plot (Cope 1989: 940). And Angela Esterhammer notes that the conjunction of social contract theory, epistemology and revolutionary discourse compelled Romantic-era writers 'to think about language in a pragmatic context ... [bringing] about the conditions for an inter-section of politics, philosophy of language and literature' (Esterhammer 2000: 67).[5] This approach also characterises studies of Rousseau. Christie McDonald discusses Rousseau's own literary works as an illustration of his philosophy: 'Julie's rejection of passionate love for her role as a member of a family unit represents the important transition from the individual to the collective society' (McDonald 1973: 130). In contrast, I argue that the relationship between political philosophy and literature does not follow the direct, practical model of positive influence or application sketched by these critics. It takes a complex, circuitous route that foregrounds conflict between the two forms. Literature impacts political theory from the bottom upwards in a relationship that cannot be conceived of as illustrative or clarifying. The line between fictional and referential language proves extremely fine in both modes of discourse. Romantic writers adopted a dissident approach to political philosophy that arises from philosophy's dissenting approach to literature. Literary criticisms of philosophy were common both within and alongside philosophical discourse. Romantic writers encountered literary elements such as figurative language, digressive first-person narration, and literary allusions which disrupted the coherence of accounts of a social collective in philosophical texts. Tales, which account for more than a third of all fictions published in the Enlightenment and Romantic periods, also disrupt values of social and conceptual coherence, foregrounding the regional, the supernatural, the fragmentary and the idiosyncratic (Jarrells 2009: 262–3). Rousseau, whose impact on late eighteenth- and early nineteenth-century audiences in Britain as the harbinger of the French Revolution is hard to appreciate fully, used literature for purposes of dissent (especially in *Julie*).

Romantic writers were astute readers of literary elements in works of political theory. Their responses to political theory, shaped by Rousseau, often take a literary form to which I refer as 'lyric'. Although lyric is generally understood as a very specific literary mode and is associated with song and expressive utterance, I draw on Andrew Abbott's discussion of lyric as a mode that brings an intense focus to the writer's private disposition towards social structures, as opposed to the historical rendition of 'the actual passage of time, marked by events' which characterises narrative (Abbott 2007: 85). Abbott's insights (addressed to sociologists) are useful for thinking about the relationship between Rousseau's political theory and accompanying accounts of fantasy and withdrawal within his texts. Rousseau's social writings are poetic as well as narrative, and often engage in affective, expressive and fantastic elements that digress from coherent analysis. Through interludes of lyric fantasy, Rousseau questions his own core ideas and values and explores the gap between private dispositions and the general will, as in his account of his withdrawal to an isolated cottage in *The Confessions* (an episode that I analyse in Chapter 2), which refracts the ambitious political theory written there. Rousseau defines sociability as a state of internal division ('One would say that my heart and my mind do not belong to the same individual') a predicament which he traces to his first 'bizarre and romantic' readings of literature (Rousseau 1995: 95, 8). Within the *Discourse on the Origins of Inequality*, Rousseau qualifies his renditions of the state of nature and of the transition into sociability as operating in a hypothetical, non-narrative mode that shares these lyric attributes. Lyric's heightened aesthetic sensibility does not rely upon the magisterial, collective values of causal and temporal coherence that characterise narrative or the general will, but upon the mediating quality of affect, which emphasises Romantic 'spots of time', and on the private perspective of the individual.

Romanticism's complex response to literary elements in Enlightenment political theory is an area that has not been thoroughly examined. Since the historicist turn of the 1980s, Romanticism has been read in highly politicised terms. Jerome McGann calls 'to return poetry to a human form' in response to 'the grand illusion of every Romantic poetry', that history can be transcended or evaded (McGann 1983: 160, 91).[6] David Simpson focuses on Edmund Burke and 1790s politics to present a politically engaged account of Romanticism and gestures towards broader debates about sociability, including Rousseau's complex model of a general will (Simpson 1993: 152, 78). Even as these studies all politicise Romanticism, and to varying degrees indicate its continuity with seventeenth- and eighteenth-century ideologies, a more direct line needs to be traced between Romanticism and Enlightenment sociability in its various discourses.[7]

A range of studies have investigated the eighteenth-century roots of Romantic sociability from intersecting temporal, generic, geographical and sociological perspectives, often in relation to the Scottish Enlightenment and to political economy.[8] Maureen McLane challenges the boundaries separating Romanticism from the eighteenth century (McLane 2008: 10). She suggests that their erosion opens up a new understanding of poetry as a form of historical discourse which has its roots in enduring aspects of pre-print rural oral media, such as songs and ballads from Scotland and the north of England (ibid. 132). Leith Davis, Ian Duncan and Janet Sorensen question the Anglocentric underpinnings of Romanticism, considering it in terms drawn from postcolonial studies and global cultures (Davis et al. 2004: 10). They emphasise a four-nations approach to Romanticism and present Scotland as a test case for challenging these borders.[9] Thomas Anhert and Susan Manning note the Scottish Enlightenment's strong ties to fiction and its interweaving of the moral self with social life (Anhert and Manning 2011: 21, 6). Essays in Gavin Budge's (2007) collection *Romantic Empiricism: Poetics and the Philosophy of Common Sense 1780–1830* question the dominance of German Idealism in Romanticism studies by examining the impact of the Scottish Enlightenment.[10] Chandler redefines the intellectual legacy of Romanticism by incorporating the Scottish Enlightenment's non-Idealist model of history, which focuses on specific locales and dates rather than universal narratives (Chandler 1998: 128).

Whereas Scotland and the Scottish Enlightenment have commanded considerable discussion, other aspects of eighteenth-century political theory have escaped comprehensive critical attention. A number of other specific studies discussed in detail in the chapters on *The Prelude* and *Frankenstein* have examined the contexts of the Enlightenment and social contract philosophy in relation to these texts, often through a focus on autobiography and Rousseau's *Confessions*. However, despite the emerging interest in Romantic sociability, scholarship has given short shrift to Romanticism's relationship to political philosophy that precedes the well-trafficked 1790s, and that looks beyond the nexus of literary and social coteries in which Romantic writers were active, another area that criticism is actively addressing at present.[11] A backward looking perspective that rethinks Romanticism in relation to seventeenth- and eighteenth-century natural law and social contract theories and attendant Enlightenment political discourses that respond to individualism – drawing on the new ground covered by scholarship on Scottish Enlightenment sociability – can support a critical redirection towards a broader understanding of the politics of Romanticism. Seen from this perspective, the Romantic movement in Britain from the late 1780s to the early 1830s criticises an emergent vision of sociability as a conflictual relationship between individuals and the social body.

This book's chapters are woven from complex interactions among philosophy, poetry and novels, which all explore, through convergent perspectives, a common crisis in the notion of community, played out thematically and formally, through questions of coherence and organisation within specific literary works and over genres and disciplines. My method involves a close reading of a common set of figural and rhetorical registers and modalities across this diverse range of texts. Romanticism's approaches to taxonomy, to the boundaries separating discourses, and to standards of coherence are extremely loose, making for texts that are necessarily tangled and discontinuous; I have in mind these points of rupture as the focus of my discussion.[12] The first two chapters of this book concentrate on the intellectual history of individualism, documented from Hobbes, its first major proponent, via the empiricism of John Locke, through the Scottish Enlightenment – with a focus on Adam Smith – to German Idealism, detouring via conservative texts of the 1790s, and finally culminating in Rousseau who is the test case for this book's argument. Because Rousseau associates philosophy with conformity to Enlightenment values of consistency argued by Voltaire and Denis Diderot, he rejects rationalism and pushes his own political theory towards the positions of self-splitting and annihilation that John Keats associates with the literary in his axiom that 'what shocks the virtuous philosopher, delights the camelion Poet' (Keats 2009: 295). Ellen Burt argues that 'from the very first, Rousseau's work has transgressed the boundaries that allow critics to stand outside the work to assess it', undermining the line between fictional and referential language (Burt 2005: 809). Rousseau's literary interludes frequently disrupt the confident, optative tone of his *Social Contract*, emphasising affect and self-doubt. Conversely, in his works of literature he engages extensively with questions of political sovereignty. His bestselling novel *Julie* taps a rich vein in analysing the ongoing conflicts between private lives and social demands, played out within the arenas of gender relations, marriage and language. In *Julie* Rousseau defines sociability as a position of irresolvable crisis and contradiction. Rousseau's philosophical fictions and theoretical literary texts develop in tandem and provide a model for Romantic writers in Britain, who follow Rousseau in bringing literature to 'judge' philosophy.

Although much has been written about the relationship between Rousseau and Romanticism, critics often handle Romantic representations of Rousseau through fixed categories which distinguish between his literary and his philosophical enterprises, conceived of as discrete entities.[13] Rousseau's literary texts – *The Confessions, The Reveries of the Solitary Walker, Rousseau, Judge of Jean-Jacques* and of course *Julie* – all question the high price of the coercion into sociability that Rousseau prescribes in his political theory. His literary writings put the central ideas of his *Social Contract* to test. Hybrid works such as the *Discourse on the Origins of Inequality* and *Emile* strictly qualify neither as literature nor as theory. Rousseau's self-consciously philosophical approach to literature and his literary approach to philosophy set a precedent for subsequent writers and represents his most challenging and enduring contribution to both areas.[14]

What is the payoff of arguing that such overdetermined synecdoches of Romanticism and literary studies as Samuel Taylor Coleridge and William Wordsworth, conceived of at large, engaged with social contract theory? Tzvetan Todorov suggests that the retrospective classification of specific genres modifies the field of literary studies as a whole, a view partially anticipated in T. S. Eliot's seminal argument that individual works have an anachronistic impact on the literary canon (Todorov 1975: 10–11; Eliot 2000: 2396). The understanding of Romanticism as a sociable movement, examined through a selection of canonical test cases representative of Romanticism's preoccupations with criticism, poetry, the novel and political theory, has centrifugal significance for understanding post-Romantic literature as part of a 'sociability of mutual dependence' – the term that Kwame Anthony Appiah coins to imagine a cosmopolitan mode of individual engagement (Appiah 2005: 268).[15] In considering Rousseau's impact on Romanticism, I begin my discussion with *The Rime of the Ancient Mariner* and *The Prelude* – hypercanonical poems at the epicentre of the Romantic tradition whose engagements with the Rousseauvian legacy of contract have not been analysed.[16] Coleridge is traditionally read through his concerns with German Idealism and Christian theology. I demonstrate the fundamental relationship of both developments to social contract theory. Coleridge's poetry and prose emphasise the unhappiness that this failed totality entails. His mariner never attains absolution and is destined to perpetual exile from his community. For Coleridge and for William Wordsworth, literary forms rely on a friction between individual and general wills in lieu of any more direct affirmation of contract. Wordsworth's early radicalism and subsequent much-maligned conservatism both engage with Rousseauvian arguments.

Romanticism studies have started revaluing the traditional boundaries separating the forms of poetry and novels.[17] Anna Wierda Rowland argues that the rise of the novel in the eighteenth century alters the generic and formal organisation of poetry to foreground its lyric aspects (Rowland 2008: 132). In this way Romantic poetry distinguishes itself from the popular but less prestigious form of the novel. Duncan notes the tendency of Romantic fiction versus poetry to emphasise dissenting and unstable perspectives, due to its greater dependence on precarious market forces, as well as the relative novelty of the concept of fiction in comparison to poetry (Duncan 2007: 29). The pressures that he identifies reverberated back upon poetry, substantiating Mikhail Bakhtin's claim that 'in the process of becoming the dominant genre, the novel sparks the renovation of other genres, it infects them with its spirit of process and inclusiveness' (Bakhtin 1981: 7). As a new genre, the novel often aligned itself with better-established poetic traditions, using poetry's terminology and citing from poems. Jillian Heydt-Stevenson and Charlotte Sussman argue that the Romantic novel shares with Romantic poems '[the] common pursuit of new modes of representing both individual consciousness and imagined communities' under the pressure of intense social change (Heydt-Stevenson and Sussman 2008: 41).[18]

Romantic novels have a different affinity to Enlightenment discourses than poetry, as writers such as Rousseau and William Godwin practised a mixed discourse in which philosophy and fiction intermingle. This was because the eighteenth-century novel was a new form, which drew on other discourses, particularly philosophy.[19] While philosophers also write novels and incorporate tales and other literary elements into their treatises, novelists write about philosophers and reflect on the relationship between the two discourses. Thanks to its easier transmission into translation, fiction is more transnational than poetry, which, as Percy Shelley observes, fundamentally resists translation. The English novel is greatly indebted to the French *roman* tradition and to Rousseau's work, so that French and German writers frequently avow their debts to Samuel Richardson and Laurence Sterne.[20] Part III of this book examines how Romantic novels oppose the traditions of social contract theory. Romantic poetry keeps a critical distance from social contract theory and seeks out alternative perspectives. This is made possible by poetry's long-standing status as a form that is traditionally distinct from political theory. By contrast, Romantic novels operate more closely within the traditions of political theory. This is due to the obvious affinity between the novel and Enlightenment semi-fictional discourses, treatises and tales, and also because of the more realistic tendencies of the novel, which often deals with historically specific characters, events and locales. Romantic novels imagine themselves and their characters as dissident elements who, unable to offer a positive alternative, must operate from within the forms and traditions of Enlightenment discourses. Although Godwin's writings have sometimes been considered chronologically as belonging to a radical political phase and then a sentimental literary one, critics now commonly read *Caleb Williams* through *Enquiry Concerning Political Justice* (Bugg 2013: 45). I suggest that a unified approach can also be brought to bear on Godwin's later sentimental novel *Fleetwood*, placing Godwin broadly but not unresistingly within the pattern established by Coleridge and Wordsworth, who engage with literary representations of a private self to dramatise the conflicts of political theory.

Godwin's novels question contract theory by pointing to its underlying gender exclusions. He fictionalises the lives of Rousseau and David Hume to question the underlying premises of their works. Godwin wrote these secret histories about philosophers in *Fleetwood* to give his readers access to the veritable boudoirs and private closets of the philosophical treatise and examine the impact of its backstage cultural norms on the day-to-day lives of individuals. His incisive view of marriage as a social contract, influenced by Mary Wollstonecraft, and his reflections on the troubled status of women, who become automatons in his novels, resonate with twenty-first-century concerns about the fraught ties between ideologies and the self. They also shed light on Mary Shelley's canonical myth of artificial life in *Frankenstein*. In interpreting *Frankenstein*'s cultural iconicity, critics often point to its extreme intertextuality and note Rousseau as one of Shelley's contexts, together with her husband, other Romantic poets, her parents, *Paradise Lost*, travel narratives and scientific discourse. However, *Frankenstein*'s relationship to social contract theory has not received adequate attention. I argue that Shelley's response to contract theory in *Frankenstein* develops from the writings of Godwin and Wollstonecraft and formulates a unique insight into the position of women as subhuman, and into a general lack of social cohesion within social contract theory as she rewrites Enlightenment philosophy. Because they are passionate and wayward, women are perceived as lacking the necessary rationality for political activity, and are hence clearly barred from membership in the body politic. Women are possessed of independent (wayward) wills and therefore remain a threat to social stability as they can potentially develop political ambitions, and thus rival men by claiming political rights. Carole Pateman emphasises that 'the new civil society created through the original contract is a patriarchal social order' which defines itself by violently excluding women (Pateman 1988: 1). Alongside her gendered critique of contract theory, Shelley also draws attention to the broader displacement of all members of society, as private wills must – in Rousseau's account – be subsumed into a greater general will. Therefore, contract theory also displaces men and is unable to concatenate even those members that should be eligible for full citizenship.

The concluding discussion turns to Thomas Carlyle's *Sartor Resartus*, which reflects on Rousseau's legacy of the social contract, on the Scottish Enlightenment, on the Godwinian mechanism of *Political Justice*, and on the popularisation of German Idealism in nineteenth-century Britain. Because German literature was still largely obscure in late eighteenth-century England, Idealism has often been related to Romanticism through parallel themes and concerns, emphasising the common insights of both movements into the structure of consciousness. Recent studies of Coleridge's, Thomas De Quincey's and Henry Crabb Robinson's transmissions of Kantian thought to England have drawn attention to the material conditions in which ideas are received as they are translated across cultures.[21] This approach also works in the other direction, as political theory travelled from Scotland, England, France and Switzerland to Germany, shaping the works of Immanuel Kant and his circle, a route that also warrants critical attention. Cathy Caruth observes a hidden homology between English Romantic poetry, German critical philosophy and empiricist epistemology in her study of Wordsworth, Kant and Locke (Caruth 1991: 133). Although British Romanticism and German Idealism both claim to overcome Lockean empiricism, this supposed transcendence works as a form of memory whereby Enlightenment ideologies are both renounced and reiterated. Caruth's comments help establish the dialogue with Lockean epistemology and political theory that made German Idealism so amenable to nineteenth-century English tastes. The themes and questions of Idealism were uncannily familiar to audiences in Britain because their original context was in local political and epistemological discourses.[22] In concluding the book, I resituate my earlier analysis of *Frankenstein* through Carlyle's reading of Mary Shelley's criticism of the body politic in *Sartor Resartus*. I suggest that Romanticism imagines a subject position which is like that of Frankenstein's monster: an element that is both necessarily political and inscribed in a network of recent discourses, while at the same time alienated from and highly critical of constitutive social cohesion; both apart from Enlightenment ideologies, while fundamentally imbricated in their values and discontents.

Notes

1. David William Bates notes the rediscovery of Aristotle's *Politics* in the thirteenth century as a landmark in political theory (Bates 2012: 38). Ernest Kantorowicz argues that medieval and early modern thought conceptualised polity, king and Church as sharing one common body (Kantorowicz 1957: 312–13).
2. Jürgen Habermas argues that a new model of sociability emerged from the mid-seventeenth to the late eighteenth centuries, which emphasises relations between private individuals instead of the former holistic model of centralised state power (Habermas 2002: 27).
3. On the ongoing impact of the social contract model, see Howard Rheingold's argument that debates about the limits of privacy and the evolving role of social media begin with the social contract's rationale that community is based on sharing collective goods for personal gain (Rheingold 1993: 13). An example of the pervasiveness of social contract theory's political narrative is the popular science fiction series *Lost*, where characters named David Hume, John Locke and Rousseau form a new society on a desert island following a plane crash (ABC 2004–10).
4. See Gillian Russell and Clara Tuite, *Romantic Sociability: Social Networks and Literary Culture in Britain, 1770–1840* and Jon Mee's *Conversable Worlds: Literature, Contention, and Community, 1762–1830*, which both explore how Habermas's public sphere theory plays out in Romantic culture. See also Mary Poovey's argument that Romantic culture moved from centralised models of power to an isotropic idea of individuals as having equal value and a sociable sense, which guaranteed self-government (Poovey 1995: 29).
5. In a similar vein, Rae Greiner suggests that the nineteenth-century realist novel expands formal aspects of Adam Smith's concept of sympathy into a literary model (Greiner 2011: 8–9).
6. For a similar argument, see also Alan Liu (Liu 1989: 515, note 3). Like Jerome McGann, Marjorie Levinson suggests that Wordsworth presents 'a negative ideal: the escape from cultural values' that she deems as a defining feature of Romanticism (Levinson 1986: 16).
7. James Chandler also draws a similar trajectory from Wordsworth and Burke to Rousseau (Chandler 1984: 69). The break between the eighteenth century and Romanticism is most clearly articulated by M. H. Abrams, who influentially argues that while the eighteenth century favoured mimeticism, Romanticism developed a new model of creative imagination (Abrams 1971: 26). In *Preromanticism*, Marshall Brown suggests that Romanticism refracts eighteenth-century concerns and style (Brown 1991: 2, 360).

8. See Miriam Wallace, who also questions the boundaries separating Romanticism from the eighteenth century (Wallace 2009a: 7–19). She argues that genres and critical approaches are often arbitrarily pigeonholed by period, whereas relations between periods and styles are actually far more fluid.

9. Beyond Britain and Germany, the Romantic movement happened later and is often associated with the 1848 revolutions, giving it an openly political agenda in Spain and Italy. Spanish Romantic literature always has a direct political context 'as a stimulant to social regeneration' and 'as a positive moral guide' (Flitter 1992: 175). I suggest that French Romanticism fundamentally precedes and shapes other Romanticisms in the four nations and elsewhere in Europe, as Rousseau – albeit a Genevan – lived in Paris for much of his life, profoundly altering Francophone culture.

10. Other critics have also analysed the enduring influence of economic theory and the works of Adam Smith and David Ricardo on Romantic and nineteenth-century literature. Robert Mitchell suggests that Smith's version of political economy provides a model for Romantic poetry and theories of the imagination (Mitchell 2007: 42). In the context of the nineteenth-century novel, Eleanor Courtemanche observes that Smith's 'economic social order, with its reciprocal relations between part and whole, is heavily dependent on a formal idea of aesthetic holism' (Courtemanche 2011: 77). Matthew Rowlinson understands early nineteenth-century literature as a response to the crisis in monetary and cultural exchange produced by the introduction of paper currencies from the early seventeenth to the late eighteenth centuries (Rowlinson 2010: 21, 192). Alexander Dick argues that Romantic literature foregrounds the shortcomings of Ricardo's economic theory, reflected in the parliamentary Gold Standard of 1816, which lacked a common standard for all. According to Dick, Romanticism supplants 'the moral deficiencies and contradictions of the economy' (Dick 2013: 35, 9). I consider the relationship between Romanticism and political economy in detail in my discussion of Wordsworth in Chapter 4.

11. Regina Hewitt analyses British Romanticism as a sociological movement which anticipates the foundation of modern sociology in the late nineteenth century. Sociologists 'saw society as prior to the individual, making it the crucible of individual consciousness rather than its product' (Hewitt 1997: 10). Nancy Yousef's *Isolated Cases* and *Romantic Intimacy* analyse Romantic critiques of the Enlightenment narrative that humans evolve independently of social relations from a different perspective to my own focus on politics and the conflict between the individual and society. Yousef analyses Romanticism's concept of intimacy, construed through the lens of psychoanalytic theory, as an alternative to the atomism of Enlightenment discourses that reify development as a radically individual process (Yousef 2013: 28). Jon Mee traces developing models of sociability in the Romantic era, which involved a complex nexus of conversations and public debates (Mee 2011: 281). Andrew Franta suggests that Romanticism needs to be considered in relation to its readership, an aspect which has been obscured by Abrams's account of Romanticism as focused mainly on the artist in *The Mirror and the Lamp* (Franta 2007: 5). Richard Eldridge reads Romantic poetry via Wordsworth as a form of philosophy that occupies a middle

ground between transcendence and shared cultural values, the latter of which are represented by temporal development and location (Eldridge 2001: 105–6, 123).

12. See Robin Valenza's *Literature, Language, and the Rise of the Intellectual Disciplines* (Valenza 2009: 34), and Michel Foucault's *The Order of Things* for parallel discussions of the vexed preoccupations with specialisation and classification in Enlightenment and Victorian cultures respectively (Foucault 2002: 224).

13. From different perspectives, Irving Babbitt and Thomas McFarland assert the importance of Rousseau's perceived concern with feeling rather than reason for British Romanticism (Babbitt 1966: 284; McFarland 1995: 268). Margery Sabin contrasts the alienated Rousseau of *The Confessions* with the exemplary Wordsworthian Romantic hero (Sabin 1976: 67). Edward Duffy suggests that first generation British Romantic writers 'came to rest in a Burkean withdrawal from all things revolutionary and Rousseauean', in contrast to Percy Shelley's direct political engagement (Duffy 1979: 53). In *Rousseau, Robespierre and English Romanticism* Gregory Dart modifies Duffy's model of withdrawal into a theory of 'transferred Idealism rather than resignation or denial' (Dart 1999: 10). Dart argues that Rousseau infuses sentiment and feeling within more traditional models of citizenship and civic humanism (ibid. 22, 58–9). Rousseau's focus on conformity through feeling, rather than Lockean values of property or reason, popularised via the *Confessions*, had a profound influence on a range of Romantic figures, including Maximilien Robespierre and Wordsworth who wrote his own form of radical autobiography in *The Prelude* (ibid. 190).

14. Paul de Man argues that the specialisation of Rousseau's writings into literature and political theory has overlooked Rousseau's important contribution to the philosophy of language, which also brings together these two aspects of his work (de Man 1979: 135).

15. In addition to M. H. Abrams's remarks on Coleridge's representative status in modern literary criticism (Abrams 1971: i), see also Ian Reid, who analyses Wordsworth and Coleridge as metonyms for the academic discipline of English as a whole (Reid 2004: 5). Appiah's concept of mutual dependence provides an alternative to Foucault's indictment of post-Enlightenment literature for creating productive forms of power which encourage conformism (Foucault 1991: 208).

16. Other examples not analysed in this book are Percy Shelley's representation of Rousseau as a figure of blasted potentiality in *The Triumph of Life*, which Edward Duffy discusses (Duffy 1979: 106–51). Paul de Man develops Shelley's reading of Rousseau in *The Triumph of Life* into a rhetorical study of a metaliterary aspect of language which he terms 'figure' – an approach to language that acknowledges the limits of its referentiality (de Man 1984: 114–15). More generally, Shelley's 'Defence of Poetry' engages extensively with the relationship of poetry to politics. Wordsworth invokes Rousseau's natural man in *Salisbury Plain* and *The Borderers*, analysed by Paul Kelley (Kelley 1976: 329). John Keats's letters, with their reflections on the chameleon poet, explore a literary model of sociability which allows for multiple and diverse perspectives as an alternative to the unitary positivism set forth by Enlightenment philosophy. Robert Merry's

poetry, immersed in material print culture, theatre and libertarianism, has also been suggested as a political model for Romanticism which counteracts Coleridge's and Wordsworth's perceived aloofness (Mee 2002: 118).

17. A parallel movement is also taking place in narrative studies. Brian McHale suggests that the tendency to dichotomise lyricism and narrative overlooks poems that are not lyrical, and lyric prose that is not poetry (McHale 2009: 14).

18. Heather Dubrow similarly proposes that the lyric mode explores the relationship between individuals and their communities and 'occupies a middle position where lyric, the genre of twists and turns, moves back and forth between private and social worlds' (Dubrow 2008: 233). Hans Robert Jauss discusses the incorporation of literary markers such as poetry within works of philosophy as representing a challenge to 'publicly sanctioned morals' (Jauss 1970: 36). Abbott suggests that lyric poetry brings an intense focus to the moment and explores the writer's disposition to social structures as opposed to sweeping histories (Abbott 2007: 85). Abbott's insights, addressed to sociologists who underestimate the writer's affective disposition, are also useful for understanding the politics of Romantic poetry, an area which Zimmerman associates with the 'potential for social engagement that has been obscured by influential critical models' (Zimmerman 2000: 74). For further cross-disciplinary approaches to the concept of the lyric, see Barbara Johnson (1998), who studies the interface between lyric and law in the concept of personhood and Brown, who associates the lyric with positions of doubt and scepticism (Brown 2004: 123).

19. Henry Fielding describes his novel *Joseph Andrews* as 'a comic Epic-Poem in Prose' (Fielding 1987: 4). In *Tom Jones*, Fielding refers to the characters of Thwackum and Square as 'a considerable Figure on the Theatre of this History' (Fielding 1995: 89). Fielding's terminology suggests that in its labile beginnings, the novel is also variously discussed as a prose rendition of the existent forms of poetry and drama, and as an imaginative version of history.

20. According to Srinivas Aravamudan, more than a third of novels read in Britain until the late eighteenth century were translations from French (Aravamudan 2011: 36). In the *Letter to d'Alembert* Rousseau praises *Clarissa* as the finest novel written in any language (Rousseau 2004: 311, note). He defines *Julie* as a commentary on Samuel Richardson's *Pamela* (Rousseau 1997: 280, note). Friedrich Schiller lists 'Fielding, Sterne, and others' as modern geniuses who have shaped his writing (Schiller 2001b: 190).

21. Monika Class notes the comparatavist bent of Romanticist discussions of Idealism which are indebted to René Wellek (Class 2012: 5). Historicist scholarship has since challenged Wellek's zeitgeist arguments by drawing attention to the complex routes of reception and of intellectual history, with its material context of editions, translations and comparisons across languages and cultures. See for example Eugene Stelzig's study of Henry Crabb Robinson's letters in the *Monthly Register*, which introduced Kantian thought to England in the early 1800s (Stelzig 2010: 65).

22. Cairns Craig suggests that twentieth-century concepts of Romanticism that privilege German Idealism oddly invert the literary politics of Europe

in the late eighteenth and early nineteenth centuries, 'reflect[ing] back upon Wordsworth and Coleridge the philosophical significance accorded to their German contemporaries' (Craig 2004: 23). Tom Toremans calls for a 'comparative reinterrogation of British Romanticism's position as mediating between the philosophical traditions of empiricism and Idealism' (Toremans 2015: paragraph 17).

Part I

Philosophy

Chapter 1

Forming a Social Contract: Hobbes to Anti-Jacobinism

This chapter and the next juxtapose natural law philosophy, the Scottish Enlightenment, German Idealism, and counterrevolutionary texts of the 1790s, together with the works of Jean-Jacques Rousseau, the most crucial political theorist for British Romantic writers who, by responding intensely to his works, also engage with the preceding century of political thought. The common ground among these otherwise varied ideologies is the new understanding that society begins with individuals in a state of nature, who form agreements to serve their private interests. The challenge of this theory of sociability is achieving cohesion among individuals, whose relationship is no longer understood as one of totality or potential harmony, and is fundamentally conflictual. In imagining sociability, political theorists identify motives for commonality that include self-interest, competition, fear and sentiment – feelings with an arbitrary basis. In contrast to the former Aristotelian idea that individuals are born into a pre-existent system, this tentative justification of commonality represents a crisis in political theory uniting an otherwise diverse range of intellectual contexts.

Following the works of Hugo Grotius and drawing on scientific methodology that undercuts traditional scholasticism, Thomas Hobbes was the first major thinker to question Aristotle's view of human nature as naturally sociable, and to consider sociability as an artificial construct devoid of a significant physiological foundation. Hobbes rejects Aristotle's dictum that 'man is an animal born fit for Society' and therefore for a predetermined social station (Hobbes 1998: 21–2). His memorable account of the state of nature as 'a time of Warre, where every man is Enemy to every man . . . And the life of man, solitary, poore, nasty, brutish, and short' is often read as an account of human belligerence (Hobbes 2003: 102). I take the view that Hobbes's description of human nature in its natural state characterises it as not actively warlike, but rather inadequately sociable. According to

Hobbes, people do have an innate desire for interaction; what they lack is the aptitude for acting on this desire in a peaceful manner. Hobbes emphasises that humans are not naturally self-sufficient, and cannot meet their needs without the assistance of others: *'infants need the help of others to live, and adults to live well. I am not therefore denying that we seek each other's company at the prompting of nature'* (Hobbes 1998: 24). Hobbes's main point is that although nature may prompt you to interact, it does not tell you how to do so. This lack of organised social structure undermines individual identities and roles; consequently, sociability must be established artificially: 'man is made fit for society not by nature, but by training' (ibid. 25).

Hobbes has a less obvious presence than John Locke or Rousseau in Romantic texts. Philip Pettit ascribes this relative downplaying of Hobbes's presence in Enlightenment Britain to his association with the violence of the Civil War, a traumatic event in a country wracked by the recent revolutions in America and France (Pettit 2008: 30). Hobbes's writings were often represented negatively in late eighteenth-century Britain, and are still treated this way by critics of this period who have recently reopened Hobbes for debate as a negative context for eighteenth-century and Romantic sociability, a figure who describes humans in radically antagonistic terms that are repugnant to values of sensibility.[1]

Writing on the brink of the Second World War, H. G. Wells expresses a popular view that fascism begins with Hobbes: 'Leviathan is the State into which the individual life is almost completely incorporated. Its will is concentrated on the sovereign' (Wells 1939: 192). The frontispiece of the *Leviathan* (Figure 1.1) illustrates the oppressive workings of Hobbes's theory of sovereignty. The Leviathan-sovereign rises organically from the hills and incorporates an undistinguished mass of individuals within a quasi-Aristotelian social body – suggesting that Hobbes does retain elements of Aristotle's model of natural sociability – the notion that *'we seek each other's company at the prompting of nature'* (Hobbes 1998: 24). This figure also repeats the hierarchical aspects of Aristotle's system. The sovereign is one man who dominates all others, recalling Hobbes's admission at the beginning of the *Leviathan* that his work is compromised by his reliance on 'too much Authority' (Hobbes 2003: 3). Hobbes explains that sovereign authority must be a singular prerogative: 'for it is the *Unity* of the Representer, not the *Unity* of the Represented, that maketh the Person *One* . . . *Unity*, cannot otherwise be understood in Multitude' (ibid. 131). Because Hobbes's theory ultimately describes a unitary individual and not a group, sociability can only be understood as an

Figure 1.1 Detail, 'Thomas Hobbes', by unknown artist. Source: National Portrait Gallery, London.

individual property – here through the figure of a single leader. Where Hobbes digresses from Aristotle is in unbinding power from the natural to the artificial; the individual will of the monarch is no longer tied to the polis as it had been in Aristotle's account, and is potentially free to violate the wills of its members. Hobbes describes society as 'an Artificiall Animal', a mechanism engineered to imitate 'that Rationall and most excellent work of Nature, *Man*. For by Art is created that great LEVIATHAN called a COMMON-WEALTH or STATE (in Latin CIVITAS)' (ibid. 9). Pettit notes Hobbes's innovative departure from the classical view of language as an innate faculty. Here language becomes a secondary property, an artefact that people develop, and a precondition for a posteriori faculties of reason, sociability and polity (Pettit 2008: 45). In *On the Citizen*, Hobbes describes society as 'an automatic Clock or other fairly complex device, one cannot get to know the function of each part and wheel unless one takes it apart, and examines separately the material, shape and motion of the parts' (Hobbes 1998: 10). Getting ahead of this book's argument and briefly looking towards the much later discussion of *Frankenstein* in Chapter 6, we will see Shelley's incisive criticism of Victor Frankenstein's ambitions to engineer a new species that can endanger his fellow humans.[2] Shelley criticises Hobbes's account of language for standing in for a weak account of sociability. Frankenstein's monster experiences language as a secondary property. Human nature, unbound from natural theories of sociability, must develop artificial social intuitions, which can only avow a partial commitment to the common good.

Hobbes's solution to this problem is to institutionalise violence through sovereignty and tyranny. The ominous sword brandished by the sovereign in the frontispiece suggests that sovereign violence can be turned against the subjects at will. Bates argues that the function of this fear is to establish stability by preventing conflict and guaranteeing cooperation (Bates 2012: 74). Pettit terms this condition of anxiety a 'second state of nature' – not one of relative social ineptness, as in the vegetative condition of *On the Citizen*, but of social anxiety, which eventually drives individuals to secure their interactions through contract (Pettit 2008: 115). Social relations must be organised by words and human invention, and guaranteed by deeds. Hobbes suggests that because all power can be abused, a singular tyrant is the least likely to fall prey to conflicts of interest (Hobbes 1998: 118). Hobbes maintains that 'the Passions of men are commonly more potent than their Reason' (Hobbes 2003: 149). The only means of containing individuals and their violent feelings is by establishing 'a Common Power, to keep them in awe, and to direct their actions to Common Benefit', thwarting violence with fear (ibid. 136). The ensuing political model is atomistic – controlled by a single sovereign and at risk of fragmenting into an angry mob of diverse constituents all vying for power, represented by the anonymous individuals embedded in the sovereign's armour. Under great duress, the rabble amalgamates and threatens to heave apart should the sovereign relax his grip. Throughout this book I will identify this imagery of a fragmented body politic held together by violence rather than volition in subsequent Romantic representations of the social body, such as Wordsworth's account of the French Revolution in book nine of *The Prelude* and Shelley's iconic account of the creature's body in *Frankenstein*.

Despite Hobbes's totalitarianism *avant la lettre* noted by his later critics, Hobbes's claim that sovereignty guarantees freedom stems from a prioritisation of individuals and the subsequent need to contain and protect a multiplicity of individuals within the social body. Hobbes himself was aware of the ambivalence of his concepts. He opens *Leviathan* by conceding that 'in a way beset with those that contend, on one side for too great Liberty, and on the other side for too much Authority, 'tis hard to passe between the points of both unwounded' (Hobbes 2003: 3). His departure from Aristotle, which leads him to contend for 'too great Liberty', produces an account of human origins as lacking a social infrastructure (ibid. 3). In his earlier *On the Citizen* Hobbes conceives of the state of nature through the metaphor of vegetation. He proposes 'to return once again to the natural state and to look at men as if they had just emerged from the earth like mushrooms and grown up without any obligation to each other' (Hobbes 1998: 102). Victoria Kahn notes Hobbes's subtle self-irony in this vegetable analogy which presents the subject as the antonym of violent passions and drives (Kahn 2004: 13). Hobbes suggests that initially people are not negatively disposed to one another, but – rather like plants – are somewhat loosely related and lack clear obligations. In this first state of nature, as Robert Bernasconi observes, individuals are not antisocial, but asocial: 'If there is no duty, no future, and especially no language in the state of nature, there is also no individuality', or no clear codes for individuals to conduct their interactions (Bernasconi 1997: 83). David Gauthier attempts to resolve the question of whether people existed before society in Hobbes's theory by suggesting that for Hobbes 'temporal priority is a metaphor for conceptual priority' (Gauthier 1977: 138). Hobbes argues that people matter more than society, not that they necessarily lived before society (ibid. 135). Gauthier's axiological reading of Hobbes overlooks the subsequently influential anthropological aspects of the Hobbesian narrative of the state of nature, which shaped popular late Enlightenment discussions of natural history. These conjectural histories, which emerge from natural law theory, support the argument of Bates and others who attribute Hobbes's minimal account of human nature to ideology rather than oversight. Hobbes's minimising of natural attributes frees him to engineer a new social body, and clears the path for subsequent theorists, whom all discard Hobbes's anachronism – his neo-Aristotelian theory of sovereignty – while retaining his idea of individuals as originally free of society.

With great acumen the Earl of Shaftesbury suggests that Hobbes's theoretical innovation consists less in his theory of the state of nature than in his reaction to Aristotle's theory of natural sociability. Shaftesbury criticises philosophers who posit human beings as asocial: 'if man be not by nature sociable, he is the foolishest creature on earth to make society or the public the least part of his real care or concern' (Shaftesbury 1900: 414). He criticises the argument that humans lack '*innate principles*', dismissing it as 'one of the childishest disputes that ever was' (ibid. 414). He further assesses that 'Tom Hobbes, whom I must confess a genius' has 'so poor a spectre as the ghost of Aristotle to fight with' (ibid. 414).[3] Shaftesbury's dismissal evokes two conflicting value systems and echoes Hobbes's own self-professedly ambivalent position. Shaftesbury suggests that Hobbes espouses a position of novel individualism, a 'childish dispute' that humans are asocial. Shaftesbury dismisses this as a moot argument because were humans really associable, they would not need to worry about society. Beneath Hobbes's argument linger the vestigial traces of Aristotelianism and of more traditional political values tangible in Hobbes's thought through the figure of ghostliness. Shaftesbury suggests that the ghosts that haunt Locke and Hobbes are 'the poor secondary tralatitious systemic of modern and barbarous schoolmen', the recent derivative expositions of Aristotle which Locke and Hobbes are targeting (ibid. 414). Were Locke and Hobbes to encounter Aristotle directly, and not in vulgar neoclassical repetitions, they would be able to appreciate that humans are innately sociable.

Katherine Rowe suggests that early contract theory often used bodily metaphors as types for political volition (Rowe 1999: 84). Read this way, dead and absent body parts such as ghosts and severed hands represent a failure to ratify rights, expressing a position of social alienation (ibid. 12). Looking briefly ahead, we will see that dismemberment remains a formative aspect of political theory and its representations in British Romanticism, so that Adam Smith's invisible hand perpetuates Hobbes's atomism and frequently appears in Romantic texts. Aristotle's ghost also recurs with uncanny persistence, eventually shifting shape and taking on Rousseauvian qualities in Romanticism. Romanticism in turn becomes a kind of ghost in modernity, a development which I consider in the book's conclusion where I draw on Thomas Carlyle's term for this search for vestigial antecedents of lost models of community as 'shadow-hunting' (Carlyle 2000: 135). Common to these ghosts are the necromancer's insight that haunting happens, as in *Hamlet*, when the polity is 'out of joint' (Shakespeare 2003: 1, 5, 188).

Hobbes emphasises that he chooses absolute power because it is a lesser evil than perpetual conflict, an effective means of protecting people and their liberties. Kahn notes the tendency of political theorists influenced by nineteenth- and twentieth-century liberalism (and its Romantic antecedents) to overlook the novelty of Hobbes's individualism (Kahn 2004: 282–3).[4] Instead of focusing exclusively on Hobbes's totalitarian turn, or on the antagonism of the state of war, it is important to assess Hobbes's contribution to political theory by attending to his influential concept of freedom. Bates notes the strategic minimalism of Hobbes's concept of individuality (Bates 2012: 13). The absence of essential qualities allows Hobbes to digress from Aristotle's antecedent of natural sociability, with its predetermined ranks and hierarchies. Human nature is unbound from universal foundations and is now open to experimentation and redefinition. If individuals are required to cede their freedom in order to become sociable, then Hobbes recasts freedom as a relative, and not an absolute, property (Pettit 2008: 140). This way Hobbes retains his focus on individual liberties, despite the individual's subordination to the sovereign. Freedom sheds its republican rationale as a property of the individual and becomes a temporary state of physical non-obstruction, a non-intrinsic aspect of movements and actions.

The liberal possibilities of Hobbes's freedom do not reassure subsequent political theoreticians, who remain troubled by the vacuousness of his individualism. Rowe argues that Hobbes conceives of freedom through voluntary motions (Rowe 1999: 11). Pettit observes that in Hobbes's revised terms, slaves held by forms of bondage that are not physical, such as verbal or legal coercion, would also be free (Pettit 2008: 139). However counterintuitive Hobbes's minimalist freedom is, he formulates freedom as a tenuous, unstable property of the individual – rather than a natural right of way. This redefinition of freedom had immense subsequent impact on accounts by Rousseau, Immanuel Kant and British Romantic writers. It endures in contemporary popular culture, music and film, which still often represent freedom as a volatile condition best understood through its absence. In 'The Mask of Anarchy' Percy Shelley repeatedly asks 'What is Freedom?' (Shelley 2002: ll. 156, 209). But all answers point to a notion that lacks positive characteristics, and can only be defined negatively. Hobbes's interpretation of human nature as incompetently sociable also had a profound influence on subsequent thinkers. Adam Ferguson observes that in Hobbes's account there is no actual basis for compact or community. He conjectures that 'men must have already been together in society, in order to form any *compact*, and must have been in practice to move in a body, before they have concerted together for any purpose whatever' (Ferguson 1978: 2.244).

Following from Hobbes, Locke presents humans as inherently free and thereby also as liberated from sovereignty. Although Lockean individuals are both freer and more rational than those of *Leviathan*, Locke's *Second Treatise of Government* still does not address the problem of how they are motivated to cooperation. If humans are already fully realised rational agents in the state of nature, then they will also lack the sole motive for sociability that Hobbes identifies – the need for self-preservation from potential harm in the face of the inevitable asociality of human behaviour. In his preface to *An Essay Concerning Human Understanding*, Locke points to a related problem. Because individuals are already fully developed in the state of nature, they are also unable to share common tastes: 'men's principles, notions, and relishes are so different, that it is hard to find a book which pleases or displeases all men . . . I plainly tell all my readers, except half a dozen, this treatise was not at first intended for them' (Locke 1993a: 6). Locke's account of individuals fleshes out the sketchy vegetable and animal origins of *On the Citizen* and *The Leviathan*, but still does not resolve the question of how individuals are to become sociable and share a common experience, leaving an urgent legacy for subsequent political thought. Bates points to the circular reasoning of Hobbes's and Locke's natural law theory: 'the state, as an institution and practice, could only ever serve the interests of the individuals who demanded its appearance in the first place' (Bates 2012: 11). Seventeenth-century political theory presents a deadlock: the state has been unbound from metaphysical legitimations of natural sociability (Aristotle's legacy), but still has not theorised the new domain of political obligation that was to replace this powerful antecedent, and can only return to the problem of a plurality of individual interests and the inevitable crisis arising from their unregulated conflicts.

Bonds of Sociability: The Scottish Enlightenment

Scottish Enlightenment and counter-contractarian philosophers such as Shaftesbury and the Anglo-Dutch Bernard Mandeville rejected Hobbes's premise that humans are not naturally sociable; they also veered away from Locke's rationalism. Instead, they returned to the premise that sociability is grounded in the senses and in feeling, a faculty which Hobbes had deemed faulty and unreliable. Francis Hutcheson returns the empiricist thesis that humans share common senses back into the arena of sociability, re-invoking elements of Aristotle's thought. Although people need the restraint of laws, they also have an innate '*moral Sense*, either of our *own* Actions, or of those of *others*' (Hutcheson 1971: 116). The moral sense renders violence a secondary concern arising from contingent conflicts rather than a primary consideration. Morality 'has this in common with our other Senses' in that it is primary, and not governed by secondary calculations of self-interest (ibid. 116). Hutcheson groups the moral sense together with sight and taste, and defines it as an inherent '*universal Determination* to *Benevolence* in *Mankind*, even toward the most distant part of the Species' (ibid. 195). Essentialist moral perceptions and feelings of benevolence form a '*Secret Chain* between *each Person* and *Mankind*' (ibid. 111). Rousseau subsequently transforms the metaphor of the chain into his momentous assertion that 'man was / is born free, but everywhere he is in chains' (Rousseau 1994c: 131). Influenced by Hutcheson, Adam Ferguson develops an anti-Hobbesian theory of innate sociability and inverts the value of these chains, turning them from an image of bondage into one of attachment. Following Hutcheson, Rousseau, Ferguson, William Godwin, Mary

Shelley and Thomas Carlyle all evoke the image of the chain to variously imagine sociability as providing both intimacy and constraint. Ferguson extends Hutcheson's chain imagery into a broader architectural edifice to demonstrate a unity of individuals within society: 'all nature indeed is connected; and the world itself consists of parts, which, like the stones of an arch, mutually support and are supported' (Ferguson 1978: 1.18). Individual and society intersect like a dogtooth arch: 'this fabric of nature, so fitly organized in the frame of every individual, is organized also in the assemblage of many individuals into one system' (ibid. 165–6). Ferguson unites the social contract's novel individualism with Aristotle's legacy, which is resurrected through these metaphors of seamless harmony.

Following Ferguson's concatenation of individualism and natural sociability, Mandeville seeks for a principle of sociability that will offer a corrective to Hobbes. In *The Fable of the Bees* and its accompanying commentary, Mandeville proposes that 'the worst of all the Multitude / [Does] something for the Common Good' (Mandeville 1997: l. 27). If self-serving actions can unwittingly benefit 'the Common Good', Mandeville is able to conclude that '*Vice is beneficial found, / When it's by Justice lopt and bound*' (ibid. l. 35). When correctly engineered by society, vice can be put to work for the general good. Through the ignoble motivations of pride, vanity and greed, people are coaxed, shamed and lured to cooperate with social goals (ibid. ll. 41, 47). It is only the dread of criticism and the desire for recognition and gain which motivate conformity (ibid. l. 209). Although Rousseau will later brand these negative dependencies and comparisons *amour propre*, Mandeville suggests that a shrewd society harnesses vices of selfish vanity and greed for the greater good. He performs this strategy by writing his social theory in the highly unusual form of epic poetry, and also draws on Virgil's *Georgics IV*.[5] Mandeville suggests that rhyme and meter, like other pleasurable arrangements, can be used to concatenate individual units, modelling values of cooperation in a larger social body through strategies of formal harmony.

David Hume extends Mandeville's literary model from the epic to encompass the genre of fiction. He dismisses the state of nature as a philosophical tale which has little credibility (Hume 1978: 493). Social contract theory is riddled with 'paradoxes repugnant to the common sentiments of mankind' (Hume 1958: 235). As a kind of fiction the social contract represents a general human tendency to regulate human interactions, filling a similar function to epic poetry for Mandeville. Hume suggests that this literary aspect is social contract theory's redeeming grace. He explains, 'when objects are united by any relations, we have a strong propensity to add some new relation to them to compleat the union' (Hume 1978: 237). The imaginative formulation of relationships enables 'the transition of the mind from one object to another, and renders its passage . . . smooth' (ibid. 254). Consciousness organises the primary phenomenological mayhem of human existence into narrative form. Likewise, society forms an imagined community from disjointed parts. On their own people have a difficult time meeting their needs: 'society provides a remedy for these . . . inconveniences. By the conjunction of forces our power is augmented. By the partition of employments, our ability increases' (ibid. 485). Whereas Hobbes posits sociability as an entirely artificial, quasi-robotic construct, Hume suggests that sociability is generated through this primary tendency of the mind to find causes and form connections. So although sociability, causality and fiction are not strictly innate properties, they still qualify as necessary ones in Hume's terms: 'I make use of the word *natural*, only as oppos'd to *artificial* . . . Mankind is an inventive species; and where an invention is obvious and absolutely necessary, it may be properly said to be natural' (ibid. 484). Fiction is a necessary invention and qualifies as quasi-natural. It not only organises but also provides an alternative to politics by preventing people from the catastrophe of acting out on violent impulses (Hume 1958: 236). Hume differs from Hobbes in classifying the state of nature as 'a philosophical fiction, which never had, and never cou'd have any reality' (Hume 1978: 493). Where 'philosophers may have been bewilder'd in those speculations, poets have been guided more infallibly', because they recognise the '*golden age*' for what it is – a necessary fiction (ibid. 494, 493). Without these quasi-natural fables of sociability, human existence devolves into a 'savage condition' (ibid. 493).

Like Hume and Mandeville, Adam Smith posits individual desires as potentially sociable. But whereas Hume presents the transition to sociability as a relatively straightforward outcome of a deep need for coherence, Smith's concept is less seamless and involves an aspect of alienation which is never really overcome. This makes Smith a particularly important figure for Romanticism and modernity in its wake. Whereas Smith's teacher Hutcheson had grounded morality in the senses, Smith's espousal of Hobbesian individualism pushes him away from accounts of natural sociability, and disposes him towards the more diffuse area of theory. People feel and suffer alone. Smith explains, 'we have no immediate experience of what other men feel' (Smith 2002: 11). He accepts Hobbes's idea that human nature is insufficiently sociable and acknowledges a difficulty reconciling parts within the whole. In a letter to *The Edinburgh Review*, Smith locates himself within the tradition of political theorists that include Mandeville, who 'suppose, that there is in man no powerful instinct which necessarily determines him to seek society for its own sake' (Smith 1980b: 250).[6] At the same time, like other Scottish Enlightenment thinkers, he also tries to see humans as inherently disposed to care for each other. These disparate positions have been mapped onto his two best-known works of political theory, *The Wealth of Nations* (1776), and *The Theory of Moral Sentiments* (1759) and termed 'the Adam Smith problem'.[7] Smith's problem draws directly on social contract theory's tension between individual and social needs. His most enduring image for the uneasy coexistence of these binary impulses is his well-known metaphor of the invisible hand. Rowe analyses the history of the hand as a type for political action in a wide range of early modern discourses (Rowe 1999: x). Glancing back at the *Leviathan* illustration, the sovereign's hands exceed the dimensions of his individual subjects and even of his own head, suggesting that the hand is a central type for social control. Locke's *Second Treatise of Government* posits the hand as a metonymy which famously configures the relationship between individuals and society as one of possession:

> Though the earth and all inferior creatures be common to all men, yet every man has a property in his own person. This nobody has any right to but himself. The labour of his body, and the work of his hands, we might say, are properly his. (Locke 1993b: 274)

Labour, figured through the hands, is an act of individuation which transmits value from the self to its environment: "tis labour that puts the difference of value on everything' (Locke 1993b: 281). Societies are formed to institutionalise and protect the primary right of the state of nature the ownership of property as an extension of the individual's body or hand. This condensation of society into a single private organ led C. B. Macpherson to suggest that Locke conceives of 'the individual as essentially the proprietor of his own person or capacities, owing nothing to society for them' (Macpherson 1962: 3).

Smith bridges between this radical self-reliance and values of community. He reconnects Locke's ultra-individualistic metonymy of the hand to the body politic. Smith explains that the rich 'are led by an invisible hand – make nearly the same distribution of the necessities of life, which would have been made had the earth been divided into equal portions among its inhabitants' (Smith 2002: 215).[8] As Albert O. Hirschman suggests, in hindsight this optimistic model was to be thoroughly disproved: 'the idea that men pursuing their interests would be forever harmless was decisively given up only when the reality of capitalist development was in full view' (Hirschman 1997: 126). Smith overcomes the absence of an innate social disposition in the individual will by positing a benign and yet vaguely defined social intuition, which guarantees that individual interests will never incur abuse, but rather promote universal wellbeing. As a result, people do not need to be motivated to sociability in order to participate in a broader social constellation:

> Regard to our own private happiness and interest, too, appear upon many occasions very laudable principles of action. The habits of oeconomy, industry, discretion, attention, and application of thought, are generally supposed to be cultivated from self-interested motives, and at the same time are apprehended to be very praise-worthy qualities, which deserve the esteem and approbation of every body. (Smith 2002: 359)

The neo-Aristotelian view of private interest as intimately tied to the common good is flawed by Smith's reliance on Hobbes's theory of minimal sociability. Smith's individuals are naturally so preoccupied with their own small misfortunes that this completely eclipses the large ones of others (Smith 2002: 97). He reflects that if 'a man of humanity in Europe . . . were to lose his little finger to-morrow . . . [he] would not sleep tonight; but, provided he never saw them, he will snore with the most profound security over the ruin of a hundred million of his brethren' if these are far from sight and mind (ibid. 157–8). You may note how Smith reduces the synecdoche of the body politic from an invisible hand to a single digit – a 'little finger' – pointing to the fragmentary nature of his own governing metaphor for sociability. A hand is only part of a body and can be further broken down into ever smaller units and digits that no longer attest to a greater whole. Smith is finally left with the vestigial organ of a vanished body politic and with humans that are fundamentally indifferent to one another.

Shaftesbury's observation that Hobbes was haunted by the ghost of Aristotle's body politic explains why the craving for a greater whole does not just disappear. Aristotle's ghostly apparition permeates Smith's account of an experience of involuntary social embodiment which transcends private experience. It also shapes Smith's Hobbesian view that human nature is potentially, while only partially, sociable. A visceral memory of the body politic remains imprinted within private bodies and finds its outlet in the complex workings of sympathy. Smith's model of the individual contains the relics of a former embodied sense of community:

> When we see a stroke aimed and just ready to fall upon the leg or arm of another person, we naturally shrink and draw back our own leg or our own arm; and when it does fall, we feel it in some measure and are hurt by it as

well as the sufferer . . . Persons of delicate fibre and a weak constitution of body complain, that in looking on the sores and ulcers which are exposed by beggars in the streets, they are apt to feel an itching or uneasy sensation in the correspondent part of their own bodies. (Smith 2002: 12)

Such experiences of sympathy are now more usually classified as a type of emotion and are hence sometimes cited as evidence that people naturally care for one another. But as T. D. Campbell emphasises, Smith's eighteenth-century use of the term pertains less to a feeling than to a kind of social tie (Campbell 1971: 94). Hence Smith observes that our own response to beggars and lacerated bodies is to recoil squeamishly, and not to assist them. Smith suggests that Hutcheson, Samuel von Pufendorf and others have 'considered chiefly the tendency of affections, and have given little attention to the relation which they stand in to the cause which excites them' (Smith 2002: 23). By this account, affections dispose people to relate themselves to others. Social sympathy – which Smith imagines through metaphors of arms and limbs that transcend the individual and are metonyms of a greater but invisible body politic – suggests a visceral endurance of commonality, which Smith terms 'fellow feeling' (ibid. 13). This can also take the negative forms of disgust and estrangement, as in Smith's example of the beggar. Smith's memorable image of an invisible hand bears the imprint of Aristotelian sociability. This invisible hand presents a complex model of commonality which, in subsequent Romantic accounts by Rousseau and Mary Shelley, is often criticised for being partial and insufficient and also gives Smith the reputation from the late nineteenth century onwards of bearing an 'Adam Smith problem'. Nonetheless, this hand binds people involuntarily to each other, in relations both good and ill, representing a theory of sociability.

Smith's problem is traditionally explained as a conflict between benevolence and self-interest, suggested by the dilemma of whether to help the beggar or to turn away from the itching and unease that he causes. Because in Smith's view people have limited intuitive access to the feelings of others, morality requires removing the self from its experience of the other. Caring for the other means avoiding the distortions caused by extrapolating private experiences into a broader account of sociability. The attempt to penetrate the foreign, often opaque experience of the other is riddled with shades of the ludicrous. Smith provides a grotesque example:

We sympathize even with the dead, and overlooking what is of real importance in their situation, that awful futurity which awaits them, we are chiefly affected by those circumstances which strike our senses, but can have no influence upon their happiness. It is miserable, we think, to be deprived of the light of the sun; to be shut out from life and conversation; to be laid in the cold grave, a prey to corruption and the reptiles of the earth . . . That our sympathy can afford them no consolation seems to be an addition to their calamity. (Smith 2002: 16)

This tendency vicariously to feel for others, while paved with the best intentions, presents a warped perspective, in line with Smith's examples of the natural tendency to prioritise the loss of one's own little finger over humanitarian catastrophe abroad, or the preference for the wellbeing of one's own itching body to that of a bleeding beggar. The dismembered body – here dead rather than partial – recurs as a metaphor for a cadaverous commonality. The vestigial traces of the invisible hand in the experience of a visceral sympathy for the dead suggests that in fact human beings are naturally primed to feel for each other and do have a fundamental sense of sociability. What we lack is the ability to form positive social interactions and, by extension, political systems from these feelings. We misdirect sympathies back upon ourselves, or lavish them upon redundant (dead) objects, wasting a primary social resource which, as Smith argues contra Hutcheson, cannot provide us with a reliable basis for governing social interactions.

Smith's theory of moral sympathy finally overcomes the problem of deficient sociability by cleaving the subject in two. He identifies a selfish agent who imagines the pain of the other, yet whose primary concern is with his own wellbeing, such as the man of humanity in Europe or the person of delicate fibre seeing the beggar on the street, and an impartial spectator who judges and determines what is best for the broader social good and is privy to the competing perspectives of this European man and of the Chinese earthquake victims, or of the delicate gentleman and the beggar. By means of alienation, the self acquires a structure that is both moral and social as it transcends private interests to consider other perspectives. Therefore, a 'man may sympathize with a woman in child-bed; though it is impossible that he should conceive of himself as suffering her pains in his own proper person or character' (Smith 2002: 374). Perhaps because he cannot feel the throes of childbirth, or because he resists identifying with the female body, this man enters the position of impartial spectatorship which allows him to establish a sympathetic, and hence a sociable, disposition. Luc Boltanski reflects that Smith's theory of sociability relies on a perspective of alienation which accounts for this counter-intuitive notion of morality as moving aside, and as involving removal from feeling (Boltanski 1999: 49). Boltanski questions Smith's confident assertion that people are unable to recognise 'the marks of the deepest affliction' in a bereaved stranger on the street, the pains of labour or the torture of the rack and feel direct sympathy (Smith 2002: 22). He locates Smith within the structure of media spectacle characteristic of humanitarianism, whereby violence and catastrophe are broadcasted far from the site of pain or of possible succour and watched impartially (Boltanski 1999: 183). This creates a 'mutual otherness of those who suffer and those who receive . . . donors in rich democracies and recipients in poor countries often with totalitarian regimes' (ibid. 189). From Boltanski's perspective impartiality objectifies the suffering of others. Spectators watch without having to intervene, partaking in a vicarious intimacy that is strangely free from responsibility, and engaging in titillated moral complacency. Boltanski points to the complex politics of Smith's model, its relation to mass media and its subsequent aesthetic legacy. This criticism of Smith is anticipated by Romantic literature's turn from immediate engagement towards the self. Mediation becomes indirect and not committed to intervention. Smith's position of moral detachment reappears in a longitudinal variety of Romantic and post-Romantic works that include Rousseau's reaction against the Enlightenment, Coleridge's literary theory and Wordsworth's formula of emotion recollected in tranquillity.[9] Romantic withdrawal – shaped by Smithian impartiality – has also shaped criticism of Romanticism, so that 'the Adam Smith problem' morphs into Jerome McGann's critique of a Romantic Ideology.

Idealist Responses: Kant, Schiller, Hegel

Anglo-French natural law and Scottish Enlightenment philosophy had an important impact on German Idealism, a philosophical movement which reformulates the tension between individuals and the community in positive terms.[10] George di Giovanni identifies German Idealism with 'the general tendency to consider human beings precisely as *individuals*' rather than within Aristotelian, Enlightenment or religious models, which all give primacy to the group (di Giovanni 2005: 2). As Karin Schutjer suggests, German Idealism is preoccupied with the difficulty that emerged in seventeenth-century political theory of negotiating between 'particular life and collective whole' (Schutjer 2001: 209). German Idealism's major initiative of devising a system from individual experience responds to the same problem that English natural law and the Scottish Enlightenment philosophies had been grappling with, and – I suggest – engages intensively with Rousseau's legacy. Kant, Friedrich Schiller and Georg Wilhelm Friedrich Hegel, as well as other central figures such as Friedrich Heinrich Jacobi and Johann Gottlieb

Fichte, variously responded to social contract theory's question of how the private self develops broader systems of meaning. To argue this is to disagree with M. H. Abrams's inscription of late eighteenth-century German philosophy within a new epoch which keeps ties with theological antecedents, but not with recent philosophical theory (Abrams 1973: 143–6).[11] However, whereas natural law and Scottish Enlightenment philosophies view this tension as a source of discontent (a position that British Romantic writers share), German Idealism regards it as a productive aspect of social development. Moral, aesthetic and historical experience, as variously defined within the German Idealist tradition by Kant, Schiller and Hegel, transcend the social contract tension between part and whole, and between the individual and society, looking towards the later developments in Friedrich Nietzsche's subsequent argument that 'we must overrule the perspective of the community, sailing straight over and *away from* morality … crushing and perhaps destroying the remnants of our morality by daring to travel there' towards an empowerment of the individual through conflict with society (Nietzsche 2002: 23).

Kant's *Groundwork of the Metaphysics of Morals* develops a model for relating the private will to a broader general will through the simile of being 'as at a crossroads', which imagines the chiastic relationship between the universal law and the individual subject conforming to it (Kant 1997: 13). Kant's concept of will bridges notions of 'universal law' with 'self law'. The universal law which the self must acknowledge is the famous categorical imperative to '*act only in accordance with the maxim through which you can at the same time will that it becomes a universal law*' (ibid. 31). The task of the will is to direct the subject towards universal, disinterested types of action that depart from the self and contribute to broader social coherence. Like Smith's position of impartial spectatorship, Kant's categorical imperative concedes to mutual standards for the common good. In his *Critique of Judgment* Kant suggests that this alienation is achieved through aesthetic experience. He presents the sublime and the beautiful as 'purposive in reference to the moral feeling', aesthetic means to a moral end (Kant 2000: 124). Schutjer emphasises that this moral aesthetic is also a theory of community (Schutjer 2001: 44). Kant enumerates the conditions whereby aesthetic judgment evolves into this *sensus communis*: '1° to think for oneself; 2° to put ourselves in thought in the place of everyone else; 3° always to think consistently' (Kant 2000: 171). Thus, sociability requires autonomy, 'think[ing] for oneself', which must be extrapolated into the categorical imperative: 'to put ourselves in thought in the place of everyone else' (ibid. 172). This is to be achieved through aesthetic judgment, which Kant regards as more reliable and stable than rational thought, the latter of which (like Rousseau) he deems as precariously subjective.

Kant's theory emphasises that the impartial spectator always remains apart from the social body. In his *Idea for a Universal History with a Cosmopolitan Aim*, Kant presents the tension between individual judgment and the broader social interest as an inherent aspect of moral experience, a position that is in line with Smith and Rousseau. He emphasises that the development of societies requires a quality of 'the *unsociable sociability* of human beings, i.e. their propensity to enter into society, which, however, is combined with a thoroughgoing resistance that constantly threatens to break up this society' (Kant 2009: 13). This tension between the desire for self-realisation and the contrary pull to conformity may appear a potential source of vainglory that must be kept in check, in line with Hobbes. But Kant dismisses any such possible objection and presents it in positive terms through a value of excellence which looks ahead to Nietzsche: 'thanks be to nature, therefore, for the incompatibility, for the spiteful competitive vanity, for the insatiable desire to possess or even to dominate!' (ibid. 14). Kant demonstrates the workings of this 'spiteful competitive vanity':

> trees in a forest, precisely because each of them seeks to take air and sun from the other, are constrained to look for them above themselves, and thereby achieve a beautiful straight growth, whereas those in freedom and separated from one another, that put forth their branches as they like, grow stunted, crooked and awry. (Kant 2009: 15)

A positive tension between the self and its social environment is at the core of Kantian aesthetic principles, so that whereas excessive freedom proves stunting, the competitive constraints of socialisation foster excellence.

In his *Letters on the Aesthetic Education of Man*, Schiller develops Kant's focus on the constructive tension between the individual and community. As Schutjer suggests, 'every time he [Schiller] sets out to mend the division, his solution contains a new fissure' (Schutjer 2001: 208). Like Kant, Schiller frames this duality and rupture in positive terms. He imagines the predicament of modern society through metaphors of fragmentation: 'one has to go the rounds from one individual to another in order to be able to piece together a complete image of the species' (Schiller 2001a: 98). People are divided between empirical sensation, 'the *sensuous* drive, [which] proceeds from the physical existence of man, or his sensuous nature' and a contrary '*formal* drive, which proceeds from the absolute existence of man, or from his rational nature' (ibid. 118, 119). In Schiller's interpretation Kant posits aesthetic experience as a resolution of the tension between the individual will and society: 'if man is ever to solve the problem of politics in practice he will have to approach it through the problem of the aesthetic, because it is only through beauty that man makes his way to freedom' (ibid. 90). The aesthetic is 'a middle disposition in which sense and reason are both active *at the same time*. Precisely for this reason, however, they cancel each other out as determining forces, and bring about a negation by means of an opposition' (ibid. 145). Schiller regards this middle state whereby the sensuous and the rational are mutually negated as a position of freedom from physical and practical considerations. Beauty makes sociability moral, because it is only through the vertiginous release of aesthetic experience that, in Schiller's account, the Kantian categorical imperative is really achieved:

> Though it may be his needs that drive man into society, and reason that plants within him the principles of social behaviour, beauty alone can confer on him a *social character* . . . All other forms of perception divide man, because they are founded exclusively either upon the sensuous or upon the spiritual part of his being. (Schiller 2001a: 176)

Aesthetic experience, and literature as a type of the aesthetic, has an important socialising function. This underlying premise of the natural law tradition which had always relied on literary elements becomes apparent in Schiller's rhetorically oriented interpretation.[12] Contracts are, after all, themselves literary texts. German Idealism helps elicit the aesthetic underpinnings of modern accounts of the self. Through Kant's transformation of impartial spectatorship into a positive relation, and in Schiller's emphasis on the cognitive dissonance of sense and reason, a gap emerges whereby individuals redefine their relationship to society. This privileging of aesthetic experience establishes literature as a site of heightened social awareness and critique.

Following Kant and Schiller, Hegel presents the tension between self and society as a positive friction which generates self-consciousness and world spirit. Smith's alienation from the self produces sympathy; for Kant alienation forms the moral will through the categorical imperative; in Schiller aesthetic experience creates freedom through the subject's simultaneous alienation from both sensuous and rational experience. Hegel transposes this familiar model into the domain of historical experience: 'it is therefore through culture that the individual acquires standing and actuality. His *original nature* and substance is the alienation of himself as Spirit from his *natural* being' (Hegel 1977: 298). Because Abrams's foundational account of Romanticism is largely based on his argument that Hegel's *Phenomenology of Spirit* transcends a naive empiricism represented by the traditions of natural law philosophy and social contract theory, Hegel's attitude towards natural law philosophy and the social contract is worthy of pause. Hegel blames the social contract for the violence of the French Revolution and objects to its sovereignty for being neither universal nor individual, and rather as grounded in arbitrary government and covert tyranny of the kind that Wells attributes to the *Leviathan*. In addition, Hegel also maintains that the social contract is a necessary phase in the development of Idealism. In order to uphold its sovereignty, the government of the French Revolution anxiously seeks proof of loyalty from its subjects. However, due to a gap between individual and general wills (which I soon consider in the chapter on Rousseau), the furnishing of this proof is impossible. Since the individual can never really be at one with the social body, power develops a paranoiac obsession with eliminating dissidents:

> The sole work and deed of universal freedom is therefore *death*, a death too which has no inner significance or filling, for what is negated is the empty point of absolutely free self. It is thus the coldest and meanest of all deaths, with no more significance than cutting off a head of cabbage or swallowing a mouthful of water. (Hegel 1977: 360)

Hegel relates the vacancy of this social body to the Reign of Terror's invention of the guillotine. Decapitation dehumanises subjects, turning them into 'head[s] of cabbage'. This vegetable metaphor echoes the atomistic register of Hobbes's *On the Citizen* which had imagined humans as mushrooms. Cabbages and mushrooms are both anthropomorphised through the synecdoche of the head, which Hegel uses to suggest that natural law and social contract philosophies bifurcate the body politic and turn its animal members into vegetables.[13] The universal values of the Enlightenment converge into the 'flat, commonplace monosyllable' of the guillotine – a standard which renders all subjects liable to the same decapitation, a principle of one for all (Hegel 1977: 360). But the guillotine actually defeats its own purpose by belabouring the schism between the social body and the individual, and grants individuality significance as the site of society's most intense vigilance. From Hegel's perspective, the French Revolution and the ideology of the social contract are important junctures in the development of spirit – negative moments that emerge when one plots a positive learning curve framed within the theological narrative of the fortunate fall. Resisting Abrams's argument that Romanticism and Idealism liberate themselves from contract and natural law means recognising Romantic literary engagements with Idealism as responses to natural law and contract theory.

The Anti-Jacobin Social Contract

Social contract theory infiltrated texts and caricatures of 1790s Britain across a spectrum of radical and conservative ideologies. In *Reflections on the Revolution in France*, Edmund Burke argued that the social contract and Rousseau's general will produced the French Revolution (Burke 1987: 45). Burke advocates a neo-Aristotelian model of natural inheritance, divine order and constitution instead of arbitrary contracts (Burke 1982: 43). This dichotomy of constitution versus contract has been reassessed in recent studies of the Romantic period which determine that Romanticism 'cannot be reduced to the formula of Jacobin vs. anti-Jacobin, or radical vs. conservative. To do so is to fall into the kind of ideological trap that the revolution itself thrust upon British citizens' (Heydt-Stevenson and Sussman 2008: 7). John Bugg similarly questions the 'categories of "Jacobin" and "anti-Jacobin" [which] have never fully comprehended the variety of politically engaged novels' (Bugg 2013: 109).[14] Charles Lloyd's *Edmund Oliver* identifies with anti-Jacobin ideology, while relying strongly on notions of contract and elements of Jacobin thought. Lloyd prefaces *Edmund Oliver* by suggesting that it is 'written with the design of counteracting that generalizing spirit, which seems so much to have insinuated itself among modern philosophers' (Lloyd 2005: 3). Lloyd identifies the 'generalizing spirit' with Godwin's attack on the institution of marriage. He suggests that instead of abstract principles, political awareness begins with individual conduct 'the human mind never will be led to interest itself with regard to a *whole*, except it have been first excited by *palpable parts of that whole*' (ibid. 3). Like Coleridge, who frames *The Rime of the Ancient Mariner* with a wedding, Lloyd regards marriage as a type for other forms of social contract. Marriage must reflect private volition rather than the external dictates of general principles, following the pattern of other forms of social contract that take the self as their starting point.[15]

The arch-conservative *Anti-Jacobin Review* criticised *Edmund Oliver* for its excessive interest in the whole rather than the part. Lloyd was accused of anti-war politics and of supporting the '*equalization of property*, and with the unusual absurd propositions, which Jacobins, for want of a better, call arguments' (Lloyd 2005: 224). Despite Lloyd's passionate and well-publicised defence of *Edmund Oliver* in his *A Letter to the Anti-Jacobin Reviewers* – where he endeavours to make his political loyalties to antirevolutionary politics clear – the reviewers were right to detect the underlying ambiguity of Lloyd's political affiliations. In his letter to his reviewers Lloyd argues against natural rights and private contracts, echoing Rousseau's contract theory: 'society is for our good, and we each of us have a right to as much good and no more, as is consistent with the greatest benefit to the greatest number' (Lloyd 1799: 26). But even as *Edmund Oliver* was, as Lloyd suggests, written with the 'utopian enthusiasm' of an inexperienced writer, it gave voice to the sometimes awkward proximity of social contract theory, Romanticism and antirevolutionary discourse in this period, which all deal with the ruptured relationship between society and its members (ibid. 21).

Edmund Oliver's conversations with Charles Maurice engage in a philosophical debate about the reorganisation of community and property. Coleridge wrote to Charles Lloyd's father in 1796, establishing his qualifications to educate his children and Lloyd, who was boarding with Coleridge at this time: 'I am anxious that my children should be bred up from earliest infancy in the simplicity of peasants, their food, dress, and habits completely rustic' (Coleridge 2002: 1.240). Through the Coleridgean character of Charles, Lloyd insists that 'human perfection is a slow process. It must go through the patient discipline of domestic duty' (Lloyd 2005: 59). Charles suggests that the 'domestic discipline' of family life represents a significant step towards a higher goal of 'human perfection' – a term which ambiguously refers either to the individual or to the species, and finally collapses the two into a common body. Much to the chagrin of *The Anti-Jacobin Review*, this included the rejection of private property. Maurice instructs Edmund that the individual always serves the greater good: 'it seemed to us, my friend, that man was merely the *steward*, not the *possessor* of these means of operating on his fellow beings' (ibid. 118). Like Wordsworth and Coleridge, Edmund bewails that 'the unnatural flocking together of the species hardens and *unsocial-izes* the heart more than uniform solitude. Human intercourse becomes so cheap that it is disregarded' (ibid. 44).

Edmund wants to abandon the narrow individualism of laissez-faire urban life and to discover a collective identity. Such a challenge will allow him to 'sink [his] own wants, and live in the happiness of others: throw aside the panoply of artificial and personal distinction, and feel a common identity with mankind at large' (Lloyd 2005: 45). Charles cautions Edmund against preferring social ideas to individual perspectives, a problem which Lloyd himself had foreseen in his prefatory warning about the dangers of the generalising spirit (ibid. 3). *Edmund Oliver* ends with Charles's and Edmund's establishment of a quasi-Pantisocratic alternative community, an enactment of social contract principles that – as I argue in the discussion of Coleridge in Chapter 3 – emerges from a direct engagement with Rousseau's political model (Wallace 2009b: 20).[16]

Broadly circulated popular prints by James Gillray blame the political instability of the French Revolution on the legacy of the social contract. They ridicule individualism and call for national solidarity, but use the imagery and often the actual texts of social contract theory, which frequently appear as quasi *mise en abyme* objects within these caricatures, functioning as satiric texts within texts. Because political caricatures were subject to intense policing and censorship during these war years, print sellers only marketed the most conservative prints (Brewer 1986: 46; Donald 1996: 147). Censorship also meant that caricaturists avoided expressing consistent political views (Donald 1996: 26); accordingly, Gillray targets left and right alike (Paulson 1983: 189). This ambivalence not only reflects prudence, but also expresses a tension between individual and collective perspectives which intertwine and fragment one another within the imagery of these caricatures and in social contract discourse, producing a vision which lacks inner coherence.

Gillray's 1798 print 'Destruction of the French Collossus [*sic*]' (Figure 1.2) visibly echoes the frontispiece of Hobbes's *Leviathan*; a superhuman sovereign emerges from the natural landscape. Gillray anatomises the forces that fragment the social body, identified as the guillotine, British attack – represented as divine intervention – and Napoleon's colonialism, suggested by the monster's attempt to straddle Europe and Egypt (an allusion to the recent Battle of the Nile). A book titled *Religion de la Nature* drops from the colossus's hand, revealing the revolution's agenda on the inscription facing its title page as 'injustice, oppression, murder, destruction', a parody of social contract values (read through the revolution) of liberty, equality and fraternity. Gillray's French colossus prefigures Mary Shelley's creature in *Frankenstein* in its superhuman composite status, natural rights education, cosmopolitanism and exposition of the ills of sovereignty.

Gillray's caricature of 1792 (Figure 1.3) 'A Family of Sans-Cullots Refreshing after the Fatigues of the Day' delves deeper into the problem of social dismemberment embodied by the figure of the colossus. Here the revolution is presented as a form of cannibalism. The private domestic sanctuary and bourgeois supper time ritual become sites of dismemberment in which the body politic is portioned-out and destroyed. Values of individual rights are grotesquely represented by its bifurcation into parts, displacing national unity. The disparate members and organs symbolise feminised feeling (the heart is served to the women), masculine rationalism, pragmatism and ownership (the men eat the eyes, heads and hands) and childish vulnerability (the infants feast on internal organs). The walls of the house are adorned with diagrams and graffiti of body parts, emphasising that this is not only the random blood thirst of the 'Mardi

Figure 1.2 James Gillray, 'Destruction of the French Collossus'. Courtesy of the Lewis Walpole Library, Yale University.

Figure 1.3 James Gillray, 'A Family of Sans-Cullots Refreshing after the Fatigues of the Day'. Courtesy of the National Portrait Gallery, London.

Gras' alluded to in the caption, but a premeditated and theory-driven assault on the social body. Values of 'Vive la Liberte [*sic*]' and 'Vive le Egalitè [*sic*]' are inscribed on the walls. Eirwen E. C. Nicholson discusses these as 'semantic enclaves' (or quasi *mise en abyme* satires-within-satires) that draw on intertextual references – here to the social contract – which are translated into the concrete social breakdown represented by this family (Nicholson 1999: 146–7). This typology of ruptured body parts draws on a crisis in models of community. Given Diana Donald's and Nicholson's arguments that the caricature constitutes a hybrid collocation of text and image, Gillray's register can be understood as an important context for Romantic literary texts which reproduce fragmentation visually, most dramatically in book ten of *The Prelude* and in the piebald body of Frankenstein's monster (Donald 1996: 142; Nicholson 1999: 146). Gillray's spatial imagery of social fragmentation provides a visual counterpart to the written text's more narrative and lyric elements, suggesting the powerful association of physical disunity with the legacy of the social contract, as well as the causal tie between works of theory and the social chaos which they produce.

In the context of the French Revolution and British responses frag-mentation becomes a purely negative social disposition, in contrast to the positive value which Kant, Schiller and Hegel place on rupture and crisis. It would take Carlyle to put a positive spin on this dark moment, reimagining it as a transitional aporia on the path to social regeneration in *Sartor Resartus*, although this regeneration remains part of a distant future that is not clearly articulated. The critical challenge, undertaken by Romanticism and its legacy, becomes reformulating the complex ties of the body politic in the advent of the departed, fractured sense of com-munity that emerges from Hobbes's elimination of natural sociability. Social contract theory and its critics try to banish Aristotle's spectre, but Aristotle leaves a lacuna which metamorphoses into the ghostly invis-ible hand in Smith's alienated model of subjectivity, into the bifurcated revolutionary body of Gillray's caricatures, into the vacant postulation of social harmony in the writings of Hutcheson and Ferguson, and into German Idealism's turn to aesthetic and historical experience as a means of healing the gaps that emerge among individuals within the social body. Aristotle's various phantom limbs all attest to his longev-ity. Modern political theory cannot readily give up the ghost of natural sociability and continues imagining the present as incomplete and fractured, a position which I explore through Rousseau, its most vocal advocate.

Notes

1. Gillian Russell and Clara Tuite suggest that eighteenth-century political theory reacted against Hobbes's extreme pessimism about human nature by promoting concepts of sensibility (Russell and Tuite 2002: 8). Nancy Yousef contrasts Hobbes's misanthropic state of nature with the utopian sympathy of the eighteenth century (Yousef 2013: 28, 33). Charles H. Hinnant's cata-logue of Hobbes's works and the WorldCat database enumerate multiple editions and commentaries on Hobbes's works in English between 1700 and 1750 (Hinnant 1980: 21–32). By contrast, in the second half of the eighteenth century there are few English publications listed on WoldCat and none in Hinnant's catalogue. Hobbes was translated into German, Italian, Russian and French, and was particularly popular in *ancien régime* France, consequently influencing Rousseau, who mediated the broader social con-tract tradition for Romantic writers (ibid. 32–43).
2. Chris Baldick argues that Hobbes's Leviathan and the creature in *Frankenstein* 'both reflect the dismemberment of the old body politic' by '[signalling] the growing awareness, hastened in the heat of regicide and revolution, of destinies no longer continuous with nature but shaped by art, by "policy"' (Baldick 1990: 16).

3. Francis Hutcheson is closer to the common view that '*Barbarity, Cruelty,* and *Fraud*; and *universal War*, according to Mr. HOBBS, would have been our *natural State*' (Hutcheson 1971: 275).

4. Like Victoria Khan, Yves Charles Zarka also regards the implications of Hobbes's formulation of the relationship between individuals and political power as greater than its totalitarian outcome (Zarka 2004: 182). He suggests that censure of Hobbes's theory of sovereignty often obscures the innovation of his individualism. Similarly David William Bates argues that Hobbesian sovereignty responds to a new era of global politics and colonial competition by grounding natural rights and pluralism beyond the traditional nation-state and considering all potential members of society (Bates 2012: 4, 25).

5. Mandeville repeats the themes of *Georgics IV*; the bee king unifies the bee world: 'He is the overseer of their industry; / they worship him and all surround him' (Virgil 2002: 132). The bees share a common origin and all spontaneously generate from the carcass of one dead bull (ibid. 148).

6. Smith develops his concept of sociability from Mandeville's idea that people can be motivated to sociability by vanity. Because people prefer themselves to others, they are also proud and conscious of how others perceive them. A passionate desire for social recognition can, according to Smith, motivate people to altruism because 'when we prefer ourselves so shamefully and so blindly to others, we become the proper objects of resentment, abhorrence, and execration' (Smith 2002: 158). Rousseau's approach to negative motivations for sociability, which he calls *amour propre* (discussed in the next chapter), is far less forgiving.

7. For further discussion of this well-known conundrum, see Doğan Göçmen (2007).

8. The invisible hand also has theological underpinnings. Peter Harrison traces it to seventeenth-century Calvinist discourses, where the invisible hand appears as a metaphor for the divine will (Harrison 2011: 36). In his *History of Astronomy*, Smith's invisible hand acquires this connotation as a synecdoche for Jupiter's intervention: 'Fire burns and water refreshes; heavy bodies descend, and lighter substances fly upwards, by the necessity of their own nature; nor was the invisible hand of Jupiter ever apprehended to be employed in those matters' (Smith 1980a: 59–60).

9. Michael McKeon traces Wordsworth's argument in the 'Preface to *Lyrical Ballads*' that the poet must achieve aesthetic distance from his object to Smith's *Theory of Moral Sentiments* (McKeon 2005: 374–6).

10. On German Idealism's underestimated debt to British literary and philosophical sources, see the introduction of Sanford Budick's *Kant and Milton* (Budick 2010: 10–11).

11. Abrams suggests that Romanticism turns from politics to the imagination, but retains its ties to religion: 'faith in an apocalypse by revolution gave way to faith in an apocalypse by imagination and cognition' (Abrams 1973: 334).

12. See for example Sheldon Wolin's argument that Hobbes draws on the epic tradition (Wolin 1970: 5).

13. Hegel's famous master–slave dialect in Chapter 4 of *Phenomenology of Spirit* reiterates Hobbes's second war-like state of nature of the *Leviathan*,

and posits violence as the origin of history as each combatant fights to gain recognition of his right to the fulfilment of desire: 'self-consciousness is thus certain of itself only by superseding this other that presents itself to self-consciousness as an independent life' (Hegel 1977: 109).

14. Similarly, Kevin Gilmartin suggests that studies of the revolutionary controversy tend to flatten revolutionary and counterrevolutionary discourses (Gilmartin 2007: 1). As M. O. Grenby observes, anti-Jacobinism is an inversion or mirror image of the Jacobinism it opposed: 'in defining itself purely in terms of what it was not ... its protagonists evaded the necessity of having to formulate any doctrine of their own' (Grenby 2001: 65). Alternative views of this relationship, closer to Burke's argument, have been offered. For example, April London argues that Jacobin novels focus on community, whereas anti-Jacobin novels emphasise the private sphere of family and sentimental concerns without dwelling on broader social models (London 2000: 75).

15. See Rousseau's analysis of marriage in *Julie*, where he presents it as a form of social contract 'the public is in a sense the guarantor of a covenant signed in its presence' (Rousseau 1997: 296).

16. Lloyd's advertisement emphasises this shift of focus in anti-Jacobin fiction, suggesting that the main point of his novel is to correct Godwin's lax morals regarding marriage (Lloyd 2005: 3). The removal of political critique to concern with proper conduct shapes the figure of the rake–philosopher, omnipresent throughout much of anti-Jacobin literature. Hence, in Elizabeth Hamilton's *Memoirs of Modern Philosophers*, political dissent is embodied by the lecherous hairdresser Vallaton who masquerades as a spokesman for the general good.

Chapter 2

Writing the Social Contradiction: Rousseau's Literary Politics

> While teaching us to think, you have learned sensibility from us, and no matter what your English philosopher says, such schooling is as good as the other; if it is reason that makes man, it is sentiment that guides him. (Rousseau 1997: 262)

Friedrich Schiller headed his *Letters on the Aesthetic Education of Man* with an epigraph from Jean-Jacques Rousseau's novel *Julie*: 'if it is reason which makes man, it is feeling which guides him' (Schiller 2001a: 86). Quotation is always excerpted, yet here the elided context of Schiller's allusion to *Julie* begs re-contextualisation. In this passage, Rousseau is not merely contrasting philosophy with feeling or sentiment, but is actually pointing to a strong affinity between the two modes. Claire addresses Saint Preux, a character whom Rousseau often uses as a mouthpiece for his own positions, and asserts 'while teaching us to think, you have learned sensibility from us, and no matter what your English philosopher says, such schooling is as good as the other; if it is reason that makes man, it is sentiment that guides him' (Rousseau 1997: 262).[1] Whereas Schiller maintains a distinction between politics and aesthetics, for Rousseau the two modes intertwine. Political philosophy contains fantastic and lyrical elements, and literature 'judges' philosophy.

Why was Rousseau so central for Romantic writers? The journals, letters and literary texts of William Wordsworth, William Godwin and Mary Shelley contain few references to German Idealism (Samuel Taylor Coleridge, of course, is the significant caveat), subtle allusions to Adam Smith, and the occasional oblique tribute to Thomas Hobbes. By contrast, Romanticism's dialogue with Rousseau is profuse and overwhelming. Rousseau is a crucial nervous centre for Romantic writers. Notably, he wasn't unique within the larger line of Enlightenment revisions of Aristotelian sociability, which all increasingly promoted a new individualism through a focus on private feeling. What is arguably different about Rousseau is that his writings can be plotted on a spectrum of discourses that range from *Julie*, a fiction, works of opera, theatre, autobiography and semi-autobiographical fragments, to hybrid texts like *Emile*, and the *Discourse on the Origins of Inequality*, and also political theory, the best known of which being *The Social Contract*. An important clue to Rousseau's influence can be found in the relationship between these aspects of his output and in the conflicted outlook which they produce in conjunction. Rousseau's writings in the double areas of fiction and philosophy channel into literary form the social tensions that had been fermenting within the preceding century and a half of political discourse. His literary writings explore the repercussions of these radical shifts in perspective on the self. An alienated persona migrates from Rousseau's political theory, through his literary texts and into Romanticism, offering an alternative to Aristotelianism and forming a more or less direct line uniting Hobbes with Wordsworth. When Wordsworth invokes Aristotle to describe poetry as 'the most philosophic of all writing', he is also, as we will later see, acknowledging the presence of Rousseau and of his new model of individualism (Wordsworth 2000b: 605).

Rousseau's concern with conflict between private and communal viewpoints explains his notorious use of paradox, an element which has troubled and intrigued generations of readers, suggested by Mary Shelley's explanation of his immense popularity in terms of a human 'fond[ness] of riddles. We delight to unravel a knotty point' (Shelley 1823: 67). Rousseau's sometimes torturous paradoxes need to be read as Shelley reads them, as a rhetorical strategy. Rousseau suggests that sociability can only be represented as a state of inherent contradiction that is best understood through literature. Rousseau's paradoxes are an imaginative expression of a major conflict in modern culture that subsequently opens up important modes of understanding for later readers – Shelley lists herself among them – and explains the overwhelming popularity of his bestseller *Julie*.

To be sure, *The Social Contract* is replete with moments of self-doubt and self-contradiction, often articulated through entangled points of self-reflection of the type that Shelley praises. But it also cultivates an optative tone, imagining how things might be under alternative, improved conditions. Within fictional writings – an area associated in the eighteenth century with the sentimental and private sphere of experience – things fall apart, and Rousseau gives voice to an alienated, individual perspective. The focus here remains political, but is dissenting rather than communal or magisterial. In using literature to pass judgment on political theory, Rousseau was drawing on a considerable tradition that had already amassed in the writings of Hobbes, David Hume, Smith and others, who use literary techniques to articulate moments of self-doubt.[2] Jacques Derrida and Paul de Man both suggest that Rousseau's reliance on figurative language is the most important aspect of his legacy. Derrida relates this to a broader conflict within the metaphysical tradition, which claims directly to represent truth and ideas without needing literary mediation and figuration, which are relegated to a secondary status (Derrida 1974: 315). De Man responds to Derrida by arguing that this is 'a fact of language over which Rousseau had no control. Just as any other reader, he is bound to misread his text' (de Man 1979: 277). According to de Man, Rousseau does not respond to a metaphysical tradition, but demonstrates the self-critical potential of aesthetic figures by performing the primacy of language over meaning. De Man identifies in Rousseau 'an introspective, self-reflexive mode which uses literary models of Augustinian and piestic origins . . . But to this are juxtaposed elements that are closer to Machiavelli than to Petrarch, concerned with political power as well as economic and legal realities' (de Man 1984: 101). This hybrid style 'has no blind spots: it accounts at all moments for its own rhetorical mode' (de Man 1983: 139). Rousseau develops a politicised, self-critical rhetoric.

How might Rousseau's literary and political uses of language be related? After Schiller, Rousseau's literary works have sometimes been analysed as mainly preoccupied with private feeling.[3] This reading of Rousseau is actually counter to the main thrust of Schiller's argument, which suggests that the aesthetic has an important socialising function. Considerable attention has been paid to the rhetorical aspects of Rousseau's political argumentation. David William Bates argues that Rousseau innovatively regards the political as a contingent historical development that may also not have happened – or in Steven Affeldt's terms a category that is produced through language, discourse and self-transformation (Bates 2012: 210; Affeldt 2000: 556). From an inverse logic, Jean Starobinski suggests that Rousseau transposes the civic value of eloquence from public life to inner feeling (Starobinski 1977: 206–7).[4] Starobinski ascribes this movement to the exigencies of despotism and censorship. Literature changes its focus and becomes concerned with the critique of power instead of the imagination of new forms. Reviewing Robert Southey's *Thalaba the Destroyer*, *The Edinburgh Review* accused Southey and his peers of emulating 'the antisocial principles, and the distempered sensibility of Rousseau – his discontent with the present constitution of society – his paradoxical morality, and his perpetual hankerings after some unattainable state of voluptuous virtue and perfection' (Francis 1802: 64). As with the *Anti-Jacobin Review*'s discussion of *Edmund Oliver*, here too prejudice mingles with astute insight into Rousseau's juxtaposition of antisocial principles with social critique. The reviewer suggests that Rousseau's conflicting attitudes produce the paradoxical morality that has corrupted Southey and his peers. Rousseau's writings foreground an irresolvable conflict between society and its constituent members, who remain fundamentally at odds with one another.

In *The Confessions* Rousseau provides an account of the conditions in which he wrote both *Julie* and *The Social Contract*, corroborating Starobinski's insight that figurative language responds to a political reality of isolation and exile. Rousseau writes of his withdrawal to a solitary cottage, where 'completely forgetting the human race, I made for myself societies of perfect creatures' (Rousseau 1995: 359). Rousseau explains:

> The impossibility of reaching real beings threw me into the country of chimeras, and seeing nothing existing that was worthy of my delirium, I nourished it in an ideal world which my creative imagination soon peopled with beings in accordance with my heart. (Rousseau 1995: 359)

Extreme isolation generates a retreat into fantasy, a viewpoint which Rousseau terms 'the country of chimeras'. This allusion to a mythical realm of grotesque beasts formed of parts of animals suggests a causal relationship between social withdrawal and the predicament of bifurcation. Being cut off from the 'human race' and 'real beings' translates into imaginings of a composite, fragmented mode of being that recalls the frontispiece of Hobbes's *Leviathan* with its splicing of individual parts, and anticipates the piebald, xenograft creature of Shelley's *Frankenstein*. Rousseau suggests that he peoples his alienated solitude with fictions of sociability which evolve into political ideals, generating the 'ideal world' and 'societies of perfect creatures' of his *Social Contract*. He reflects 'I passed hours, days there without counting, and losing the remembrance of all other things; hardly had I eaten a bite' (Rousseau 1995: 359). His major works of social theory thereby respond to a state of extreme isolation.

Rousseau's political theory turns loneliness into a social vision; his literary works explore the underpinnings of discontent that motivate civilisation. *Julie* and *The Social Contract*, written in tandem, develop parallel concerns. Rousseau focuses on the unhappiness of the varied individuals that actually form society.[5] From this potentially tragic model, he derives an influential theory of sociability. In the appendages to the letters which constitute *Julie*, Rousseau establishes an editorial persona identified as '*Jean Jacques Rousseau*' who reflects on the function of literature. This persona would fragment a decade later into '*J.J.*' and '*Rousseau*' in Rousseau's dialogue *Rousseau, Judge of Jean-Jacques* (Rousseau 1990: 19).[6] Rousseau took pains to distinguish the editorial persona from his own implied positions. Following the pattern of Samuel Richardson's *Pamela*, which this editor persona in *Julie* occasionally cites (ibid. 280, note), Rousseau / the editor claims that *Julie* is not a novel, but 'real' letters which he has found (ibid. 8–9). He prefers calling these letters 'a long ballad' rather than referring to them as a novel (ibid. 12), avoiding the terms of fiction and expressing what James Grantham Turner calls an eighteenth-century 'fear of novel-induced automatism' (Turner 1994: 79). The editor asserts, 'great cities must have theaters; and corrupt peoples, Novels. I have seen the morals of my times, and I have published these letters. Would I had lived in an age when I should have thrown them into the fire!' (Rousseau 1997: 3). Julie's husband, the austere Monsieur de Wolmar, suggests that children need to be protected from their propensity to enjoy violent spectacle that 'entertains them, seduces them, and makes them like what they should fear' (ibid. 606–7). The editor seconds Wolmar's position with a footnote explaining that 'that is why we all like the theatre, and quite a few of us novels' (ibid. 607, note). Coming from Wolmar and the editor, characters that Rousseau associates with excessively conservative positions, this anti-literary bias, which dates as far back as Plato's expulsion of the arts from the ideal republic, calls for an ironic reading.

Saint Preux, with whom Rousseau identifies more clearly, comments that in Paris novels inure readers to corrupt morals and adultery (Rousseau 1997: 222). But through Saint Preux's comments, Rousseau also suggests that this formative quality of novels can still be put to productive use, as 'novels are perhaps the ultimate kind of instruction remaining to be offered to a people so corrupt that all other is useless' (ibid. 227). Because novels are widely read and easily assimilated, they are potentially able to reform their impressionable readers. But can such examples really change Rousseau's jaded audience, given his previous remarks that books can only have a salutary impact on their readers away from large cities, or that only a few readers will understand his fiction? (Rousseau 1992c: 184–5; Rousseau 1997: 13) And why is philosophy – another major form of Rousseau's output – unable to do this work? These questions are complicated by Rousseau's references to literature and philosophy as closely related and interchangeable discourses, contrary to the popular view that they belong to separate spheres. The editor explains that Saint Preux is a philosopher, who 'makes of moral conscience a sentiment and not a judgment, which goes against the definitions of the philosophers. I think however that in this their putative colleague is right' (Rousseau 1997: 561, note). The editor's comments suggest that sentimental literature and philosophy essentially perform a similar function, so that philosophy has an important fictional component. The editor adds, 'it is a mania common to philosophers of all eras to deny what is, and to explain what is not', much like writers of fiction (ibid. 597, note). Saint Preux comments that literature and philosophy also share a common readership: 'Poetry, Literature, history, philosophy, even politics, one must notice right away by the style of all books that they are written to amuse pretty women' (ibid. 226). Rousseau repeatedly suggests that the anathema of these varied and catholic forms of female entertainment is reason, espoused by Wolmar who confronts Saint Preux with this opposition:

> Such, he interrupted me, are Julie's seductions. She always puts sentiment in the place of reasons, and renders it so touching that the only answer is always to give her a kiss: might it not be from her master of philosophy, he added with a laugh, that she has learned this manner of argumentation? (Rousseau 1997: 487)

Saint Preux with Wolmar represent sentimental and Enlightenment approaches to philosophy respectively.

In the 'Preface to a Second Letter to Bordes' Rousseau gives a plausible explanation as to why he favours Saint Preux's sentimentalism to Wolmar's Enlightenment rationalism. Rousseau prophesies that only a handful of readers will actually understand his arguments, since most readers have 'found my discourses badly connected and almost entirely rambling, for lack of perceiving the trunk of which I showed them only the branches' (Rousseau 1992c: 184–5). Rousseau suggests that if there is meaning in his fragmented texts, it must be gathered from interpreting the branches rather than in seeking out a coherent trunk. These branches are a visual metaphor for the cruxes of contradiction, suggesting a circular form of argumentation. The rambling quality of Rousseau's discourse is a ruse to shake off lazy readers, who seek explicit and literal meaning and can't see the wood for the trees (ibid. 184–5). In *Rousseau, Judge of Jean-Jacques*, Rousseau returns to the metaphor of trunkless branches to describe his paradoxical writing style. Lured by the promise of philosophical truth, a fictional reader of his works complains of their difficulty: 'such sublime virtues aren't found by themselves. They are only branches of virtue. I looked for the trunk and didn't find it' (Rousseau 1990: 208). He comes to see J.J.'s convoluted discourse as 'a trap which J.J. enjoys setting for careless readers' (ibid. 131). The Rousseau persona retorts, 'if that is so, he is well punished for it by readers of bad faith, who pretend to be caught in order to accuse him of not knowing what he is saying' (ibid. 131). These readers do not recognise that truth has a circular, indirect quality. In the Socratic 'Conversation about Novels' that prefaces *Julie*, the editor persona asserts, 'you want people always to be consistent; I doubt that is possible for man; but what is possible is for him always to be true: that is what I mean to try to be' (Rousseau 1997: 20). Rousseau questions Enlightenment values of consistency and coherence – espoused by the implied readers of the 'Preface to a Second Letter to Bordes', by the Frenchman in *Rousseau, Judge of Jean-Jacques*, and by Wolmar in *Julie* – and distinguishes them from truth, which he associates with a convoluted, ramifying, elliptical rhetoric. Precisely because it is indirect, the literary work and Saint Preux's brand of sentimental philosophy are truer than political theory.[7]

In *The Confessions* Rousseau connects his tendency to paradox to the inner division produced by social tensions: 'I have never been able to keep a mean in my attachments and simply fulfil the duties of society. I have always been everything or nothing' (Rousseau 1995: 437). *Rousseau, Judge of Jean-Jacques* takes this conflict into the arena of aesthetic form, producing a literary work that is internally split: 'his life is divided into two parts that seem to belong to two different individuals, with the period that separates them – meaning the time when he published books – marking the death of one and the birth of the other' (ibid. 14). These Doctor Jekyll and Mister Hyde personas respond to a political climate which has misread Rousseau's writings and demonised their author, casting him into exile. J.J. evolves when Rousseau's works are published and misread. This inner division generates a Fata Morgana apparition of sociability, as the character Rousseau solipsistically reads his own writings to alleviate his loneliness: 'this solitary state was sad. J.J. rescued me from it. His books strengthened me against the derision of free-thinkers. I found his principles so compatible with my feelings' (ibid. 53).The absurd prospect of finding a twin soul in oneself is rendered somewhat less strange when read vis-à-vis Smith's model of sociability, which involves the splitting of the self into sentient and impartial aspects. Rousseau presents himself as an impartial spectator looking on at J.J., counteracting 'the noisy assertions of passionate people by the peaceful but certain observations of an impartial man' (Rousseau 1990: 107). Rather than the passionate mob that hunts down J.J., the impartial position allows for sympathy, a sociable virtue. J.J. prefers this impartial stance of isolation to direct interaction:

> J.J. did not always flee from men, but he has always loved solitude. He enjoyed himself with the friends he believed he had, but he enjoyed himself

still more alone. He valued their society, but he sometimes needed to withdraw, and he would perhaps have preferred to live always alone than always with them. His fondness for the Novel *Robinson Crusoe* made me judge that he would not have thought himself as unhappy as Crusoe did confined to his desert island. (Rousseau 1990: 117–18)

Like Crusoe on his desert island, who befriends Friday, Friday's father and a Papist Spaniard, J.J. finally forms a miniature society in exile at the end of *Rousseau, Judge of Jean-Jacques*. He imagines these two parts of himself, together with the Frenchman, as a mini-community that echoes the holy trinity. J.J. finds solace in 'the sweetness of seeing two decent and true hearts once again open themselves to his own. Let's temper in this way the horror of that solitude in which he is forced to live in the midst of the human race' (Rousseau 1990: 245). The individual is no longer alone, but has become a company of three, consisting of the writer (Rousseau), his works (J.J.) and the intended reader (the Frenchman). Literature replaces the society which has produced such a passionate need for fragmentation and aesthetic withdrawal, forming a new contract among its members. Rousseau exposes the split self as a parody of the social contract, pushing its logic to a grotesque extreme as society finally emerges as a company of one, exposing the sociability of individualism as a deathly singularity.

Julie and *The Social Contract*

Julie presents a virulent critique of Rousseau's social contract theory. Through the themes of unrequited love and domestic servitude Rousseau emphasises the price which conformity exacts by alienating individual desire, as well as a more specific focus on the abuse of women in forming the social body. He presents Julie as free to choose between marriage and an asocial agenda, represented by her forbidden tryst with Saint Preux. But finally the marital and social contracts prevail over the private individual. Rousseau emphasises that marriage is a social contract 'the public is in a sense the guarantor of a covenant signed in its presence' (Rousseau 1997: 296). Julie explains,

> One does not marry in order to think solely about each other, but in order to fulfil conjointly the duties of civil life, govern the household prudently, raise one's children well. Lovers never see anyone but themselves, are endlessly occupied with each other alone, and the only thing they can do is love each other. That is not enough for Spouses who have so many other duties to attend to. (Rousseau 1997: 306)

In this discussion of political economy Rousseau connects marriage to social duty. Shoshana Felman notes that '*épouser*' means both to marry and to promise, belonging to J. L. Austin's 'commissives / espousals' which enact duty (Felman 2003: 20).[8] Julie's marriage to Wolmar is a social agreement between men, rather than an expression of individual volition: 'so my father has sold me? He is making merchandise, a slave of his daughter with his friend' (Rousseau 1997: 77). Wolmar seeks to reconcile Julie and Saint Preux within the ideal society of his estate in Clarens. But the collective society of Clarens is founded on the suppression of its private constituents and finally breaks down.

Hence, far from reinforcing the social contract, Julie's relationship with Saint Preux subverts the tyranny of the general will. On her deathbed Julie suggests that desire and duty belong to separate spheres which cannot be brought together, reiterating a central dilemma of the romance tradition. She explains that her love for Saint Preux is

> involuntary, it has cost my innocence nothing; everything within the power of my will was for my duty. If the heart, which is not in its power, was for you, that was a torment for me and not a crime. I have done what duty required; virtue remains to me without spot, and love has remained to me without remorse. (Rousseau 1997: 608–9)

Saint Preux expresses a similar view of desire as an innate quality independent of socially constructed positions like duty:

> so it would be vain to pretend to remold a variety of minds on a common model. You can coerce them and not change them: you can prevent men from showing themselves as they are, but not make them become other. (Rousseau 1997: 463)

Conformity finally kills Julie. She drowns rescuing her son Marcellin, who Rousseau presents as a metonymy of her loveless marriage to Wolmar. This resolution is contrasted with her subversive attachment to Saint Preux, which resurfaces toward the end of the novel when Julie's misgivings about her marriage begin emerging. At this point, the editor persona comments: 'ah! I quite fear, devout charmer, that you are not, not even you, too much of one mind! Besides, I confess that this letter looks to me like the swan's song' (Rousseau 1997: 566). Through the letters that constitute *Julie*, Rousseau suggests that desire cannot be stifled, but only killed along with its subject. Wolmar realises that the dying Julie has never really been part of Clarens: 'I have figured you out; you are delighted to be dying; you are more than happy to be leaving me' (ibid. 590). And Julie herself comes to a similar realisation shortly before her fatal accident: 'that is part of what I have been experiencing since my marriage, and since your return. All about me I see nothing but causes for contentment, and I am not content' (ibid. 566).

The utopian mini-society of Clarens, where servants and masters cultivate the land in unison and share its fruits and individual desire is transformed into social harmony, proves to be a lie. At times, Clarens appears to be a matriarchal society, presided over by Julie. Saint Preux remarks on Julie's '[envy] of sovereigns only by the pleasure of making themselves beloved. Envy nothing, her husband said in a tone of voice he should have left for me; we have all long been your subjects' (Rousseau 1997: 457). Wolmar's uncharacteristically humorous tone in this repartee marks the limits of Julie's sovereignty as a joke that cannot be taken seriously, a matter of affection rather than authority. These limits are made most vividly tangible in Rousseau's account of her sanctuary, her private garden Elysium. The Elysium is a quasi-natural garden planted by Wolmar to distract Julie from the memory of her former trysts with Saint Preux, which happened nearby. When he visits the Elysium, Saint Preux is initially overcome by the presence of nature: 'I thought I was looking at the wildest, most solitary place in nature, and it seemed to me I was the first mortal who had ever set foot in this wilderness' (ibid. 387). On closer inspection, however, the verdant forest turns out to be 'creeping, parasitic plants that, trained upon the tree trunks, surround their crowns in the thickest foliage' (ibid. 389). Birds flock to Elysium only because Wolmar feeds them (ibid. 391). When Saint Preux remarks on the absence of footprints, Wolmar explains that these are all carefully erased (ibid. 393). Elysium at first appears deceptively Edenic, but is finally revealed as an alternative to passion; a rococo parody of natural desires displaces real nature.

Julie's pseudo-natural garden, her Elysium, is a *mise en abyme* which reflects on the problems of patriarchy, somewhat like the complex status of *Julie* itself within Rousseau's corpus (or like Rousseau's own anomalous figure within the Enlightenment tradition as a whole).[9] Rousseau's complex literary works emerge as a looking glass through which the ethical underpinnings of a new era of individualism come apart. Rousseau introduces the language of poetry into *Julie* to question reason. Repeatedly citing Petrarch and Tasso, Saint Preux suggests that figurative language is necessary for reflecting on political realities. He councils Julie 'to read little, and reflect much on our reading' (Rousseau 1997: 46). When Julie accuses Saint Preux of artificial wit, he insists that 'metaphors and figurative expressions are necessary to make oneself understood' (ibid. 195, 198). Poetry, novels, rococo landscaping, and other aesthetic forms such as the Socratic dialogues of *Rousseau, Judge of Jean-Jacques*, provide the only means of articulating an individual perspective, often through irony and from a position of extreme coercion, in a society which consumes its members by subjecting them to arid Enlightenment standards of coherence.

Rousseau credits his novel with the ability to question Enlightenment ideology and scrutinise its underlying dilemmas, and with the preference of the individual to the general social body. Charles Griswold reads *Julie* as a commentary on Smith's *Theory of Moral Sentiments* (Griswold 2010: 76). Wolmar articulates the alien purview of Smith's impartial spectator:

> I enjoy observing society, not taking part in it. If I could change the nature of my being and become a living eye, I would gladly make that exchange. Thus my indifference of men does not make me independent of them; though I care not about being seen, I need to see them, and though I do not cherish them I find them necessary. (Rousseau 1997: 403)

Griswold suggests that from Rousseau's perspective, impartial spectatorship cannot produce a shared community (Griswold 2010: 77). Anticipating Luc Boltanski's critique of Smith through the character of Wolmar, sympathy appears as a guise for voyeurism.[10] Perceiving suffering does not translate into moral action, but in this case presents a kind of emotional vampirism. Wolmar is like the parasitical creepers that he plants in Julie's Elysium. He vicariously feeds on the suppressed love of Julie and Saint Preux, taking possession of their secret correspondence unbeknown to them. Rousseau suggests that instead of the diffuse bonds of sympathy, which can conceal a multitude of antisocial motivations such as Wolmar's perverse *Schadenfreude* at Julie's and Saint Preux's unrequited loved (Rousseau terms this *amour propre* in the *Second Discourse*), society needs a stronger rationale for holding individuals together. In this light, the Smithian community of one that emerges towards the end of *Rousseau, Judge of Jean-Jacques* appears all the more ironic. Rousseau has not found a new social modus vivendi, but rather undermines existent forms of individualism.

Free from Desire

Rousseau's *Social Contract* imagines sociability as a fall from freedom to servitude. Rousseau opens *The Social Contract* with the famous assertion that 'man was born free, and everywhere he is in chains' (Rousseau 1994c: 131).[11] His political theory seeks to ameliorate duty and to redefine obligation as a virtue, transforming freedom from an individual into a social property. Yet *Julie* makes it clear that Rousseau never really meets this goal; duty remains inimical to freedom, as social relations are invariably structured around domination and coercion. The *Discourse on the Origins of Inequality* imagines the state of nature as a hypothetical condition that precedes socialisation. At the heart of Rousseau's understanding of sociability, and of literature's rhetorical power to represent the social, is a gaping aporia. The state of nature operates within a fantastic mode and qualifies as a fiction. These are events 'which no longer [exist], which perhaps never existed, and which probably never will exist, and about which it is nevertheless necessary to have precise Notions in order to judge our present state correctly' (Rousseau 1992a: 13). In Rousseau's political theory the fissure is more subtle than the vast chasm that separates Julie's false happiness from her secret suffering. But for this reason Rousseau's political work allows a more precise identification of the fault line where individuals part ways with the social body, and where natural desires devolve into Elysium's dystopia.

Rousseau's *Discourse on the Origins of Inequality* presents a powerful vision of natural man as a totally self-sufficient being, wanting only readily available resources to meet very basic needs: 'doing only the things he knows and knowing only those things the possession of which is in his power or easily acquired, nothing should be so tranquil as his soul' (Rousseau 1992a: 86, note 9). As a self-contained entity Rousseau's 'savage lives within himself' (ibid. 66). Simple wants and natural abundance render him blissfully autonomous: 'I see him satisfying his hunger under an oak, quenching his thirst at the first stream, finding his bed at the foot of the same tree that furnished his meal; and therewith his needs are satisfied' (ibid. 20). Man does not need others in 'the solitary way of life prescribed to us by Nature' (ibid. 23). Through the state of nature, Rousseau presents a powerful idea of people as independent entities, happiest when alone. In this fantasy, human nature has no innate social principle or faculty. Rousseau disqualifies the family or a need for external authority as possible motivations for socialisation, arguing against Locke and Aristotle respectively (Rousseau 1994c: 132–4).

A move from simple needs to complex desires brings a violent end to this autonomy. Rousseau conjectures: 'the first person who, having fenced off a plot of ground, took it into his head to say *this is mine* and found people simple enough to believe him, was the true founder of civil society' (Rousseau 1992a: 43). The manipulation of nature suggested by the 'fenced off plot of ground' implies the creation of an artificial desire for property, which is no longer spontaneously satiable. This desire is formed randomly and is distinct from innate needs. It becomes entrenched in human interactions.[12] People must now both encroach on others and try to manipulate their environments in order to secure their wellbeing. Even those who abstain from property are forced to protect themselves in order to survive. As humans now function co-dependently, they cease being autonomous. Rousseau explains the irreversible nature of this fall:

> A man who wanted to regard himself as an isolated being, not depending at all on anything and sufficient unto himself, could only be miserable. It would even be impossible for him to subsist. For, finding the whole earth covered with thine and mine and having nothing belonging to him except his body, where would he get his necessities? By leaving the state of Nature, we force our fellows to leave it too. (Rousseau 2010: 342)

In society, people become controlled by external sources. Roger D. Masters traces Rousseau's abrupt termination of the state of nature to his attack on Denis Diderot's *Droit naturel*. Arguing against Diderot and the French Enlightenment, Rousseau suggests that there is no concept of natural law without an attendant notion of civil society (Masters 1968: 269). He criticises philosophers such as Diderot who '[carry] over to the state of Nature ideas they had acquired in society; they spoke about savage man and they described Civil man' (Rousseau 1992a: 19). Diderot, the prototype for Wolmar, cultivates a vision of nature to compensate for an oppressive social environment. Instead, Rousseau presents the state of nature as a hypothetical condition which probably 'never existed' (ibid. 13). He disdains 'destroy[ing] Societies, annihilat[ing] thine and mine, and go[ing] back to live in forests with Bears' (ibid. 79, note 26). The state of nature belongs to a mystic, optative past which can never bear a direct relation to social realities.

In his commentary on Rousseau, Louis Althusser raises the problem of how sociability can emerge *ex nihilo* from this fantasised state of nature. Althusser explains that contracts always involve two pre-existing entities and therefore are inherently sociable and not individualistic in structure:

> in every contract the two Recipient Parties [RP1 and 2] exist prior to and externally to the act of contract. In Rousseau's Social Contract only the RP1 conforms to these conditions. The RP2, on the contrary, escapes them. It does not exist before the contract for a very good reason, it is itself the *product* of the contract. (Althusser 1982: 129)

If every contract must have two pre-existing parties, how can a community be formed from a state of nature in which there are only isolated private individuals? Can political activities such as agreements emerge from an asocial abyss?[13] Christie McDonald suggests that Rousseau's state of nature is an idealised inversion of his disturbing experience of modernity and as such is inherently social in structure:

ideal nature is the antithesis of corrupt society. In fact, it responds point by point to each evil in society; chaos is replaced by order, discord by harmony, and agitation by tranquillity. That is to say, *ideal nature is the negative counterpart of evil society.* (McDonald 1973: 57)

This common source gives nature and society a shared set of images and themes. Rousseau's negative view of society leads him to develop a fantasy of savagery as the antonym of decadent civilisation, but one which effectively collapses these oppositions. Hence, the sexual freedom available to natural man is a development of modern sexual excess; the uniformity of individuals in the state of nature reflects a contemporary tendency to conformity. As Julie's tragic story suggests, all forms of dependencies, upon others or upon resources not immediately available, alienates people, driving them from autonomy to coercion.[14]

Instead of resorting to fantasies of a primitive existence, Rousseau explains that once people have left the state of nature, they must work in groups to protect their wellbeing and, by extension, their property (Rousseau 2010: 341–2). He asserts: 'the basis of the social compact is property, and its first condition that each person continue in the peaceful enjoyment of what belongs to him' (Rousseau 1992b: 163). Property even overrides freedom, because it is more easily seized and more fundamental to survival (ibid. 157). But as in Hobbes's *Leviathan*, this right peacefully to enjoy property is threatened by distorted desires and unequal prospects of meeting them. Rousseau laments the compromises incurred by leaving the state of nature: 'having formerly been free and independent, behold man, due to a multitude of new needs, subjected so to speak to all of Nature and especially to his fellows, whose slave he becomes' (Rousseau 1992a: 51). Because independence is no longer possible, the challenge becomes managing the unnatural reality of dependence, the sudden scarcity of resources, and the excess of new needs as best possible. These needs are responsible for the malaise that Rousseau perceives around him. Once they have departed from self-sufficiency and independence, people form addictions to the vices of comfort and luxury. They become sensitive to inconveniences of which natural man would have been blissfully ignorant. They also suppress their most basic human needs. It is these stifled needs ('*besoins*') that resurface with a vengeance in *Julie* and destroy Clarens's civilised façade at its end. In exchanging basic needs for decadent appetites and desires, people become dependent and thus incomplete. Rousseau suggests that 'our greatest ills come from the efforts made to remedy the smallest ones' (Rousseau 1994b: 40). He describes socialisation as the 'mutilat[ion of] man's constitution' in order to 'transform each individual, who by himself is a perfect and solitary whole, into part of a larger whole' (Rousseau 1994a: 101). This mutilation is effected by the arts, by industry and commerce and by the sciences, which all merely perpetuate the destructive cycle of appetites and suffering.[15] Rousseau's special antipathy for cities is based on the view that societies become corrupt as they become sophisticated. In the preface to *Julie* he argues that only away from 'the bustle of great cities, from large gatherings' can books avail their incontinent readers (Rousseau 1997: 13).

Human needs have changed so radically from the hypothetical state of nature that 'men like me . . . can no longer nourish themselves on grass and nuts, nor do without Laws and Chiefs' (Rousseau 1992a: 79). Instead Rousseau seeks to reframe this loss as a virtue. He explains: 'men become wicked and unhappy in becoming sociable . . . let us attempt to draw from the ill the remedy that should cure it' (Rousseau 1994b: 20). Rousseau posits a binary opposition between nature and society: 'every attentive Reader cannot fail to be struck by the immense space that separates the two states' (Rousseau 1992a: 65). He explains,

> Good social institutions are those that best know how to denature man, to take his absolute existence from him in order to give him a relative one and transport the *I* into the common unity, with the result that each individual believes himself no longer one but part of the unity and no longer feels except within the whole. (Rousseau 2010: 164)

Social problems can only be resolved by further socialisation, by the establishment of ever-more-sophisticated institutions that address society's shortcomings. Hence, Rousseau proposes to heal society through the root cause of all social ills: dependence on others. If people now need each other, they must define a basis of mutuality that overrides mere self-gratification. Tracy B. Strong observes,

> what worries Rousseau about society as it is experienced in the contemporary world (his world and to a great degree still that of the West) is that the actuality of the common, the actuality of my existence *as* your existence (and yours as mine), needs to be reclaimed. (Strong 2002: 34)

This common ground is absent because of what Arthur Melzer calls Rousseau's 'rigorous and sweeping reinterpretation of the political world from the standpoint of the belief in man's asociality' (Melzer 1990: 198). Society must develop from a situation of mutual co-dependence which lacks grounding in human nature.

The first step toward establishing a common social platform is liberation from the unnatural desires that society has formed, which enslave human beings to themselves and each other in the redundant and abusive pursuit of fulfilment. Rousseau refers to this destructive condition as *amour propre*, contrasting it with the natural state of *amour de soi*. In *Rousseau, Judge of Jean-Jacques*, Rousseau defines *amour propre* as 'a relative feeling by which one makes comparisons . . . whose enjoyment is purely negative, and it no longer seeks satisfaction in our benefit but solely in the harm of others' (Rousseau 1990: 9). In the state of nature people are absorbed by immediate needs. In the state of society they become sociable and thereby corrupt: 'as society becomes more closely knit by the bond of mutual needs, as the mind is extended, exercised, and enlightened, it becomes more active, embraces more objects, grasps more relationships, examines, compares' (ibid. 113). Melzer emphasises the imperative to overcome self-gratification in relations of co-dependence, so that socialisation can steer clear of this inevitable course of corruption:

> If men cannot be completely separated they must be completely united. They must never live with others while caring only for themselves. Hence the mission of the political solution is quite simply this: to find a form of association that completely eliminates man's natural selfishness. (Melzer 1990: 94)

Because people are no longer self-sufficient, they must cede their selfishness to find value in each other's company. To make a virtue of the necessity of sociability, Rousseau returns to Hobbes's concept of freedom as a temporary condition or feeling, rather than an innate quality. In *Julie* Saint Preux criticises the need for external sources of freedom: 'I frequently hear people reasoning against man's freedom, and I despise all such sophisms, because it makes no difference if a reasoner proves to me that I am not free; inner sentiment, stronger than all his arguments, constantly belies him' (Rousseau 1997: 561). In justifying her love for Saint Preux, Julie explains that freedom is a state of mind. This way she can be loyal to Wolmar and still love Saint Preux. In the state of society Rousseau redefines freedom as a private feeling, a negative disposition towards one's environment, rather than the positive attribute that it had represented in the state of nature.

Rousseau presents freedom in the state of society as the overcoming of appetite and the false desires of socialisation: 'the impulse of appetite alone is slavery, and obedience to the law one has prescribed for oneself is freedom' (Rousseau 1994c: 142). Through this formulation, one of the first advantages of leaving the state of nature emerges. In having developed exorbitant needs, people also have the challenge of overcoming them and become free. In the state of nature people never needed to obey laws or abstain from appetites, but never acquired a will either. And for Rousseau the will develops through the restraint of desire. He asserts,

> It is not so much understanding which constitutes the distinction of man among the animals, as his being a free agent. Nature commands every animal, and the Beast obeys. Man feels the same impetus, but he realizes that he is free to acquiesce or resist; and it is above all in the consciousness of this freedom that the spirituality of his soul is shown. (Rousseau 1992a: 26)

Only in the state of society can free will be cultivated. Notably, rather than the standard Enlightenment view of reason as a primary social value, Rousseau argues that becoming social means being 'free to acquiesce or resist' desires. This is the upside of the challenge posed by insatiable desires. The greater the urge, the greater the opportunity to rise above it.[16] The very act of leaving the state of nature corresponds to Rousseau's definition of freedom; people resist the beast within themselves, trading a primitive obedience to nature for a possible standpoint of greater servitude, but also potentially of greater self-mastery.

Thus, people transcend their new situation of dependence by asserting their autonomy over appetite and *amour propre*. This prevents various kinds of abuse among members of society, who now no longer assault each other's property or persons in pursuit of fulfilment. But it still does not guarantee a positive basis for mutual coexistence and dependence, which Rousseau has yet to reinterpret as a virtue. Moreover, in an early draft of *The Social Contract*, Rousseau suggests the aetiology of a new variety of suffering caused by inner division between the conflicting pulls of autonomy and sociability:

> What causes human misery is the contradiction between our condition and our desires, between our duties and our inclinations, between nature and social institutions, between the man and the citizen. Make man united and you will make him as happy as he can be. Give him entirely to the state or leave him entirely to himself; but if you divide his heart you tear him to pieces. (Rousseau 1994b: 41)

As humans can no longer be sufficient unto themselves, they must be transformed into consistently sociable creatures, devoted entirely to the state. This requires a radical overhaul of human nature. Rousseau explains:

> One who thinks he is capable of forming a People should feel that he can, so to speak, change human nature. He must transform each individual, who by himself is a perfect and solitary whole, into a part of a larger whole from which this individual receives, in a sense, his life and his being . . . He must, in short, take away all man's own, innate forces in order to give him forces that are foreign to him and that he cannot make use of without the help of others. (Rousseau 1994a: 101)

By substituting asocial human nature with foreign needs that require the help of others, people will be forced to recognise that needing others precludes autonomy. Rousseau thereby addresses the double standard noted by Melzer whereby people 'live with others while caring only for themselves' (Melzer 1990: 94). Rousseau suggests that this dependence on others can be further sublimated into reliance on political institutions. He explains, 'dependence on men, since it is without order, engenders all the vices, and by it, master and slave are mutually corrupted. If there is any means of remedying this ill in society, it is to substitute law for man' (Rousseau 2010: 216–17).

Through the mediating faculty of the general will Rousseau is able to channel self-interest into a broader concern for society. This general will is the foreign element that forces people to recognise themselves as social entities. It replaces the vices of dependence and the *Schadenfreude* of *amour propre* with the virtues of society. Rousseau describes the general will as the mean of all private wills: 'just as it has been said that beauty is only the combination of the most common traits, it can be said that virtue is only the collection of the most general wills' (Rousseau 1994b: 22). Following the Enlightenment ideal of beauty as 'the image of the whole race, which floats among all the variously different intuitions of individuals', the general will represents an assembly of private wills, united by a free-floating common spirit (Kant 2000: 87). In joining society, people convene around shared values of '*freedom* and *equality*' (Rousseau 1994c: 162). They trade their natural liberty for the more sophisticated deferrals of desire which civil freedom provides: '*each of us puts all his power in common under the supreme direction of the general will; and in a body we receive each member as an indivisible part of the whole*' (ibid. 139). Man exchanges his 'natural freedom and an unlimited right to everything that tempts him and that he can get' for 'civil' and 'moral freedom, which alone makes man truly master of himself' (ibid. 141). Because Rousseau equates licence with servitude to appetites he presents the loss of natural freedom as a gain. He suggests that the general will transcends selfish appetites and reinforces civil freedom by addressing people's desire for autonomy.

Through the general will, Rousseau strives to reconcile the dependence of social existence with individual freedom. In turning toward society, people turn away from the needs and appetites which would otherwise hold them in thrall. Melzer observes that this notion of dependence on others does not reflect 'egalitarian moralism or obedience to some preexisting metaphysical or ethical imperative' (Melzer 1990: 158). Rather, it represents a 'horizontal' understanding of virtue as a property which does not reside in higher ends, but in the sphere of interpersonal relations (ibid. 103). Instead of resorting to an external source, people must discover collectivity from within and fashion themselves toward a communal existence. Rousseau presents sociability as an ad-hoc construct rather than an ideal or preordained entity, drawing on the varying needs of differing groups of individuals who live together more from necessity than choice. From this perspective, the general will is a practical, proto-utilitarian device that secures the greatest good for the greatest number of people under the far from perfect conditions of a mutual existence. Its main function is to contain individual appetites and *amour propre*, replacing them with a disposition that is no longer enslaved to appetites and thereby more sociable, and turning dependence from a vice into a virtue.

But even after the foundation of this general will, individuals remain at odds with their social situation, which is counter to a naturally self-centred disposition which they never really shake off. Hence Julie's recognition that despite her decision to marry Wolmar, 'a secret languor worms its way into my heart; I can feel how empty and oppressed it is' (Rousseau 1997: 566). Rousseau suggests that the only freedom that individuals retain in joining the social contract is the right to leave and relinquish their social identity through death as demonstrated by Julie's final plunge into Lake Geneva. Those who cede their wills to the social body are never in complete accord with the general will either. Rousseau ascribes the field of politics to a constant gap between the private and general aspects of the will and the consequent need perpetually to redirect errant 'different interests' toward 'the common interest' (Rousseau 1994c: 147, note). At times, Rousseau seems to suggest that in joining society, people are only obliged to cede those aspects of their wills that pertain to society and can retain other private aspects (Rousseau 1994a: 95). Elsewhere, however, he insists that there is no real distinction between the private and social selves, and that citizens must regard themselves and the state as one (Rousseau 1992b: 155). Rousseau remains sceptical about ever achieving this cohesion, which could only take place in a utopia. Clarens is a fiction. This fictionalisation, when closely pursued in Clarens, proves dystopic. Rousseau does not give any concrete examples of how this cohesion would work in his political theory. And ever practical in his approach, Rousseau emphasises that the general will cannot represent all aspects of society. It is not the sum total of private wills in a community, as the majority is ignorant of its best interests (Rousseau 1994c: 147). Individuals are also usually unable to grasp 'overly general views and overly remote objects', precluding the ability for strategising, abstraction and broad social analysis necessary for determining the common good (ibid. 156). Rousseau suggests that even despotism, which purports to subordinate a multitude to one individual, merely represses this gap between the individual and society rather than overcoming it (ibid. 137). Because individuality remains fundamentally asocial, socialisation must rely on conformity – on the coercion of individual volition in the name of a greater good, a reiteration of Adam Smith's 'problem' – the notorious conflict between individual and collective perspectives, which also becomes Rousseau's problem.

As the general will is constantly besieged by divergent individual wills, Rousseau argues that the common interest needs to be secured through a social contract. The social contract is 'a form of association that defends and protects the person and goods of each associate with all the common force, and by means of which each one, uniting with all, nevertheless obeys only himself and remains as free as before' (Rousseau 1994c: 138). Instead of collapsing individual wills into a common body the social contract – an agreement among individuals to adhere to the general will – purports to maintain the freedom of its constituents. Yet Rousseau's definition of freedom as the surmounting of private appetite in the interests of 'common utility' renders this a less liberating proposition than it might otherwise appear (Rousseau 1994a: 94). In overcoming personal volition but still retaining their freedom, individuals are actually required to cede all vestiges of autonomy: 'properly understood, all of these clauses come down to a single one, namely the total alienation of each associate, with all his rights, to the whole community' (Rousseau 1994c: 138). The social contract thereby demands the unreserved relinquishing of individual volition. Its freedom is really tantamount to conformism, as each member of society is called upon to '[alienate] . . . all his rights, to the whole community' (ibid. 138). Instead of bringing individuals together, institutions that are formed to protect private individuals actually keep them apart.

In struggling to transform naturally asocial human beings into functioning members of society, Rousseau reverses his former priorities. If individuality was anterior to sociability, now the individual becomes entirely subordinate to society. In joining the social contract, the political subject undergoes an immediate and dramatic transformation from which (as Rousseau suggests in *Julie*) there is no return:

> Instantly, in place of the private person of each contracting party, this act of association produces a moral and collective body, composed of as many members as there are voices in the assembly, which receives from this same act its unity, its common *self*, its life, and its will. (Rousseau 1994c: 139)

This transformation of the various members of society into a collective embodiment of the general will is meliorated by Rousseau's suggestion that the general will and the social contract enhance personal freedom and independence.[17] Nonetheless, two related problems emerge in the sublimation of individual wills into the general will. The first is how to resolve conflicts between the individual and general will when personal interest clashes with the greater good. This type of problem is frequent, because of the perpetual gap between naturally asocial human nature and the socially constructed general will, as suggested by Julie's dilemma between love and duty. And the second concerns the nature of the collective body established by the social contract and how it differs from either its individual constituents or its individual ruler.

Addressing these questions, Affeldt suggests that Rousseau is less concerned with conflict between the individual and general wills than with preventing the total collapse of the private will into the general will (Affeldt 1999: 310). The general will must remain active in terms of its constituents in order to retain its status as a will. It relies entirely on individual volition and participation for its existence, 'receiv[ing] from this same act its unity, its common *self*, its life, and its will' (Rousseau 1994c: 139). Therefore, according to Affeldt, 'the possibility of society . . . depends upon the work of individuation', on the active involvement of individuals in the general will (Affeldt 2000: 556). Society requires 'a continuous effort of self-transformative work . . . [with] individuation as its central principle' (ibid. 588). If people flag in this task by locating the responsibility for their existence beyond themselves, they must be redirected to freedom through philosophy and education, which will give them a more active role in the general will (Affeldt 1999: 317–18). Affeldt's argument helps elucidate Rousseau's view of the relationship between the individual and general wills as one of fruitful conflict, along the lines that Kant would develop in his categorical imperative. In *Emile*, where Rousseau provides a programme for training the will, he explains,

> It is . . . hard to see how we one can be certain that a particular will always will agree with this general will. One ought rather to presume that the particular will will often be contrary to the general will, for private interest always tends to preferences, and the public interest always tends to equality. (Rousseau 2010: 654)

This friction between personal and common interests is healthy for the will. Rousseau suggests that 'virtue belongs to a being that is weak by nature and strong by will. It is in this that the merit of the just man consists' (Rousseau 2010: 633). Kant's development of Rousseau's view of human beings as complex agents who must work on self-transformation to become moral agents has coloured subsequent readings of Rousseau's general will (Schneewind 1998: 507). Yet it is here that Kant and Rousseau part ways. Rousseau posits that 'whoever refuses to obey the general will shall be constrained to do so by the entire body; which means only that he will be forced to be free' (Rousseau 1994c: 141). Affeldt invokes Kant to apologise for this notorious solution. He concedes that the verb 'force' is stronger than necessary to connote the mere guidance of stray wills and ascribes this to emphatic purpose, drawing attention to the urgent vigilance with which society must protect the freedom of its members (Affeldt 1999: 315). Yet Rousseau's main use of rhetoric in this passage is neither emphatic nor hyperbolic but in fact oxymoronic. The collocation of forced freedom undermines Rousseau's most cherished values in terms of the nature of freedom and the illegitimacy of force, drawing his discourse back to the familiar figure of paradox and to the Smith problem.

In the opening of *The Social Contract*, Rousseau asserts freedom as an inalienable human essence: 'to renounce one's freedom is to renounce one's status as a man' (Rousseau 1994c: 135). He also questions the authority of force: 'force is a physical power. I do not see what morality can result from its effects. Yielding to force is an act of necessity, not of will' (ibid. 133). Rousseau premises the general will – the cornerstone of his political theory – on an immoral action contradictory to his conviction that 'force is . . . not of the will' (ibid. 200). Rousseau acknowledges this problem: 'it is asked how a man can be free and forced to conform to wills that are not his own' (ibid. 200). He deems 'the question . . . badly put. The Citizen consents to all the laws, even to those passed in spite of him' (ibid. 200). Because the individual is entirely absorbed within the general will, holding an opinion contrary to the general will is a threat to one's freedom – to one's conformity to society – and must be met with force (ibid. 201). Rousseau follows Hobbes in redefining freedom as the fulfilment of social duty, so that forcing someone to conform to social expectations would, in a very peculiar sense, safeguard their freedom. But individuals lack an inclination toward the general will and need to be coerced into compliance. And force must be interpreted as freedom in order to support this argument. Rousseau's reliance on a form of power that he deems both immoral and ineffectual points to a deficiency in the basis for cohesion among individuals. As Rousseau observes toward the beginning of *The Social Contract*, slaves come to 'love their servitude' and the chains that coerce them (ibid. 133). Yet instead of justifying slavery, this merely attests to the power of force to pervert the individual will.

Similar difficulties contort Rousseau's discussion of government. Although Rousseau clearly exonerates sovereigns from individual interests and desires, he concedes that 'the vices that make social institutions necessary are the same ones that make their abuse inevitable'

(Rousseau 1992a: 62). The extent to which the sovereign embodies society as a whole, or his own personal agenda, remains a concern. To avoid despotism, Rousseau proposes the institution of a great legislator who will mediate between the sovereign and the people. But this great legislator's necessary separation of powers renders him unable to enforce order: 'one finds combined in the work of legislation two things that seem incompatible: an undertaking beyond human force and, to execute it, an authority that amounts to nothing' (1994c: 156). The great legislator is unable to reconcile individual and collective interests and provides a moot solution to the deep-set problem of cohesion.

Because Rousseau understands socialisation as a secondary property of human nature, society remains no more than the sum of its parts. Rousseauvian society can only be secured through repressive practices of forceful leadership which Rousseau strongly condemns in other contexts. In *The Social Contract*, he resists social disintegration by suggesting that individuals must relegate their freedom and be forced into compliance. Yet, as he observes in *Emile*, the members of society subsequently become internally divided to the point of ineffectuality:

> Always in contradiction with himself, always floating between his inclinations and his duties, he will never be either man or citizen. He will be good neither for himself nor for others. He will be one of these men of our days; a Frenchman, an Englishman, a Bourgeois. He will be nothing. (Rousseau 2010: 164)

This limbo between self and society has a paralysing effect.

> Swept along in contrary routes by nature and by men, forced to divide ourselves between these different impulses, we follow a composite impulse which leads us to neither one goal nor the other. Thus, in conflict and floating during the whole course of our life, we end it without having been able to put ourselves in harmony. (Rousseau 2010: 165)

Human nature's asocial origins and constitution lead to a profound disjuncture between self and society. Instead of resurrecting fragments of the ghost of Aristotle to fill the gap, as does Smith, or a Kantian transcendence of self (Affeldt's reading), Rousseau moves to a more fractured understanding of the subject position, which is internally divided by the conflicting exigencies of private and communal needs. The sense of self-division and of an ensuing self-consciousness parallel to that of Smith made Rousseau particularly appealing to Romantic-era writers in Britain, faced with post-revolutionary disappointment and its frustrated vision of sociability. Subsequently in the works of Coleridge, Godwin and Shelley, Rousseau's ghost exorcises and replaces Aristotle's.

Notes

1. In *Rousseau, Judge of Jean-Jacques*, Rousseau describes Saint Preux as a younger version of himself (Rousseau 1990: 90). The English philosopher is the fictional Milord Edward Bomston, who represents a position of narrow empiricism which Rousseau contrasts with Saint Preux's liberal outlook.
2. See for example David Hume's use of autobiography at the end of book one of *A Treatise of Human Nature*. Having just rejected 'the most usual conjunctions of cause and effect', Hume describes the impact of this theory on his own sense of identity, which becomes fractured and at times incoherent (Hume 1978: 267). Through this self-portrait, Hume casts doubt on the scepticism which he has just set forth. Another example discussed in the previous chapter is Smith's invisible hand. Smith mitigates his position by using a literary figure instead of direct argumentation to question Aristotle's dominant legacy.
3. See, for example, Thomas McFarland (McFarland 1995: 50–1) and David Marshall (Marshall 1988: 152). This tendency to read Rousseau as an apolitical, sentimental writer has been noted by Gary Kelly (Kelly 1982: 93) and by Eugene Stelzig (Stelzig 2000: 41–2).
4. And from an inverse perspective to Starobinski's, Christopher Kelly reads Rousseau's literary works as political theory, suggesting that 'historical accounts of particular events can be read as moral fables', so that in *The Confessions* individual experience functions as an exemplary account of human nature and as a model for political citizenship (Kelly 1987: 47).
5. Tragedy has been questioned as a model for reading Rousseau. Rowan Boyson argues that readings of Rousseau as a tragically isolated figure are anachronistic, and represent values of Anglophone liberalism; instead, Rousseau needs to be understood through an alternative concept of pleasure (Boyson 2012: 65–6). Sandra Macpherson classifies contract theory within an emergent eighteenth-century anti-tragic tradition that emphasises legal rights rather than the potentially tragic predicament of liabilities (Macpherson 2010: 7).
6. In addition, Rousseau's extremely lengthy and digressive footnotes to the *Discourse on the Origins of Inequality* establish a similar ironic distance from the main text by developing an editorial persona who invites his readers to withdraw and reflect on alternative lines of thought. For example, Rousseau deviates from his discussion of natural man to develop a lengthy five-page taxonomy of monsters observed by travellers (Rousseau 1992a: 81–6, note). Through this sojourn Rousseau implicitly invites his readers to compare natural man with monsters, casting further doubt on the conjectural history set forth in the main body of the *Second Discourse*.
7. Rainer Warning reads the Enlightenment genre of the *conte philosophique*, to which *Julie* belongs, as aporias which reflect on the limits of Enlightenment ideology (Warning 1992: 142).
8. In the original Rousseau refers to spouses as '*des époux*' (Rousseau 1970: 453).
9. Lisa Disch remarks on a tension between 'the virtue story and the friendship story [which] exemplifies a more general tension in Rousseau's corpus,

between Rousseau the Enlightenment theorist and Rousseau the romantic' (Disch 1994: 22). I disagree with Disch's argument that Claire represents passion and a subversive concern with female friendships. Rather, the character of Claire, counterbalanced by Edward Bomston, fills the function of comic relief, offsetting the tragic story of Julie and Saint Preux.

10. On the critical relationship between Rousseau and Smith, see Dennis Rasmussen, who argues that they represent opposed Enlightenment and counter-Enlightenment positions on major questions of progress and liberty (Rasmussen 2013).

11. The gendering of this assertion is not incidental. Mary Wollstonecraft famously criticises Rousseau for viewing women as lesser individuals than men in her *Vindication of the Rights of Woman*. In Rousseau's *Discourse on the Origins of Inequality*, natural man is clearly gendered as male. Rousseau describes reproduction from a male vantage point, explaining that natural man had

> one appetite that invited him to perpetuate his species, and this blind inclination, devoid of any sentiment of the heart, produced only a purely animal act. This need satisfied, the two sexes no longer meant anything to each other, and even the child no longer meant anything to his mother as soon as he could do without her. (Rousseau 1992a: 43)

Here the emphasis is clearly on the father and child, whom Rousseau imagines as oblivious of biological dependence, rather than on the gestating mother. These attitudes are supported by Rousseau's comments on his own children in *The Confessions*, whom he placed in a foundling hospital immediately after birth (Rousseau 1995: 299–300). Yet in *Julie*, Rousseau foregrounds questions about the relationship between gender and autonomy. Julie appeals to St. Preux to 'consider the situation of my Sex and yours' in terms of her recent pregnancy and miscarriage (Rousseau 1997: 173). Rousseau also frames his novel with the argument that 'if there is some reform to be attempted in public morals, it must begin with domestic morals' (ibid. 17).

12. Rousseau clearly distinguishes between *besoins* and desires. Whereas needs are primary, passion/desire expresses corrupting secondary dependencies: 'the less natural and urgent the needs, the more the passions augment' (Rousseau 1992a: 75, note 7). These passions produce a craving for destructive luxuries, such as 'corrupted foodstuffs, falsified drugs' (ibid. 76, note 7).

13. This criticism of the state of nature also emerges in Coleridge's reading of *Leviathan*. Coleridge reasons that 'fear presupposes conquest, and conquest a previous vision and agreement between the conquerors' (Coleridge 1968: 64).

14. Hina Nazar emphasises that *Julie*'s ending subverts values of citizenship and domesticity as Julie is not effectively rehabilitated by Wolmar from her fallen state (Nazar 2012: 97).

15. In 1749, Rousseau wrote his first political treatise, a *Discourse on the Sciences and Arts*, in response to the Academy of Dijon's proposed topic: 'has the restoration of the sciences and arts tended to purify morals?'

(Rousseau 1994d: xi) His negative response won the first prize and launched a lifelong critique of Enlightenment notions of progress.

16. In *Emile*, Rousseau presents a somewhat less magnanimous answer to this question. Rather than proposing the overcoming of desires, he prescribes their abstention:

> From where does man's weakness come? From the inequality between his strength and his desires. It is our passions that make us weak, because to satisfy them we would need more strength than nature gives us. Therefore, diminish desires and you will increase strength. (Rousseau 2010: 309)

17. Neil Saccamano explains that the socially constructed social contract must be presented as natural, rather than human-made. Rousseau sees the people as too unreasonable to be swayed by argumentative discourse; violent imposition is equally ineffective in obtaining genuine consensus. Consequently, 'the legislator must wrest consensus while troping its violence as an imminent, self-moving force' (Saccamano 1992: 746). People must be led to believe that the social contract reflects their own natural predilections and a broader natural order, which are both in fact socially constructed by its legislator.

Part II

Poetry

Chapter 3

Coleridge's Exile from the Social Contract, 1795–1829

Ending in Mere Nothingism: Pantisocracy to Idealism

In the *Biographia Literaria* Samuel Taylor Coleridge cites his 'Satyrane's Letters', recording his voyage from England to Germany of 1798, which was marred by anticlimax. Coleridge explains: 'I had associated such an immensity with the ocean, that I felt exceedingly disappointed, when I was out of sight of all land, at the narrowness and *nearness*, as it were, of the circle of the horizon' (Coleridge 1983: 2.169).

This sense of being hemmed in by the sea is familiar from Coleridge's *Rime of the Ancient Mariner*. In his letters, the ideological underpinnings of the feeling of confinement become apparent. Coleridge had expected the sea to encompass infinitude, representing his hopes that Idealism would exceed the bounds of his early Pantisocracy and Hartleyan empiricism.[1] But these traditions converge vertiginously; Coleridge's intellectual horizons – represented by the sea – prove narrower than he had hoped. Instead of representing disparate ideologies, the philosophical tensions of Coleridge's engagements at home anticipate those awaiting him in Germany. Such states of angst and unease, common in Coleridge's writings, have been interpreted ideologically since the 1980s, and connected to the historical transition from revolutionary to bourgeois epochs.[2] Changes in the social body alter Coleridge's sense of his own private body. I suggest that Coleridge's inner tensions draw on the strains between individuals and the social body in the social contract tradition.

Coleridge often describes the individual and social bodies as closely interrelated, linking personal distemper to social unrest. In his letters, he writes to John Morgan that his opium addiction has the effect of severing him internally, finally pushing him away from the social body:

> my Volition (by which I mean the faculty *instrumental* to the Will, and by which alone the Will can realize itself – its Hands, Legs, & Feet, as it were) was completely deranged, at times frenzied, dissevered itself from the Will, & became an independent faculty. (Coleridge 2002: 3.489)

Opium fragments the individual into disparate fractions, so that Coleridge's legislative and executive functions (to which he refers as 'the will' and the 'volition') are separated – like the parts of Rousseau's general will. Coleridge describes opium addiction to Lord Byron 'as a specific madness which leaving the intellect uninjured and exciting the moral feelings to a cruel sensibility entirely suspended the moral will' (Coleridge 2002: 4.626). Opium does not damage Coleridge's 'moral feeling' – his self-awareness of his character and of his behaviour; what it impairs is his ability to act on his judgments, ensuing in both frenzy and humiliation. Finally the loss of the will leads to a sense of vacancy. Coleridge's reduced volition led him to mirror the views of his addressees in his letters, and extends to the subjects that he wrote about (McFarland 1995: 119).[3]

Central among these subjects of Coleridge's identification is Rousseau. Coleridge's engagement with Rousseau's legacy and with social contract theory has not been significant to ideological readings of his works, which usually focus on 1790s politics and on German Idealism.[4] In addition to his political engagements, Coleridge wrote extensively about Rousseau over his long and varied career. He published an article comparing Rousseau to Luther in his journal *The Friend* (1809). He discussed Rousseau in works as far apart as his *Lectures 1795 on Politics and Religion* of 1795 and *On the Constitution of the Church and State* of 1829. Coleridge frequently mentions Rousseau in his letters, dated from the early 1790s to the late 1820s, suggesting his ongoing preoccupation with Rousseau in a career traditionally polarised into radical and conservative phases. These writings on Rousseau have been relatively neglected but shed light on Coleridge's preoccupation with the fragmented social body.[5]

Coleridge began his career with the short-lived dream of forming a Pantisocratic community on the banks of the Susquehanna River with Thomas Poole, Robert Southey and John Thelwall, as recounted by Charles Lloyd in the dialogue between the protagonist and Charles Maurice in his novel *Edmund Oliver*.[6] Coleridge adopts Adam Smith's view that society has an underlying political-economic infrastructure, repeating *The Wealth of Nations*' postulation that the rich will support the poor by providing employment and other resources that eventually trickle down the social ladder to benefit all (Smith 1993: 9).[7] Poole's exposition of Pantisocracy follows Smith's proto-utilitarian principles, but redistributes its surplus to benefit the literati. Poole calculates that because 'there is not above one productive man in twenty . . . if each laboured the twentieth part of his time it would produce enough to satisfy their wants' (Poole 1888: 97–8). This would mean that 'each man should labour two or three hours in a day, the produce of which labour would, they imagine, be more than sufficient to support the economy' (ibid. 97). In the remaining time, 'a good library of books is to be collected, and their leisure hours to be spent in study, liberal discussions, and the education of their children' (ibid. 98). This alternative social model, which Poole formulated in collaboration with Coleridge and his circle, redefined writing, which had been understood as a precarious occupation, as something sustainable and productive.

To be sure, the dream of making it in poetry played its part. Coleridge reports that a man recently returned from America says 'that literary characters make *money* there' (Coleridge 2002: 1.99).[8] But Coleridge's plan of immigration, with its attendant hasty marriage and shared property, defined Pantisocracy by actively negating Smith's vision of luxury and commerce: Pantisocracy requires 'an abolition of individual property' (ibid. 1.96). Instead, of laissez-faire capitalism, Coleridge advocates a collective social model: 'I have positively done nothing but dream the System of no Property every step of the way' (ibid. 1.90). Thus, Coleridge retains Smith's concept of an underlying system uniting individuals, but does not assume that individual property will find its way back to the community. Instead, he merges Smith's notion of system with eclectic anti-materialist sources drawn from Rousseau and his Christian heritage.[9] Coleridge uses Rousseau's language of contract theory, referring to the need 'to sketch out the code of contracts necessary for the internal regulation of the society' (ibid. 1.96). To Thelwall, Coleridge explains that

> the real source of inconstancy, depravity, & prostitution, is *Property*, which mixes with & poisons every thing good – & is beyond doubt the Origin of all Evil . . . Yes! Thelwall! the disciples of Lord Shaftesbury & Rosseau [*sic*], as well as of Jesus. (Coleridge 2002: 1.214)

In his Bristol coffeehouse lectures, given to raise funds for Pantisocracy, Coleridge presents Christ and Rousseau as kindred spirits, separated only by the atheism of Rousseau's times, which Coleridge dismisses as the contingent legacy of 'the political and moral philosophy of English Free-thinkers re-modelled by *Parisian Fort Esprits*' (Coleridge 1969a: 142–3). In all other respects, Coleridge suggests that Rousseau and Christ live in comparably corrupt materialistic societies. Christ grows up 'untinged with one prejudice of that most prejudiced people among whom he was educated', immune to the alleged Jewish love of money, a mainstay of anti-Semitic stereotypes (Coleridge 1969b: 159–60). Like Christ, Rousseau is educated in a society corrupted by materialism, but remains a Christian at heart: his 'reasonings would not suffer him to believe the miracles of Jesus, but . . . [his] heart had too much of Man, too little of Atheist in it, not to feel and profess, that the God of Love was in him' (ibid. 160).

Extending the comparison, Coleridge suggests that Christ and Rousseau respond to their toxic environments in a similar manner, by chiselling out social covenants that counteract prejudice by protecting individual rights. Coleridge's Bristol lectures echo the main arguments of Rousseau's political theory. Coleridge praises a Jewish 'Original Contract', which he defines as a principle of communal property that distinguished Jews from polytheists as precursors of Christianity (Coleridge 1969b: 118).[10] Like Rousseau, he justifies this theory of collective property by denouncing materialism:

> As Manufactures improved and the artificial Want[s] of Life increased, inequality of life became more mark'd and enviable and the motives to mutual Injury numerous. From their undisciplined Passions as Individuals and as Communities, private Vices and Public Wars became frequent – and the influence of Kings and Chieftains increased with Despotism. Thus the jarring Interests of Individuals rendered Governments necessary and governments have operated like quack Medicines; they have produced new diseases, and only checked the old ones – and the evils which they check, they perpetuate. (Coleridge 1969b: 219)

Because political institutions and governments only worsen the cycle of material dependence and inequality, Coleridge searches for an egalitarian alternative. He reiterates Rousseau's *Discourse on the Origins of Inequality* to attack the slave trade. 'whence arise our Miseries? Whence arise our Vices? From artificial Wants' (Coleridge 1969b: 235). These wants enslave individuals to artificial needs and eventually produce a trade in human lives, so that commodity culture turns people into things, a position that we can recall from Rousseau's attack on luxury. Coleridge's comments present a complex view of the social body as a plastic organism, which both fashions individual desires and modifies in response to them – one in which people are subject to social forces but can resist automatisation by impacting and shaping their environments.

Because individual desires and the social body reciprocally form one another, Coleridge suggests that full political citizenship must begin with changes to the private body.[11] In *The Social Contract*, Rousseau describes the general will as an instantaneous and permanent chemical change to the private body, a 'formula' from which there is no reprieve (Rousseau 1994c: 139–41). David William Bates notes that 'the difficult and seemingly magical transformation of independent, isolated individuals into a new unitary political whole must be understood as analogous to a chemical process', drawing on developments in eighteenth-century science (Bates 2012: 190). The rules governing this transformation of matter into an organised structure, like those governing the transition from the individual to the general will, remain perplexingly vague to the late eighteenth-century imagination. Coleridge's Pantisocracy involves a bottom-up model, whereby change begins with the individual. Therefore, 'those of us whose bodies, from habits of sedentary study or academic indolence, have not acquired their full tone and strength [should] learn the theory and practice of agriculture and carpentry' (Coleridge 2002: 1.97). Coleridge associates agriculture with a return to the land and to the state of nature, and carpentry with religion; after all Christ was 'the son of a carpenter' (Coleridge 1969b: 160). While Pantisocracy repeats the Puritan fantasy of leaving Europe and forming a new state of nature in America, Coleridge adopts Rousseau's construction of the peoples of North and South America as the antithesis of *fin-de-siècle* European decline. In the *Second Discourse*, Rousseau had asserted that 'the reports of travellers [to South America] are full of examples of the strength and vigour of men in barbarous and Savage Nations' (Rousseau 1992a: 72). Close to God and nature, and far from European luxury, Coleridge anticipates forming an alternative rural community on egalitarian principles in America.

Coleridge uses the symbol of the body politic to express this aspiration to sociability. Ernest Kantorowicz explains that by conceptualising the state as a body, early modern theorists of the body politic aligned political authority with the mystical power of the church (Kantorowicz 1957: 271).[12] Coleridge's Pantisocracy letters draw on this traditional political theology, which brings together state, religious authority and the self within the overarching figure of community:

> Pantisocracy – O I shall have a scheme of it! My head, my heart are all alive – I have drawn up my arguments in battle array – they shall have the *Tactician* Excellence of the Mathematician with the Enthusiasm of the Poet – The Head shall be the Mass – the Heart the fiery Spirit, that fills, informs, and agitates the whole. (Coleridge 2002: 1.103)

In this extended comparison, Coleridge conceives of his own body as a miniature society which he divides and marshals into constituents with discrete vocations (mathematics and poetry), and identifies through its various organs (the head and heart). In his later treatise, *On the Constitution of the Church and State*, Coleridge explains why the commonplace type of the body politic has mattered to him:

> It would be difficult in the whole company of language, to find a metaphor so commensurate, so pregnant, so suggesting so many points of elucidation, as that of *Body Politic* . . . The correspondence between the Body Politic to the Body Natural holds even in the detail of application. (Coleridge 1976: 84–5)

Explaining a parallel use of metaphor to politicians in *The Statesman's Manual*, Coleridge suggests that 'the elements of necessity and free-will are reconciled in the higher power of an omnipresent Providence that predestines the whole in the moral freedom of the integral parts' (Coleridge 1972: 31). The body politic and omnipresent providence both emphasise an interdependence between parts and whole, individual body and higher power – the system that breaks apart in Coleridge's opium addiction. Coleridge discusses Andrew Marvell's poem 'On a Drop of Dew' to demonstrate this model of reciprocity:

> Are we struck with admiration at beholding the Cope of Heaven imagined in a Dew-drop? The least of the animalcula to which that drop would be an Ocean contains in itself an infinite problem of which God Omni-present is the only solution. (Coleridge 1972: 50)

Coleridge envisions the self as a part of a larger whole through registers in which the literary, the political and the theological mutually reinforce and refract one another. Increasingly his understanding of this relationship emphasises the tension between disparate concepts of freedom and sovereign authority. In the *Biographia Literaria* Coleridge rejects David Hartley's argument that the mind is mechanically produced through the act of perception, referring to Hartley's theory as internal division 'between the despotism of outward impressions, and that of senseless and passive memory' (Coleridge 1983: 1.110). Instead, of obeying the senses the will must precede the environment and the subjects perceiving it (ibid. 1.112). Coleridge's use of the political language of despotism indicates that the argument for epistemological independence is also an argument for individual freedom.

Coleridge's support of Pantisocracy breaks down when he discovers Southey's withholding of private funds from their joint account for establishing their settlement. Coleridge accuses Southey of being 'one who had fallen back on ranks ... Your Sun was Set: your Sky was clouded' (Coleridge 2002: 1.166). He conceptualises Southey's corruption through imagery of natural decline, expressing the demise of his former fantasy of returning to the state of nature. Coleridge now modifies his approach to the social contract and the body politic, regarding them in hierarchical rather than egalitarian terms:

> Mind hath a divine right of sovereignty over Body – But who shall dare to transfer the reasoning 'from Man to Brute' to 'from Man to Man[']! To be employed in the Till of the Field while *We* are pursuing philosophical Studies – can Earldoms or Emperorships boast so huge an inequality? (Coleridge 2002: 1.122)

The fantasy of working only several hours a day and devoting the rest to writing relies on the labour of large groups of society, degraded to the status of beasts of burden. Southey's selfishness reveals the foundation of this model of sociability on oppression and inequality rather than mutual agreement, a pattern anticipated by Hartley's despotic empiricist epistemology. The social contract of Pantisocracy breaks down.

It is here that Coleridge turned to German Idealism and began planning his voyage to Germany. His concern with Idealist philosophy is usually dated to approximately 1801, after his famous collaboration with Wordsworth and the initial drafting of his major poetry. But this leaves critics with a puzzle: Coleridge's major poetry seems to enlist German Idealism proleptically, before Coleridge had actually read any of its works.[13] It has recently been established that Coleridge developed his Idealist views through direct avenues of reception, traced by Monika Class who has demonstrated Coleridge's familiarity with Kant's student, F. A. Nitsch (Class 2012: 40–5). Nitsch published and lectured on Kant's theory of the will as an autonomous faculty to British rational dissenting and radical circles in the mid-1790s (ibid. 192–3). From Nitsch's perspective, echoed in Coleridge's comments on Hartley, Kantianism was as much a political position as it was an Idealist abstraction, an alternative to the conservatism and determinism that Nitsch associated with British empiricism (ibid. 73). Coleridge's engagement with Kant was heavily determined by his previous exposure to Rousseau's arguments for individual freedom articulated in *The Social Contract* and the *Second Discourse*, and played out in the Pantisocracy scheme. Following the 1794 Pantisocracy crisis, Coleridge proposed 'studying German, & in about six weeks, [hopes to] be able to read the language with tolerable fluency' (Coleridge 2002: 1.209). He foresaw that this would enable him '[to translate] all the works [of] Schiller' and also 'of Kant, the great German Metaphysician' (ibid.1.209).[14] These comments follow on the heels of his previous disappointment with Rousseau's theory of equality and with Hartleyan empiricism, suggesting that Coleridge associates his earlier engagements with his subsequent interest in German Idealism.

In *On the Constitution of the Church and State* Coleridge cites

Rousseau's note on François Prévost's *Histoire generale des voyages* in the *Discourse on the Origins of Inequality*, voicing his disdain for the 'state of nature, or the Ouran Outang theology of the origin of the human race' (Coleridge 1976: 66; Rousseau 1992a: 186, note 85). Radically dismissing the objection that language distinguishes humans from animals, Rousseau speculates that orang-utans may be humans still living in a primitive state of nature (Rousseau 1992a: 81–2, note 8). Primates, Africans and Europeans share common origins, by Rousseau's account reflecting an egalitarian potential. Coleridge rejects this radical hypothesis, and Rousseau's postulation of the individual as the originary social unit.[15] He argues against Rousseau that humans do not originate in a state of nature. Instead, Coleridge searches for continuity and refers to history as 'the great drama of an unfolding providence' (Coleridge 1976: 32). He draws a contrast between his own progressive theological model and Rousseau's contract, determining

> Every reader of Rousseau, or of Hume's Essays, will understand me when I refer to the Original Social Contract, assumed by Rousseau and by other wiser men before him, as the basis of all legitimate government ... I shall run little hazard at this time of day, in declaring the pretended fact a pure fiction, and the conception of such a fact an idle fantasy. It is at once false and foolish. For what if an original contract had actually been entered into, and formally recorded? Still I cannot see what addition of moral force would be gained by the fact. The same sense of moral obligation which binds us to keep it, must have pre-existed in the same force and in relation to the same duties, impelling our ancestors to make it. (Coleridge 1976: 14)

Coleridge's opinion on Rousseau and the times that have formed him alters dramatically. While the Bristol lectures compare Rousseau to Christ, and suggest that both reacted to analogous forms of prejudice by forming social contracts, Coleridge now presents Rousseau as foolish and misled. He rejects all models of contract outright, including Hume's more conservative modification of contract. Coleridge's objection to Rousseau's theory of contract anticipates Adam Ferguson's (and Louis Althusser's) criticism that any contract presupposes the pre-existence of parties and interests (Ferguson 1978: 2.244; Althusser 1982: 129).

In *The Friend* Coleridge further develops his objection to Rousseau by establishing a negative analogy to Luther, the great church reformer. The relative dearth of commentary on Coleridge's response to social contract theory may be due in part to the vehemently negative quality of what Coleridge has to say about Rousseau in this context. In *The Friend* Coleridge expresses open disgust with

> the crazy ROUSSEAU, the Dreamer of lovesick Tales and the spinner of speculative cobwebs; shy of light as the Mole, but as quick-eared too for

every whisper of the public opinion; the Teacher of stoic *PRIDE* in his principles, yet the victim of morbid *Vanity* in his feelings and conduct! (Coleridge 1969a: 132)

Coleridge suggests that Rousseau's subterraneous antisocial disposition compromises his integrity. Rousseau becomes consumed with *amour propre* and is excessively vain and anxious to please public tastes. And his judgment is impaired by 'the strange influence of his bodily temperament on his understanding', states of disintegration which recall Coleridge's own opium-induced angst (Coleridge 1969a: 134).

In considering Rousseau, Coleridge reflects on the role that politics have played and speculates how different Luther would have been had he been born 'a citizen of Geneva': 'we [would] lose the great reformer' (Coleridge 1969a: 142–3). Being a scapegoat no longer guarantees that one can speak up against the crowd. Social conditions now assume a more deterministic function. Yet as a result, Coleridge also understands Rousseau as more sinned against than sinning, and identifies with his persecuted status, conceiving of himself within Rousseau's porous legacy. He shares Rousseau's 'constitutional melancholy pampered into a morbid excess by solitude', with his embittered political ambition and sense of redundancy (ibid. 134). Coleridge regards both himself and Rousseau as victims of a revolutionary era in which individuals have been granted autonomy but not the means for cooperation, effecting a crisis between the various legislative and executive functionings of the will.

Coleridge locates Rousseau within the breakdown of Smithian political economy and the disappointment of broader aspirations to social unity and coherence, impacted by the collapse of Pantisocracy and the French Revolution. Reassessing Rousseau's legacy, Coleridge maintains that 'the whole ground work of Rousseau's philosophy ends in mere Nothingism' (Coleridge 1969a: 159). He criticises 'the falsehood and nothingness of the whole system' (ibid. 193). Coleridge's frequent repetition of 'nothingness' and 'Nothingism', expressing the empty, arbitrary 'system' that Coleridge attributes to Rousseau, points to a catachrestic gap in political terminology, which has no vocabulary for talking about a common social body. Thomas McFarland connects Coleridge's coinage of 'Nothingism' to the nihilism of Friedrich Jacobi, who regarded the Enlightenment passion for unitary explanation as a vacant project that masked an underlying emptiness and covert atheism (McFarland 1995: 261; di Giovanni 2005: 11–12). Better to be born in Luther's Saxony than to be a citizen of Geneva, or of 1790s England. This unease anticipates Coleridge's subsequent endorsement of German Idealism as a theory which rewrites autonomy in positive terms.

Coleridge also conceptualises his shared emptiness with Rousseau in literary terms, as a preference for theory rather than poetry.[16] Turning away from society also means '[turning] away from . . . all the flowers & herbs that grow in the Light and Sunshine – to be meanwhile a Delver in the unwholesome quick-silver mines of abstruse Metaphysics' (Coleridge 2002: 2.1178). In the *Biographia Literaria* Coleridge uses similar language to write about the positive influence of William Lisle Bowles's sonnets on his own poetry: 'well were it for me perhaps, had I never relapsed into the same mental disease; if I had continued to pluck the flower and reap the harvest from the cultivated surface, instead of delving in the unwholesome quicksilver mines of metaphysic depths' (Coleridge 1983: 1.17). Coleridge contrasts his own attraction to obscure philosophy with Wordsworth's powerful vocation as 'a great, a true Poet – [while] I am only a kind of metaphysician' (Coleridge 2002: 1.658). Hence, Coleridge clearly associates poetry with sociability, and philosophy with withdrawal. He writes,

> From my very childhood I have been accustomed to *abstract* and as it were unrealize whatever of more than common interest my eyes dwelt on: and then by a sort of transfusion or transmission of my consciousness to identify with the Object – and I have often thought, within the last five or six years, that if ever I should feel once again the genial warmth and stir of the poetic impulse . . . I should venture on a yet stranger and wilder Allegory than of yore – that I would *allegorize* myself, as a Rock with its summit just raised above the surface of some Bay or Strait in the Arctic Sea. (Coleridge 2002: 4.975–6)

The term 'genial warmth' describes the poetic impulse as a feeling of sympathy for others that can overcome the gulf of Rousseau's nothingness.[17] In his critique of Coleridgean Romanticism Paul de Man suggests that Coleridge uses symbols to transcend historical specificity (de Man 1983: 192). By contrast, de Man regards allegory, the most fundamental type of language (de Man 1983: 135), as a figure that 'designates primarily a distance in terms of its own origin . . . In so doing, it presents the self with an illusory identification with the non-self, which is now fully, though painfully, reorganized as a non-self' (de Man 1983: 207). Rousseau's general will is a symbol in de Man's terms, because it prescribes the identification of the part with the whole. By contrast, allegories retain the painful distinction between the self and its representations within the social body.[18] Coleridge's poetry explores a non-self which cannot be wholly absorbed into a symbolic reciprocity, the alienated nothingness that Coleridge associates with Rousseau's writings.

Through the dialogue with social contract theory, Coleridge's poetry questions whether a common social body can really unite its diverse members. Coleridge describes himself in his letters through the image of the 'tip of an iceberg', the metonymy of a greater body largely absent from view and detached from a landmass. In *Letters Written During a Short Residence in Sweden, Norway and Denmark* (1796), which Coleridge read and admired, Mary Wollstonecraft uses similar imagery to express her experience of marginalisation:[19] 'how frequently has melancholy and even misanthropy taken possession of me, when the world has disgusted me, and friends have proved unkind. I have then considered myself as a particle broken off from the grand mass of mankind' (Wollstonecraft 1989: 248–9). After Wollstonecraft, the voyage to the frozen north (or south, in Coleridge's *Rime*) becomes a major topos in British Romanticism.[20] Wollstonecraft's *Letters* relate the voyage northwards explicitly to her rejection of 'Rousseau's golden age of stupidity', a pejorative allusion to the state of nature in the *Discourse on the Origins of Inequality* (ibid. 298).

Coleridge's Conversation Poems

Before turning to Coleridge's *Rime of the Ancient Mariner*, his major poetic engagement with exile, I turn to consider Coleridge's conversation poems, where he explores the possibilities of sociability within the post-Rousseauvian alienation from a stable concept of society. Unlike Coleridge's more obscure prose reflections on Rousseau and sociability, these poems occupy a central position in the Romantic canon, and have been labelled by M. H. Abrams as a microcosm for 'the greater Romantic lyric' that culminates in Wordsworth's *The Prelude* (Abrams 1965: 528–9). Although Coleridge's conversation poems are standardly taught this way, as an introduction to the Romantic lyric, for readers versed in the lyric tradition, conversation poetry may appear as something of an oxymoron. After all, what kind of conversation can anyone have with 'a nightingale who sits in the darkness, and sings to cheer its own solitude with sweet sounds' (Percy Shelley 2002: 516)? Abrams argues that the conversation is between parts of the self over different periods of time, emphasising themes of loss and moral dilemma. In *The Mirror and the Lamp* Abrams presents a triangular scheme of artist, universe and audience (Abrams 1971: 6). He argues that the audience and environment are secondary to the artist in Romanticism, making poetry into a solitary affair not much concerned with its environment. Paul Magnusen expands Abrams's model to include the French

Revolution and Coleridge's dialogue with Wordsworth (Magnusen 2002: 41–3). Jon Mee argues that the purpose of the conversation is to establish a universal democratic sphere (Mee 2011: 200). By contrast, Ewan Jones emphasises the points of interruption, giving pause for self-reflection, in the conversation poems (Jones 2014: 54). This critical emphasis on the self means that Coleridge's most frequently taught and discussed conversation poems have been regarded as his most introspective works, further de-contextualised by being considered in isolation from one another.[21] But read as a poetic sequence, they present a sustained concern with developing a poetics of sociability, and with understanding the self in relation to a changing political environment.

Coleridge presents his conversation poems as an interim form between poetry and prose, echoing Wordsworth's rallying cry for a colloquial poetics in the 'Preface to *Lyrical Ballads*'. Coleridge opens 'Reflections on Having Left a Place of Retirement' with the epigram 'more appropriate to prose' from Horace (Coleridge 2001: 261). To 'Fears in Solitude' he adds a postscript: 'the above is perhaps not Poetry ... but rather some sort of Middle thing between Poetry & Oratory – Sermoni propior. – Some parts are, I am conscious, too tame even for animated prose' (ibid. 469). In considering the relationship between poetry and philosophy, Coleridge indicates their common goal of modifying the imagination and fostering values of sympathy, which Coleridge emphasises as a sociable virtue (Coleridge 1983: 2.5). What matters about the figure of conversation is its Horatian dialectic between individual retirement and socialisation. Coleridge's conversation poems stage states of inner division that recall the divided selves of *Rousseau, Judge of Jean-Jacques* and of *Julie*'s 'Conversation about Novels'. Like Rousseau, Coleridge understands solitude as a form of sociability. The fragmented self becomes its own society, and reflects on the forces of war and revolution that redefine this passionate need for retreat as a social disposition.

A close look at 'Reflections on Having Left a Place of Retirement' shows that Coleridge's model of sociability formulates a dilemma between active political involvement and the temptations of retreat from society. The poem opens in 'the VALLEY of SECLUSION' at a cottage in Clevedon (Coleridge 2001: l. 9). The speaker cleaves to his wife, but away from society, drawing on the contranymical denotations of cleaving. The enjambed description of the cottage foliage expands this ambiguity into a larger thematic concern with the boundaries between the inwards and the outer, and the self and society:

>   across the porch
> Thick Jasmins twin'd: the little landscape round
> Was green and woody and refresh'd the eye. (Coleridge 2001: ll. 6–8)

Coleridge carefully deploys lineation to create the impression that the jasmines are growing around the cottage. But punctuation and a caesura midline disrupts this illusion. The refreshing green surroundings, rather than the twining jasmines, are in fact the referent of round. The plants seem alive, but Coleridge implies that this is only an appearance fostered by subjective perspective, as in Wolmar's contrived Elysium. Rei Terada notes Coleridge's fascination with optical illusions, which displace his anxiety about a lack of distinction between the internal and external into a playful blurring of the boundaries of the self (Terada 2009: 37). Coleridge explores an ambiguous zone between the mind and its perceptions, toying with the appearance of natural sociability. Thus, the 'tallest Rose / Peep'd at the chamber-window' anthropomorphises the rose and gives it prominence as the subject of the poem's opening gambit, while entertaining the sceptical possibility that this is all just good tempered banter, games that the mind plays in its interaction with an inherently alien and asocial world (Coleridge 2001: ll. 1–2).

Mee notes that the poem, originally published in *The Monthly Magazine* as 'Reflections on Entering into an Active Life', gravitates away from its manifest social vocation to a final state of withdrawal (Mee 2002: 117). Differing from Mee, I regard the dilemma between sociability and withdrawal as its central preoccupation. In the cottage Coleridge notes hearing 'the Sea's faint murmur' at the points of 'silent noon, and eve, and early morn' (Coleridge 2001: ll. 3–4). Wordsworth echoes Coleridge's 'murmur' two years later, in 'Lines Composed a Few Miles above Tintern Abbey', which he opens with the 'sweet inland murmur' of the River Wye, and ends with the affirmation that he no longer 'mourn[s] nor murmur[s]' the loss of direct contact with nature (Wordsworth and Coleridge 2008: l. 87). 'Murmur' forms a connecting sound which enables the mind to elicit subtle points of overlap between city and country, and England and France, and also to take pleasure in things half perceived or heard. In Coleridge's 'Reflections', the sound of the murmuring sea is a metonymy for the cottage's ties to its broader environment, which are ubiquitous even in the places of most secluded retirement. An episode of Rousseauvian *amour propre* reinforces Coleridge's view that this place of retirement is not a state of nature, but a socialised condition that operates by forming comparisons with others. As Regina Hewitt observes, Coleridge's reported conversation with a Bristol businessman on a Sunday walk contrasts his own communal values of family with the merchant's individualistic pursuit of wealth (Hewitt 1997: 67):

> Once I saw
> (Hallowing his Sabbath-day by quietness)
> A wealthy son of commerce saunter by,
> Bristowa's citizen: Methought, it calm'd
> His thirst of idle gold, and made him muse
> With wiser feelings: for he paus'd, and look'd
> With a pleas'd sadness, and gaz'd all around,
> Then eyed our cottage, and gaz'd around again,
> And sigh'd, and said, *it was a blessed place.*
> And we *were* blessed. (Coleridge 2001: ll. 9–18)

The businessman's register of wealth, commerce, citizenship and idle gold clashes with the Sabbath quiet that he seeks and the blessing that he gives. This tourist from the city makes Coleridge feel virtuous, but only through a negative comparison which ironically underscores their many points of similarity.

In a letter recalling the Nether Stowey cottage where he lived a year later, Coleridge remembers Thelwall criticising him for raising his son Hartley to recite the Lord's Prayer, and also for his unkempt garden.[22] Coleridge reports answering Thelwall with a zeugma, 'I intended to educate it strictly on the ROUSSEAU PLAN, and to have preserved it from all artificial Semination' (Coleridge 2002: 4.880). Coleridge's anecdote connects the overgrown cottage landscapes of 'Reflections on Having Left a Place of Retirement' and 'The Eolian Harp' to Rousseau's writings on botany, education and politics. Rousseau reacts against the rigidity of neoclassical nurseries and models of sociability by encouraging freedom. Yet, as in Julie's Elysium, freedom proves to be illusory. Botany and education are able to recapture elements of the state of nature, but remain heavily theorised and constructed. The Clevedon garden in 'Reflections on Having Left a Place of Retirement', like its Stowey counterpart in Coleridge's anecdote, forms a subtle parody on the 'philosophical faith' of 'the eloquent philosopher of Geneva', who wants to see nature as wild, society as free, children as naturally good, the plants as alive and the cottagers as partaking in a natural sociability (ibid. 4.880). In actuality, all of this turns out to be as deliberately constructed as the workaday world of Bristol business, anticipating the interruption of another businessman two years later while writing 'Kubla Khan', the person from Porlock who fractures Coleridge's reverie in yet another isolated cottage (Coleridge 2001: 512).

The realisation that withdrawal is an illusion, brought home to Coleridge by the intruding businessmen, shifts the poem's perspective towards scepticism; immediate and direct imagery replaces the muted scenery and blurred boundaries between the self and its environment. The landscape is no longer concealed by foliage which had obscured the relationship between the parts. Instead, it is laid before the speaker, exposing a Pisgah sight:

> naked banks;
> And seats, and Lawns, the Abbey, and the Wood,
> And Cots, and Hamlets. (Coleridge 2001: ll. 31–5)

In cataloguing the landscape, Coleridge emphasises a tension between his assertion that the world 'seem'd *imag'd*', which emphasises the mediated aspect of the world's appearance through the mind's tendency to establish connections, and the claim of immediacy and nakedness suggested by 'vast circumference' (Coleridge 2001: ll. 38–40). This sense of doubt leads the speaker to reject a series of formerly held attitudes. He asks how he could have withdrawn in wartime and reposed on 'rose-leaf Beds, pamp'ring the coward Heart / With feelings too delicate for use' (ibid. ll. 46–8). The Rose peeping at 'the chamber-window' at the beginning of the poem evolves into an image of irresponsible withdrawal and stunted political agency (ibid. l. 2). Coleridge rhymes 'coward' with 'Howard', contrasting himself to philanthropist and prison reformer John Howard (ibid. l. 49). Coleridge was familiar with Howard's work through Bowles's two poems on Howard (Coleridge 2004: 53, note 7). His allusion to Bowles as a positive social influence, in contrast to his own unwholesome taste for metaphysics, suggests Coleridge's own sense of isolation in contrast to Howard's / Bowles's philanthropy and sociably oriented poetry (Coleridge 1983: 1.17). In a letter to Thelwall written later in the same year (December 1796) Coleridge quotes an unpublished poem written to Poole with ironic allusions to Bowles that recall his reference to Howard in 'Reflections':

> Such Verse as Bowles, heart-honoured Poet, sang
> That wakes the Tear yet steals away the Pang,
> Then or with Berkeley or with Hobbes romance it
> Dissecting Truth with metaphysic lancet. (Coleridge 2002: 1.295)

Bowles and Howard both foster stoicism. Coleridge suggests that Bowles's poetics take the pang out of human relations and thereby promote social indifference. Indifference can then be theorised and romanced by 'Berkeley or . . . Hobbes', via abstract metaphysical distinctions that alienate innate connections. In 'Reflections on Having Left a Place of Retirement' the speaker retreats to a position of isolation, 'while my unnumbered Brethren toil'd and bled' (Coleridge 2001: l. 45).

He comes dangerously close to cold beneficence and the social indifference of 'my Benefactor, not my Brother man', one who helps from afar and lacks kinship (ibid. l. 53). Such a benefactor sheds a well-meaning tear that 'chills me while he aids' (ibid. l. 52). Coleridge reserves his greatest disdain for those who conceal their indifference under the disingenuous guise of sympathy:

> Who sigh for Wretchedness, yet shun the Wretched,
> Nursing in some delicious solitude
> Their slothful loves and dainty Sympathies! (Coleridge 2001: ll. 57–9)

By alliteratively linking 'sloth' with 'love', Coleridge undermines the loving sympathies of Clevedon (Coleridge 2001: l. 22). Writing 'On Sensibility' in *Aids to Reflection*, he emphasises that 'sensibility is not necessarily Benevolence. Nay, by rendering us tremblingly alive to trifling misfortunes, it frequently prevents it' (Coleridge 1993: 58–9). Coleridge supports this argument by quoting the attack on sympathy in 'Reflections on Having Left a Place of Retirement'. He critiques the Smithian theory that sympathy involves impartial spectatorship as counter to human intuitions of kindness and kinship. Direct engagement with suffering presents a more socially responsible alternative in Coleridge's terms anticipating Luc Boltanski's criticism of Smith.

Coleridge's revulsion from self-centred and withdrawn perspectives leads the poem to its conclusion in 'the bloodless fight / Of Science, Freedom and the Truth in CHRIST' (Coleridge 2001: ll. 61–2). Through 'honourable toil' Coleridge is able to clear his conscience of the risks of excessive sentiment (ibid. l. 63). He can then revisit Clevedon in his waking dreams, pleasurably recalling 'thy Jasmin and they window-peeping Rose', free from guilt (ibid. l. 66). Home should represent a communal prerogative rather than a private sphere:

> Sweet abode!
> Ah – had none greater! And that all had such!
> It might be so – but the time is not yet.
> Speed it, O FATHER! Let thy kingdom come! (Coleridge 2001: ll. 69–71)

Coleridge begins with the individual, but finally emphasises the need for a universal kingdom. The ties between the self and this wider community still remain strained. Reform and sympathy are inept to the task, and often slip into empty benevolence. Coleridge introduces Christ as a means to this end, but emphasises that his time has not arrived either, looking back on his earlier idea of Christ as limited by social prejudice and incomprehension in his Bristol lectures. Religion, a sociable disposition, cannot placate the lure of social withdrawal that Clevedon poses; therefore, millennial times remain a dream deferred.

The Beauties of the Anti-Jacobin; or, Weekly Examiner published a satirical poem, 'New Morality', which lampooned Coleridge's carefully constructed political identity, accusing Coleridge of having an 'equalizing spirit and eccentricities', which in their account rendered Coleridge susceptible to the perceived atheism and lax morals of the French Revolution (Canning and Ellis 1799: 306, note 17). The editors note, 'he has since married, had children, and has now quitted the country, become a citizen of the world, left his little ones fatherless, and his wife destitute' (ibid. 306, note 17). This footnote is glossed as an allusion to Rousseau, notorious for abandoning his five children, as told in *The Confessions* (Coleridge 2004: 113, note 8). Coleridge responds to these criticisms in the marginalia of his conversation poem 'Fears in Solitude', suggesting the need to distinguish himself from the Rousseauvian neglect of duty by emphasising his loyalties.[23] He complains of being called 'a runagate from his Country, who had denounced all patriotic feelings', and quotes this poem as proof of the contrary (ibid. 113, note 8):[24]

> There lives nor form nor feeling in my soul
> Unborrow'd from my country. O divine
> And beauteous island! thou hast been my sole
> And most magnificent temple, in the which
> I walk with awe (Coleridge 2001: ll. 194–7)

By forming a pun of 'soul' with 'sole', Coleridge emphasises national pride. He suggests that, like the British Isles, he is set apart from Europe and its political havoc. In these lines Coleridge turns 'which' from a pronoun into a proper noun, emphasising the value of his location. The grammatically irregular 'in the which / I walk' draws attention to the mundane as a place of heightened moral insight (Coleridge 2001: ll. 196–7). Coleridge emphasises his new values by locating the self after the domestic: 'Homewards I' (ibid. l. 211). But this concluding vision of domesticity is symbolically blocked from sight by Poole's house, a metonym for their joint Pantisocratic movement. Coleridge indicates that Pantisocracy no longer dominates his understanding; he is now ready to form an alternative vision of home. Solitude has granted him a social standing and has sanctioned his retirement as a political choice, one which he can cite in his painful dispute with *The Beauties of the Anti-Jacobin; or, Weekly Examiner* and with its widely read source, *The Anti-Jacobin: Or Weekly Examiner*. The political aspect of the pattern that Coleridge's conversation poetry establishes is rooted in Rousseau's own complex dialectic of retreat and engagement. It is important for understanding both Coleridge and Wordsworth, and the Romantic movement associated with their writings. The murmur that makes its way from 'Reflections on Having Left a Place of Retirement' into 'Tintern Abbey' is the muted sound of war in France, closely bound up with questions about the nature of liberty and the relationship of the self to its environment which Coleridge inherits from Rousseau's own cottage retreat, where he wrote his major works of political theory.

Scepticism and *The Ancient Mariner*

Coleridge's *Rime of the Ancient Mariner* is framed by a marriage ceremony. Coleridge is reported to have said that 'marriage belongs to society; it is a social contract' (Allsop 1836: 171).[25] In removing the guest from the wedding, the mariner not only tells his tale of isolation, but also performs it, breaking the guest's ties with the social contract and with his 'next of kin' (Coleridge 2001: l. 6).[26] The wedding takes place and the contract is formed, but the focus is on those outside it. Repeatedly, Coleridge contrasts the 'merry minstrelsy' and 'loud uproar' of the wedding party to the solitary voice of the mariner telling his tale outside (ibid. ll. 36, 591). The mariner takes the guest from the wedding and burdens him with interlocution, making him 'a sadder and a wiser man' at the poem's end (ibid. l. 624). He is left as 'one that hath been stunned, / And is of sense forlorn', a predicament that is relayed from the mariner to the guest and then to the reader, in a centrifugal chain of interlocutive trauma, reproducing the tale of social breakdown potentially ad infinitum (ibid. ll. 623–4). The mariner starts out as a member of a large crew, consisting of two hundred of his peers and at least one relative, 'my brother's son' (ibid. l. 341). Cheered on its departure (ibid. l. 21), the ship is overtaken by storm once it leaves the mainland of sociability, changes course and reverts to a state of nature. The mariner never truly returns from this voyage.

Coleridge expresses the breakdown of traditional models of community through form. He writes most of the *Rime* in relatively stable tetrameter and trimeter quatrains, conforming to the ballad measure convention. In the *Biographia Literaria*, Coleridge discusses metre and rhyme as a means of transmitting cultural memory and a stimulant to the reader's attention (Coleridge 1983: 2.67–9). Albert Friedman discusses the ballad as reflecting a 'homogenous community, one in which there is a high degree of social cohesion, uniform social attitudes, a common cultural background and only vaguely individuated tastes' (Friedman 1961: 24–5). In the later eighteenth century the ballad developed into a sentimental genre that imagined a simple, happy past (ibid. 178). Much like the mariner who keeps apart from the minstrels at the wedding, Coleridge flouts ballad convention with a dramatic flourish at key points in the poem. He disrupts its meter, adding extra lines and beats to describe liminal states associated with the supernatural, religious salvation, and lyrical affect. To this effect, Coleridge enacts the driving force of the storm and its assault on the ship's social standing, as it is expelled from its itinerary and driven away from its homeland:

> With sloping masts and dipping prow,
> As who pursued with yell and blow
> Still treads the shadow of his foe,
> And forward bends his head,
> The ship drove fast, loud roared the blast,
> And southward aye we fled. (Coleridge 2001: ll. 45–50)

This unusually long six-line Burns stanza (or 'standard Habbie'), the first of Coleridge's many digressions from the ballad form, enacts the ship's loss of control. The internal rhyme of 'fast' and 'blast' and the successive rhyming of 'prow', 'blow', and 'foe' kinaesthetically mimic the sound of the storm. Coleridge adds extra lines to a later stanza evoking the dead shipmen's cursing of the mariner: 'Seven days, seven nights, I saw that curse, / And yet I could not die' (Coleridge 2001: ll. 261–2). Here the additional lines enact the mariner's protracted experience of time over the course of that week, interrupting the poem's measure and prolonging its duration. Coleridge also represents the mariner's absence of rest through an exceptional anapaestic tetrameter that digresses from the regular pattern of iambic tetrameter: 'For the sky and the sea, and the sea and the sky / Lay like a load on my weary eye' (ibid. ll. 251–2). Repetition and irregular meter enact the protracted sense of time created by insomnia and the mariner's tossing and turning. The wedding guest fears that the mariner is a ghost, but the mariner reassures him in an extra fifth line that his salvation was the result of divine intervention, and not death. Irregular form expresses irregular occurrences and is juxtaposed with the regular, sociable ballad framework, foregrounding Coleridge's theoretical concern with the tension between part and whole within the social body.

Stanley Cavell reads *The Ancient Mariner*'s digressions as an exploration of noumenal aspects of knowledge, which Kant locates beyond the mind's access (Cavell 1988: 50). He assumes that Coleridge was unaware of Kant when writing *The Rime of the Ancient Mariner* (ibid. 47). But Coleridge was familiar with Kantianism through his exposure to Nitsch, and associated Kant with political freedom. When

Coleridge crosses Kant's epistemological dividing line between the phenomenal and the noumenal, he is thereby also probing the underlying limits of the social body. Through the mariner's encounter with the albatross, the poem's pivotal event, Coleridge pursues the ambiguous divide between civilisation and a fantastic state of nature, which Coleridge associates with the supernatural. He introduces the albatross with an internal rhyme: 'at length did *cross* an Albatross' (Coleridge 2001: l. 63, emphasis added). The albatross is a figure of crossing and transgressing boundaries. Cross is also a pun on crucifixion, which Coleridge associates with prejudice and intolerance in his Bristol lectures. As an otherworldly entity, a type for Christ and for the transgression of boundaries, the albatross challenges the limits of human tolerance: '*As if* it had been a Christian soul, / We hailed it in God's name' (ibid. ll. 65–6, emphasis added). By using a conditional clause, Coleridge emphasises that the albatross is in fact not a Christian soul, even if it is finally crucified by the mariner's crossbow, which Coleridge prefigures through the iconic image of the albatross's perch on the mast for prayer gatherings (ibid. l. 76). Like Christ, the albatross seeks acceptance, but is betrayed by a society lacking basic values of hospitality towards beings from outside the community.

In the *Discourse on the Origins of Inequality*, Rousseau had argued that animals and humans essentially share one community; hence orang-utans may be humans in a state of nature (Rousseau 1992a: 81, note 8). In *The Social Contract*, Rousseau's argument gestures towards exclusion. Society cannot embrace all creatures; it forms contracts to define its boundaries and excise pernicious members. Coleridge repeats Rousseau's ambivalence. If this section of his poem extends hospitality to non-human creatures, the marriage that frames the poem distinguishes another kind of community which is clearly not extended to animals. The albatross pursues companionship with the mariner: 'every day, for food or play, / Came to the mariner's hollo!' forming this bond by '[eating] the food it ne'er had eat' (ibid. ll. 73–4, 66). In the 1798 version of the poem, Coleridge specifies that 'the Marineres gave it biscuit-worms', rotting remains of human food (Coleridge 2001 [1798]: l. 67). The hybrid image of 'biscuit-worms' collocates human artifice (biscuits) with the natural world, symbolising a disturbing relapse that always threatens civilisation and perhaps explaining Coleridge's need to excise this disturbing image in the process of revision, following criticism that the poem was too ghoulish.[27] This worm-like imagery resurfaces in the pivotal scene of the mariner's repentance, which is catalysed by the biblical yet still ungainly spectacle of water snakes undulating in the moonlight.

Coleridge marks the fragile divide between the state of nature and the state of society, and between freedom and civilisation, through the serpentine imagery of biscuit worms and water snakes as well as the later transition of the dead sailors from corpses to seraphs. This divide appears as a mysterious magical transformation – a chemical change which, in Rousseau's terms, cannot be reversed. In his *Discourse on the Origins of Inequality*, Rousseau reflects on the new appetites that socialisation generates – the albatross's desire for 'food it ne'er had eat', which exposes previously self-sufficient individuals to dependence on others, and on such artificially modified food as biscuits which expose the albatross to abuse and degeneration, the addictive behaviours and habits of modernity in the Pavlovian relationship that the albatross forms with the mariners. The mariner treats the albatross with hospitality, considers it a Christian soul, tames it as his pet, and then kills it, essentially repeating Rousseau's account of civilisation, which anticipates this destructive cycle of domestication. Rousseau suggests that animals,

> all have a more robust constitution, more vigour, more strength and courage in the forest than in our houses. They lose half of these advantages in becoming Domesticated, and it might be said that all our cares to treat and feed these animals well only end in their degeneration. It is the same even for man. In becoming sociable and a slave, he becomes weak, fearful, servile. (Rousseau 1992a: 24)

By killing the albatross the mariner violates the natural order, and introduces new and corrupting social needs. He eventually learns to love 'both man and bird and beast' (Coleridge 2001: l. 613). But this recognition does not reinstate the equilibrium of the state of nature that the mariner has disrupted, and does not restore him to the community that he has lost or the status that he had enjoyed. After his repentance, the mariner remains on the threshold of society. He is rescued by the hermit, the first in a line of interlocutors that lead from the wedding guest and extend to the implied reader. In his *Table Talk*, Coleridge is reported to have discussed the mariner as 'the ever-lasting wandering Jew – had told this story ten thousand times since the voyage which was in early youth and fifty years before' (Coleridge 1990: 1.273–4). The mariner himself becomes a hermit-like figure, excluded from the community and associated with religious marginalisation and persecution. Conversations with hermits and wandering Jews do not generate sociability in Coleridge's terms, but rather enact ceaseless repetition and permanent dislocation. As Cavell suggests, killing the albatross means 'being driven to deny my internal, or natural, connection with others, with the social as such' (Cavell 1988: 60). Feeding the albatross is a social act, establishing a kind of contract. And killing it is a breach of contract. The ice, with its pun on isolation, emphasises the stakes of this crisis in terms of the ensuing loss of community.

Alongside his narrative of crime, punishment, atonement and belief, Coleridge presents a parallel negative axis of interpretation through the mariner's peregrinations and ceaseless repetitions. Coleridge's response to Anna Barbauld's criticism that the poem is excessively didactic presents its main fault as an

> obtrusion of the moral sentiment so openly on the reader as a principle or cause of action in a work of pure imagination. It ought to have had no more moral than the *Arabian Nights'* tale of the merchant's sitting down to eat dates by the side of a well and throwing the shells aside, and lo! a genie starts up and says he *must* kill the aforesaid merchant *because* one of the date shells had, it seems, put out the eye of the genie's son. (Coleridge 1990: 2.149)

David Perkins comments on *The Rime of the Ancient Mariner*'s 'status of omnisignificance, like *Hamlet*', which has ultimately disrupted the possibility of arriving at any coherent interpretation of this complex poem through the multiple possible readings that it generates (Perkins 1996: 425). Coleridge's flouting of meaning ruptures causality. At crucial junctures of causal sequencing in the narrative, Coleridge erases temporal and spatial transitions. The killing of the albatross is explained in terms of its domestication. By contrast, the mariner's motivation remains opaque and cavalier. His punishment is determined by a game of dice (Coleridge 2001: ll. 195–7). Although the odds of winning do seem weighted in favour of Life-in-Death, who overshadows 'the naked hulk alongside', the dice nonetheless suggest an arbitrary logic governing the poem's main events (ibid. l. 195). Like the mariner, the reader is privy to supernatural forces which remain unexplained. A mysterious polar spirit oversees Life-in-Death's mission, and the spirit's emissary 'fellow dæmons' hold a Socratic dialogue about the mariner's repentance (ibid. 403). Other causal nexuses are entirely missing, such as the ship's unknown mission and voyage into uncharted seas.

The Rime of the Ancient Mariner questions the coherence of individuals within larger orders of social, natural and metaphysical meaning. This scepticism is congruent with Rousseau's ambivalent discourse of a state of nature and of a social contract which is lost and which leaves individuals without a governing principle of sociability, or even a clear moral distinction between the human and the animal, ending in mere 'Nothingism'. Coleridge is quick to observe in *The Friend* that Rousseau's unhappiness is not merely personal; the shortcomings of his theory arise from a broader conflict between an age of individualism and the ongoing need for a theory of community. Luther and Rousseau share the same desires, but not the same moment of faith in the coherence of religious and social systems. Enlightenment scepticism, which Coleridge compares to the prejudices that led to Christ's crucifixion, undermines modern social covenants and finds its outlet in Coleridge's recourse to supernatural forces as types for the arcane and the unknowable.

In the *Biographia Literaria* Coleridge formulates a theory of poetic faith as an alternative to scepticism. He famously refers to poetry's sublime moment of aesthetic pleasure, derived from his readings of Friedrich Schiller, as 'that willing suspension of disbelief for the moment, which constitutes poetic faith' (Coleridge 1983: 2.6). Poetry is freer than philosophical or political arguments in its ability to tolerate the conflict between individual and collective values which characterises post-Enlightenment culture. Because it does not need morals or a determinate agenda, and steers clear of 'a restless desire to arrive at the final solution', in Coleridge's chillingly proleptic turn of phrase in the *Biographia Literaria*, poetry is better suited to sceptical times than expository discourse, which remains potentially coercive in its insistence on the sovereignty of reason (ibid. 2.14). Jerome McGann invites his post-Romantic readers to 'inaugurate our disbelief in Coleridge's "poetic faith". This Romantic ideology must be seen for what it is, a historical phenomenon of European culture, generated to save the "traditional concepts, schemes, and values" of Christian heritage' (McGann 1981: 65). Read through Coleridge's double negative, whereby disbelief is suspended, this watershed moment in literary theory sounds more like an invitation to call ideologies into question, a position of Romantic irony already anticipated by Christian values which, in Coleridge's view, responded to a culture of persecution and misunderstanding much like that of the Enlightenment. Coleridge's use of hybrid literary forms that combine poetry and philosophy, encompassing the lyrical / theoretical prose of *The Friend*, his conversation poems, and *The Rime of the Ancient Mariner*, suggests his concern with gaps between individuals and the social body which he does not try to mend into a greater whole. Coleridge's tolerance of rupture and insights into the underlying tensions and chemical changes in the social and private body that generate the need for fiction render him a subsequently crucial figure for an emergent post-Romantic position of alienation.

Notes

1. Margaret Cohen suggests that for Coleridge and other Romantic writers the sea is associated with transgressing epistemological boundaries to achieve a sublime state of imagination, usually represented through the spectacle of boundlessness, as in the paintings of William Turner (Cohen 2010: 117).
2. See Jerome McGann's argument that 'Coleridge's views developed out of his revisionist study of the Enlightenment movement which centered on the historical study of classical and biblical texts' (McGann 1983: 5). Alan Liu traces the dramatic sway in Wordsworth's and Coleridge's ideologies to a dialectic in politics whereby the private self takes precedence over history (Liu 1989: 426–7).
3. Monica Class discusses a similar blurring of boundaries in Coleridge's position as a reader who readily absorbed and reorganised his materials, complicating the view of him as a plagiarist (Class 2012: 178). Coleridge referred to this intersubjective style of reading as 'genial criticism'. See also Julie Ellison, who argues that Coleridge identifies with Rousseau 'as the victim of an age that could not discipline or contain his hysterical tendencies', which Coleridge adopts and repeats through Gothic idioms (Ellison 1989: 420).
4. For arguments on the 1790s, see John Barrell's *Imagining the King's Death* (Barrell 2000: 644–53) and Nicholas Roe (1988: 113–45). David Simpson argues that British nationalism develops from French radicalism and German sensibility (Simpson 1993: 77). There have been many studies of Coleridge and German Idealism. See Rosemary Ashton's *The German Idea* (1994), James Engell's *The Creative Imagination* (1981), and Mark Kipperman's *Beyond Enchantment* (1986).
5. Existing discussions focus on Coleridge's article in *The Friend*. Ellison notes Coleridge's identification with Rousseau's tendency to hysteria and Gothic excess (Ellison 1989: 419–20). Edward Duffy argues that Coleridge expresses empathy towards Rousseau in *The Friend* and does not engage with the political context of revolution (Duffy 1979: 67). Andrea Timár suggests that Coleridge identifies with Rousseau because, unlike Luther, Rousseau's writings have been misinterpreted, leading to effects which he could not have foreseen (Timár 2007: 173–4).
6. The character of Edmund Oliver is often identified as a representation of Coleridge – see Richard C. Allen (Allen 1996: 269).
7. See Robert Mitchell, who argues that radicals and conservatives alike were influenced by Smith's view that society is held together by an underlying invisible infrastructure (Mitchell 2005: 59–60).
8. There has been significant critical attention to Coleridge's understanding of writing as a financial enterprise. Richard Adelman discusses the proximity of poetry to manual labour for Coleridge as both a moral and productive activity, a spirit which pervades much of the 'Preface to *Lyrical Ballads*' (Adelman 2011: 105). Mitchell argues that Romanticism engages in a one-sided borrowing from economic discourse, of the kind demonstrated by Poole's reliance on Smith (Mitchell 2007: 128). As a result of this borrowing, Romantic writers are able to reinvest their labours with economic value and present them as productive, so that

Catherine Gallagher suggests that Coleridge's later discourse of unhappiness borrows from the ennobling suffering of the labourer (Gallagher 2006: 27–8). These works of new economic criticism all point towards a convergence of capitalist and revolutionary discourses in Coleridge's Romantic ideology.

9. Coleridge is recorded to have borrowed all fifteen volumes of Rousseau's *Collection complete des oeuvres* for one day from the Bristol Library in 1797 (Wu 1994: 180–1). Duncan Wu notes that the brevity of his loan means that he was already familiar with it. Coleridge probably also took out *The Confessions* and *Reveries of the Solitary Walker* for Joseph Cottle in the same period (ibid. 185).

10. Coleridge suggests that Jews were unable to practice these republican principles due to their excessive materialism (Coleridge 1969b: 127–8). He complains that on a coach journey to London 'a horrible stinking Jew crucified my nose the whole way' (Coleridge 2002: 2.880). For more on Coleridge's ambivalence about Jews, see Chris Rubinstein's (2004) 'Coleridge and Jews'.

11. Margaret Jacob identifies this as a post-revolutionary republican theme of 'the kind of personal transformation needed to create the democratic subject' (Jacob 2002: 25). Her argument echoes Steven Affeldt's reading of Rousseau's general will as relying on the ongoing active participation and self-transformation of its members (Affeldt 2000: 556).

12. See also Christopher Hill, who argues that the feudal model of the body politic dominated seventeenth-century theology and influenced social contract philosophy through the idea that both God and his subjects could be held to a contract (Hill 1997: 239).

13. Explaining this conundrum, M. H. Abrams suggests that Coleridge's relationship to German philosophy is based on a common bible-based culture. The concurrence in topics and design among Coleridge and the Germans was 'less the result of mutual influence than it was of a common experience in the social, intellectual, and emotional climate in the post-Revolutionary age, and a grounding in a common body of materials – above all the Bible' (Abrams 1973: 256). More radically, Stanley Cavell argues that because Coleridge read Kant after writing his most Kantian poems, any similarity between them cannot be based on influence, but rather on a parallel understanding of the structure of consciousness (Cavell 1988: 47).

14. Coleridge's second related plan 'is to become a Dissenting parson and abjure Politics & carnal literature' (Coleridge 2002: 1.210). He considers 'the first impractical – the second not likely to succeed' (ibid. 1.209).

15. In the late eighteenth century, travel narratives like Prévost's speculated about the possibility of evolution. Geologists of this period were replacing models of sudden change with a gradualist view of evolutionary continuum (Wyatt 1995: 104).

16. In 'The Eolian Harp' of 1795 Coleridge reports Sara Fricker admonishing his poetics musings as

> . . . shapings of the unregenerate mind;
> Bubbles that glitter as they rise and break
> On vain Philosophy's aye-babbling spring. (Coleridge 2001: ll. 55–7)

17. Coleridge's term geniality describes an intuitive insight into the spirit in which a work is written (Class 2012: 178).
18. Critics have often noted Coleridge's insistence on figures of dissimilitude. Seamus Perry discusses Coleridge's 'needy impulse to cross self-constraining boundaries, in a way that seems to work against the unitary pieces of the poetic theory' (Perry 2001: 263). Susan Wolfson similarly argues that for all his claims to logocentricity, 'Coleridge is more prone to a skepticism about figures than to a poetics of blithe equivalence' (Wolfson 1997: 86). Hewitt comments on Coleridge's turn from similarity as a principle of social cohesion in Pantisocracy to a political position which emphasises difference (Hewitt 1997: 73).
19. Coleridge disliked Godwin, but frequently praised Wollstonecraft (Coleridge 2002: 1.549).
20. Siobhan Carroll notes the fascination with polar exploration 'from the seventeenth century onward … the poles were often conceived as a type of fictional space, as areas over which the imagination reigned supreme' (Carroll 2015: 21).
21. Primarily 'Frost at Midnight', and also 'Dejection: An Ode', 'The Eolian Harp' and 'This Lime-Tree Bower My Prison'. The engagement of these poems with sociability becomes apparent when the conversation poems are read as a sequence. Magnusen suggests that political themes are present throughout all of the conversation poems, but are sometimes raised indirectly through domesticity, which becomes an expression of nationalism (Magnusen 2002: 41).
22. The incident is reported to have taken place about a year later in 1797, and is recalled in 1818 (Coleridge 2002: 4.879).
23. 'Fears in Solitude' continues where 'Reflections on Having Left a Place of Retirement' leaves off. Coleridge focuses on an allegorised 'humble man' in a liminal space of reverie, half within the sensory world and half outside it (Coleridge 2001: l. 14). From this threshold position, the humble man finds

    > Religious meanings in the forms of nature!
    > And so, his senses gradually wrapt
    > In a half sleep, he dreams of better worlds. (Coleridge 2001: ll. 25–7)

24. Coleridge wrote these comments in the margins of a manuscript copy of 'Fears in Solitude', dated approximately 1807 (Coleridge 2004: 109, 113, note 8).
25. This account of marriage as a social contract is reinforced by Coleridge's view of marriage as a condition for joining the Pantisocratic community. When his own marriage broke up, he blamed Southey but also furnished this loveless marriage as 'proof to me that my name is not ignoble' in his self-purportedly altruistic dedication to communal values rather than selfish desires (Coleridge 2002: 1.1156).
26. Unless otherwise indicated in the parentheses, references are to the 1817 version of *The Rime of the Ancient Mariner*. Poem references are indicated by line numbers, and gloss references are indicated by page number. I have chosen the 1817 version because Coleridge's addition of the editorial gloss integrates prose elements and an alternative historical perspective, creating

a more complex text than the 1798 version (McGann 1981: 50). Critics associate the gloss with questions of coherence which relate to this book's concern with sociability. Huntington Brown compares the gloss to the chorus of ancient Greek drama (Brown 1945: 324). By contrast, Wendy Wall argues that the gloss subverts the poem's main didactic concerns from its margins (Wall 1987: 182).

27. See Southey's assessment of the poem's Gothic elements as 'a Dutch attempt at German sublimity' (Wordsworth and Coleridge 2008: 149).

Chapter 4

Individual Sovereignty and Community: Wordsworth's *Prelude*

A choice that from the passions of the world
Withdrew, and fixed me in a still retreat;
Sheltered, but not to social duties lost,
Secluded, but not buried. (Wordsworth 2007: ll. 5.52–5)

Given the pivotal role that the French Revolution plays in *The Prelude*, it is surprising that William Wordsworth's engagement with Jean-Jacques Rousseau – the prophet of the revolution – has not received more attention.[1] Much has been published on Wordsworth's apostasy from revolutionary to counterrevolutionary ideologies.[2] By this account, Wordsworth's poetry turns from its early faith in revolutionary possibility to seek refuge in the private imagination. In particular, his later poetry (of approximately 1807 onwards) and revisions of his earlier works are often dismissed as a decline into reactionary torpor.[3] I propose reframing *The Prelude* within a broader history of ideas that goes beyond the impasse of Wordsworth's ideological reprobacy and quietism, to reclaim his later developments as integral to his thought. Understanding Wordsworth's response to Rousseau in a framework that looks beyond *The Confessions* relates *The Prelude*'s politics to the problems of social contract theory. And conceiving of Wordsworth's reaction to the French Revolution through the social contract's theoretical conflicts frames Wordsworth within an ongoing modification of contract theory rather than a flight from politics.[4] *The Prelude*, read across its 1805 and 1850 versions through Wordsworth's allusions to Rousseau's social contract, emerges from this perspective as an epic poem about the fraught status of individuals within a new configuration of civilisation rather than an apotheosis of private imagination created by political disillusionment.

Recent studies of Wordsworth's engagements with political economy have gone a considerable way towards modifying this standard view of Wordsworth.[5] Philip Connell suggests that readings of Wordsworth and Coleridge as Tory reactionaries do not reflect 'their abiding reputation as

the first, prophetic critics of high capitalist society' (Connell 2001: 125).
Mary Poovey notes that literature and political economy defined one
another dialectically over the long eighteenth and nineteenth centuries,
often through a pattern of mutual repudiation whereby literature
affirmed itself as the antithesis of economy, and economy – in turn –
undercut values of humanism (Poovey 2008: 28). Wordsworth attached
prefaces and instructions to his poems to define literary value as a 'new,
nonmarket model of value', an alternative to political economy (ibid.
290).[6] As Catherine Gallagher points out, the common ground uniting
literature and political economy is a post-Enlightenment assessment of
human nature as inherently irrational (Gallagher 2006: 7–8). Gallagher
proposes,

> with the subtle prodding of political economy, British organicism, even in
> its Romantic form, underwent a transition from imagining the nation on the
> model of a unified single organism to imagining it as a vital autotelic system,
> not only tolerating but also requiring conflict. (Gallagher 2006: 33)

David Simpson observes that Romanticism translates the new political economy of early capitalism into a haunting sense of ontological
vacancy (Simpson 2009: 2). Gallagher's and Simpson's arguments
offer a platform for considering Wordsworth's response to Rousseau's
post-Aristotelian theory of society as a constitutive disruption of the
individual and the social collective.

Although not much attention has been paid to Wordsworth's
engagements with Rousseau's political theory, Cathy Caruth, Nancy
Yousef and Alan Bewell have established a clear relationship between
Wordsworth's Romantic subjectivity and other Enlightenment models
of epistemology and sociology.[7] Reading *The Excursion* through John
Locke's *Essay Concerning Human Understanding*, Regina Hewitt
suggests that Wordsworth does not so much retreat from society
through his poem as chronicle the more general decline of a unifying
concept of society (Hewitt 1990: 189). *The Prelude* – a text now far
more frequently read and taught than *The Excursion* – needs to be
considered within a related context as a response to changing models in
political economy. I glean references to Rousseau and to his theory of
contract from within the 1805 *Prelude*, from its revised 1850 version,
and its sequel *The Excursion*, as well as from a variety of theoretical
arguments about the function of poetry that Wordsworth wrote across
his long and varied career. In addition to Rousseau, Wordsworth
also responds to the works of Adam Smith and William Godwin who
seek to combine a pragmatic focus on proto-utilitarian principles of
a general good and on social planning respectively with principles of

individualism. Wordsworth's works subsequent to the 1805 *Prelude* develop his earlier engagements with the tension between individual sovereignty and community. Across its long and diverse compositional history, Wordsworth's *Prelude* and *The Excursion* resist contract theory and explore the friction between social contract theory's powerful concept of individual sovereignty, and the concurrent need to produce a new model of community. Instead of breaking from politics, I suggest that what happens in Wordsworth's later version of *The Prelude* and especially in *The Excursion* is a reflection on the potential deadlock of utopian ideologies.

At this point, a sketch of Wordsworth's ideological development across his career may help to establish where I identify these lines of continuity. Wordsworth's *Prelude* looks back to his 1793 'Letter to the Bishop of Llandaff', which admires Rousseau and praises the influence of *The Social Contract* on events in France. When the revolution becomes corrupt, Wordsworth questions whether Rousseau's individualism is compatible with values of community. By the time he began writing *The Prelude*, Wordsworth had come to reject Rousseau, whose ideology seemed to have failed as a political project. In the *Tract on the Convention of Cintra* (1808) Wordsworth comments that Rousseau, Condillac and Voltaire are 'plants which will not naturalize' on British soil (Wordsworth 1915: 177). This dismissal itself retains aspects of Rousseau's legacy – suggested in this instance by the horticultural metaphor, a register which Gallagher traces to Scottish Enlightenment vitalist physiology and natural law theory, which conceptualise society as an organic unity (Gallagher 2006: 20). Wordsworth imagines Rousseau's lack of endemicity in Britain through a central trope for social cohesion, indicating his ongoing concern with post-Enlightenment models of community in this later chapter of his career. Wordsworth's revised *Prelude*, finalised in 1839 and published posthumously in 1850, and his *Excursion* of 1814 explicitly depart from Rousseau to explore alternative social models, while addressing the question of how to equilibrise individual and collective needs, a delicate balance, as we will see, because of the threat that communitarianism poses to individual sovereignty.

Wordsworth's return to England from revolutionary France marks the beginning of a lengthy crisis and revaluation of his earlier principles. Initially, he strives to rescue individuality from contract theory by privileging memory – expressed in his famous meditation on 'spots of time' – and poetry, voiced in the *The Prelude*'s crowning vision of aesthetic vocation. Wordsworth contrasts his own position with Godwin's more radical dismissal of social institutions, and with Smith's attempt to conceptualise individualism within a broader social system. These negative comparisons express Wordsworth's discomfort with Godwin's and Smith's versions of individualism. In the 1850 *Prelude*, Wordsworth modifies some of his more defiant assertions of individualism to integrate a communitarian ideology. *The Excursion* takes communitarianism one step further and subordinates the individual to society. Wordsworth's poem dwells on the ill fate of individuals who withdraw from traditional forms of sociability and turn to revolution and self-destruction.

Social Nature

Wordsworth begins *The Prelude* by repeating the pattern of Rousseau's *Confessions*, where retreat to a rural setting is the basis for redefining the foundations of society. More than midway through the poem, at the beginning of book eight, Wordsworth identifies his governing theme as the 'Love of Nature leading to Love of Mankind' (Wordsworth 1991: 211). This insight both develops gradually, and is implicit from *The Prelude*'s inception.[8] Nature performs a socialising function, preparing the poet as an individual fit to join society. Wordsworth's homecoming to the Lake District in book one invokes Rousseau's account of natural man in the *Second Discourse*, who 'know[s] only those things the possession of which is in his power or easily acquired, nothing should be so tranquil as his soul' (Rousseau 1992a: 86, note 9). In the *Second Discourse*, natural man 'satisf[ies] his hunger under an oak, quench[es] his thirst at the first stream, find[s] his bed at the foot of the same tree that furnished his meal' (ibid. 20). Similarly, Wordsworth 'drink[s] wild water, and ... pluck[s] green herbs, / And gather[s] fruits fresh from their native bough' (Wordsworth 1991: ll. 1.37–8). He celebrates being

> Chear'd by the genial pillow of the earth
> Beneath my head, sooth'd by a sense of touch
> From the warm ground, that balanced me. (Wordsworth 1991: ll. 1.89–91)

Unlike Rousseau, who posits a breach between nature and society, for Wordsworth nature remains a fundamentally social concept. He subsequently assumes an easy passage 'through nature to the love of human Kind', anthropomorphising nature and ascribing it an ethical, social consciousness (Wordsworth 1991: l. 8.588).

Nature castigates Wordsworth when he goes poaching; when he steals a boat, it appears to reprimand him. Nature disciplines Wordsworth and installs a social structure in his otherwise pre-social and inchoate mind, which comes to be framed by

> a dark
> Invisible workmanship that reconciles
> Discordant elements, and makes them move
> In one society. (Wordsworth 1991: ll. 1.353–6)

This social infrastructure provides the necessary training for the poet's later interest in external social institutions. Wordsworth eventually discovers

> My thoughts . . . attracted more and more
> By slow gradations towards human Kind,
> And to the good and ill of human life:
> Nature had led me on, and now I seem'd
> To travel independent of her help. (Wordsworth 1991: ll. 8.760–4)

Wordsworth presents the nature of his youth as a preliminary stage in becoming sociable.

Although he grows up in an isolated rural community, Wordsworth emphasises that he had always understood himself and nature in potentially sociable terms. And accordingly, he explains, his 'creative agency' had always taken precedence over analytic reasoning. Wordsworth's argument draws on the Scottish Enlightenment notion of sympathy as a structural relation rather than an affective bond (Campbell 1971: 94). Wordsworth describes his imagination as developing through sympathy:

> . . . [an] interminable building rear'd
> By observation of affinities
> In objects where no brotherhood exists. (Wordsworth 1991: ll. 2.401–4)

Wordsworth represents the bonds connecting the self to its social and natural environment through the architectural metaphor of a building. He also employs images drawn from social and urban registers to define nature as the 'great social principle of life' (Wordsworth 1991: l. 2.408). On returning from the Lake District to London, Wordsworth explains that sociability is still a latent potential which has yet to become manifest:

> My Fellow-beings still were unto me,
> Far less than she was; though the scale of love
> Were filling fast. (Wordsworth 1991: ll. 8.867–9)

Although it takes time for nature to reveal itself as a fully social concept, the germ and the promise of this metamorphosis – suggested by social imagery in Wordsworth's account of his developing mind and of nature – is there from the start. The tutelage of urban dystopia in London and of revolutionary upheaval in France are necessary to render this latent potential manifest.

Education: London and Europe

The first significant opportunity to exercise values of sociability derived from nature arrives when Wordsworth moves to London.[9] But the chaotic and heavily populated city confounds his individualistic social vision. On arriving in London, Wordsworth is initially eager

> [to pitch] my vagrant tent,
> . . . at large, among
> The unfenced regions of society. (Wordsworth 1991: ll. 7.60–2)

He expects society to be an extension of the socialising nature of his childhood, a site for him to 'pitch [his] vagrant tent' and occupy 'unfenced regions'. Counter to this expectation, the unfenced quality of London violates individual autonomy and eclipses Wordsworth's earlier sense of himself as united mysteriously with society by nature, like a planet orbiting the sun and 'mov[ing] / In one society' (Wordsworth 1991: ll. 355–6). Because London confounds Wordsworth's social vision, he envisions it as the antithesis of society, as a violent and threatening urban jungle. If nature constitutes the 'great social principle of life', his sense of himself away from nature becomes that of a vagrant (ibid. l. 2.408). London's indifference to the private individual eclipses the poet's earlier sense of himself as contained by socialising nature. The profusion of natural metaphors in Wordsworth's rendition of London suggests the common origin of these accounts of nature and society. Wordsworth eventually decamps from London to the Lake District, disappointed with the social vision that he had ascribed to nature during childhood. He remarks on the painful absence of social cohesion in London:

> O blank confusion! and a type not false
> Of what the mighty City is itself
> To all except a Straggler here and there,
> To the whole swarm of its inhabitants;
> An undistinguishable world to men,
> The slaves unrespited of low pursuits,
> Living amid the same perpetual flow
> Of trivial objects, melted and reduced
> To one identity, by differences
> That have no law, no meaning, no end. (Wordsworth 1991: ll. 7.696–705)

As 'no law' guarantees the discreteness and dignity of the individual, all are 'melted and reduced / to one identity', eliding the cherished autonomy of Wordsworth's childhood. In the 1850 *Prelude*, which emphasises the community more than the 1805 version, Wordsworth nonetheless retains his critique of the loss of individuality in the city. He refers to London as

> thou monstrous ant-hill on the plain
> Of a too busy world! Before me flow,
> Thou endless stream of men and moving things! (Wordsworth 1985:
>   ll. 7.149–51)

The monstrosity of this anthill results from the 'endless stream of men and moving things' which violates individual dignity. In this flow, men are no longer clearly distinguishable, and lose their autonomy and identity.

Wordsworth's account of London is shaped by Rousseau's malevolent cityscapes. Wordsworth echoes Rousseau's view that 'men are not made to be crowded together in ant-hills, but scattered over the earth to fill it. The more they become massed together, the more corrupt they become. Disease and vice are the sure result of over-crowded cities' (Rousseau 2010: 18). Marcel Hénaff comments on Rousseau's comparison of city dwellers 'to ants (an economic model of large masses abandoned to servile tasks)' (Hénaff 1992: 18). This metaphor suggests that *'when men are too close, they devour each other'*, losing their discrete identities (ibid. 23). It is only on his subsequent visit to revolutionary France that having 'one identity' and being part of a swarm start acquiring positive significance for Wordsworth. When Wordsworth visits Europe in the early stages of the revolution, his horrific experience of London is initially transformed. Wordsworth presents early revolutionary France as a direct inversion of London's Rousseauvian dystopia. He transforms London's negative 'swarm of . . . inhabitants' from an image of chaos to one of pleasurable commotion that echoes Mandeville's *Fable of the Bees* and its antecedent, Virgil's *Georgics IV*. Wordsworth describes 'a merry crowd' of citizens celebrating the anniversary of the revolution, 'swarm[ing], gaudy and gay as bees' (Wordsworth 1991: ll. 6.393, 398). Albeit clearly positive in this context, the image still bears traces of its negative predecessor. Mandeville's bees are sociable, but motivated by potentially antisocial self-interest and malice. Although the swarm now inspires revelry rather than horror, suggested by the switch from monstrous ants to festive bees, Morton Paley comments on its pervasively threatening connotation for Wordsworth, who echoes the swarming army of fallen angels in *Paradise Lost* (Paley 1999: 174).

A similar reversal transforms gaudiness, which is vulgar in Wordsworth's account of London and becomes gay rather than degrading in France. Having 'one identity' also comes to connote cohesion instead of the loss of autonomy. Much as Clarens compensates for the shortcomings of

Paris in *Julie*, revolutionary France redeems London from its multitude of sins. Wordsworth accomplishes this transformation through the image of the '*fête*', the communal gathering which rectifies the mayhem of urban society (Hénaff 1992: 23). Subsequent to this metamorphosis, he wonders at 'how bright a face is worn when joy of one / Is joy of tens of millions' (Wordsworth 1991: ll. 6.359–60). The 'joy of tens of millions' celebrating the anniversary of the revolution is the positive counterpart of the 'endless stream of moving things' witnessed in London. Where Wordsworth had previously been appalled by the absence of a collective principle that could safeguard the identity of individuals in society, he is now enraptured by its discovery in revolutionary theory and by its recuperative effect on his former experience of alienation in London. The 'joy of tens of millions' now complements 'the joy of one', inspiring awe in its apparent capacity to maintain the discrete identities of its constituents.

Wordsworth initially perceives post-revolutionary Europe as the perfect venue for effecting a seemingly harmonious transition from the state of nature to a condition of natural society. He explains that at any time nature's 'mighty forms' would have been sufficient cause to visit the Alps (Wordsworth 1991: l. 6.351). The revolution combines these natural resources with individual and political rejuvenation:

> . . .'twas a time when Europe was rejoiced,
> France standing on the top of golden hours.
> And human nature seeming born again. (Wordsworth 1991: ll. 6.352–4)

Wordsworth's imagination becomes captivated by the notion of revolutionary society as an extension of the values of nature, founded on the same communal and ethical principles instilled in his mind in childhood. At this initial stage, Britain embraced the French Revolution as the inevitable counterpart of parliamentary reform, part of a trajectory of progress that would soon terminate arbitrary power.[10] The reinvention of society through the revolution is subsequently conflated with the rebirth of nature, so that Wordsworth finds

> . . . benevolence and blessedness
> Spread like a fragrance every where, like Spring
> That leaves no corner of the Land untouch'd. (Wordsworth 1991:
>   ll. 6.368–70)

Not only are nature and society reborn, but also Wordsworth's sense of himself: 'Bliss was it in that dawn to be alive, / But to be young was very heaven' (Wordsworth 1991: ll. 10.692–3). Natural, social and individual rejuvenation – dawn, revolution and youth – seamlessly coincide. Wordsworth subsequently resolves to make social life 'as just in regulation, and as pure / As individual in the wise and the good', extending what had previously been a concern with his own individual knowledge and virtue into a regard for society as a whole (ibid. ll. 9.370–1). The transition is effortless, as from the start nature had raised and prepared Wordsworth to conceive of himself within a broader social context.

General Wills, Individual Ills: The Life and Death of Social Bodies

During his visit to France in 1792, Wordsworth's friend and mentor Michel Beaupuy introduced him to Rousseau's *Discourse on the Origins of Inequality* and *Social Contract* (Wu 1994: 119). *The Prelude* echoes Rousseau's political writings, recounting Wordsworth's pivotal discussions with Beaupuy on the extension of private happiness into social rejuvenation whereby Rousseau's ideas are radicalised in the context of the French Revolution. Wordsworth and Beaupuy consider

> . . . How, together lock'd
> By new opinions, scatter'd tribes have made
> One body spreading wide as clouds in heaven.
> To aspirations then of our own souls
> Did we appeal; and finally beheld
> A living confirmation of the whole
> Before us in a People from the depths
> Of shameful imbecility upris'n
> Fresh, as the morning star. (Wordsworth 1991: ll. 9.392–400)

Wordsworth's reference to scatter'd tribes suggests an intermediate grouping which straddles private individuals and a broader 'confirmation of the whole'. James Chandler argues that Wordsworth draws on a chivalric, tribal register derived from Edmund Burke's concept of tradition (Chandler 1984: 205–6). Burke conceives of tradition as a middle ground between binary concepts of nature and society (ibid. 72). Chandler regards this middle ground as a site of disingenuousness, whereby Burke and Wordsworth in his wake can present their ideologies as natural. But Wordsworth's identification of a ground located midway between the state of nature and the state of society also serves as a site for potential empowerment, whereby the individual is able to change the social body. In this regard, we will see, Wordsworth is unique among Romantic writers. If the middle ground between nature and civilisation and extremes of individual freedom and institutional coercion eludes Rousseau and Coleridge (as I suggest in the coming chapters that it likewise eludes Godwin, Mary Shelley and Thomas Carlyle), Wordsworth is able to postulate his local social environment as a place of productive tension between individual and communal needs in *The Prelude*. Wordsworth derives this tertium quid from the new political account of society as existing to serve individual needs, and as not an inherent characteristic of human nature. For Rousseau, and Wordsworth after him, the individual precedes social arrangements.

In *The Prelude*, Wordsworth traces a movement from private, individual wills to one general will which Rousseau describes in *The Social Contract*. In his account of his discussions with Beaupuy, Wordsworth re-enacts Rousseau's vision that *'each of us puts all his power in common under the supreme direction of the general will; and in a body we receive each member as an indivisible part of the whole'* (Rousseau 1994c: 139). Wordsworth demonstrates his familiarity with the general will in the 'Letter to the Bishop of Llandaff', where he deems that 'it seems madness to expect a manifestation of the *general* will, at the same time that we allow to a *particular* will that weight which it must obtain in all governments, that can, with any propriety, be called monarchical' (Wordsworth 1974b: 41). In *The Prelude*, Wordsworth employs Rousseau's terminology to criticise monarchy in *ancien régime* France for disempowering citizens, registering 'hatred of absolute rule, where will of One / Is law for all' (Wordsworth 1991: ll. 9.514–15). After seeing a 'hunger-bitten Girl', the victim of despotism, Wordsworth blames 'sensual state and cruel power / Whether by the edict of the one or few' (ibid. ll. 9.512, 9.529–30). As in the 'Letter to the Bishop of Llandaff', here too Wordsworth suggests that 'the edict of the one or the few' is harmful to the greater good. He hopes to 'see the People having a strong hand / In framing their own Laws' and forming a more democratic government (ibid. ll. 9.543–4). Following Rousseau's argument in *Emile* that political liberation operates via education, Wordsworth suggests that democracy redeems private individuals 'from the depths / Of shameful imbecility' by providing education and political rights (ibid. ll. 9.398–9). In the 'Letter to the Bishop of Llandaff', he quotes Rousseau's *Social Contract*, 'every man born in slavery is born for slavery; nothing could be more certain. Slaves lose everything in their chains, even the desire to be rid of them. They love their servitude as the companions of Ulysses loved their brutishness' (Rousseau 1994c: 133).[11] Wordsworth admires Rousseau's attempt to reclaim people from the brutishness of slavery through education.

But despite his enthusiastic employment of Rousseauvian language and concepts, in *The Prelude* Wordsworth admits that his own education has been remiss in failing to master the underlying principles of political economy. He confesses having been

> . . . untaught by thinking or by books
> To reason well of polity or law
> And nice distinctions, then on every tongue,
> Of natural rights and civil. (Wordsworth 1991: ll. 9.208–11)

This naivety provides him with

> . . . a sounder judgment
> Than afterwards, [I] carried around with me yet
> With less alloy to its integrity
> The experience of past ages. (Wordsworth 1991: ll. 9.346–9)

Wordsworth suggests that he adopts corrupting social theories 'of natural rights and civil' without really understanding them (Wordsworth 1991: l. 9.204). Although he had 'skimm'd and sometimes read / With eagerness the Pamphlets of the day', he lacks a more thorough command of recent events in France (ibid. ll. 9.105–6):

> . . . Having never chanced
> To see a regular Chronicle which might shew,
> If any such indeed existed then,
> Whence the main organs of the public Power
> Had sprung, their transmigrations when and how
> Accomplish'd, giving thus unto events
> A form and body, all things were to me
> Loose and disjointed. (Wordsworth 1991: ll. 9.108–15)

This fractured state reflects Wordsworth's disjointed ideological affiliations. Initially, he mixes with aristocrats and royalists; in these circles

> . . . all discourse, alike
> Of good and evil, in the time, was shunn'd
> With studious care. (Wordsworth 1991: ll.9.120–2)

He then shifts to a desultory interest in the revolution,

> . . . and thus did soon
> Become a Patriot, and my heart was all
> Given to the People, and my love was theirs. (Wordsworth 1991:
>   ll. 9.123–6)

What unites these transitory, polarised ideologies is an uninformed grasp of historical events and an attendant lack of ideological grounding.

As revolutionary France degenerates into violence, Wordsworth grows increasingly aware of its proximity to a chaotic, anarchic state of nature, to which it can suddenly relapse without warning, as there is no real division between nature and society. Following the September massacres, he begins to perceive revolutionary society disintegrating into a pre-civilised state of nature that resembles Hobbes's war of all against all, rather than Rousseau's pre-social idyll. Wordsworth describes a night at the Place de Carrousel – a name that implies the fickle changeability of revolutionary society, which has turned from peaceableness to violence overnight. At this site where a month previously Republicans had massacred royalists, Wordsworth observes that Paris

> . . . at the best . . . seemed a place of fear,
> Unfit for the repose of night,
> Defenceless as a wood where tigers roam. (Wordsworth 1991: ll. 10.79–81)

He imagines the members of this new society as predatory tigers rather than cohesive bees (Wordsworth 1991: l. 6.403). Wordsworth reflects on this collapse of these 'scatter'd tribes', which no longer form one body (ibid. l. 9.393):

> . . . To Nature then
> Power had reverted; habit, custom, law
> Had left an interregnum's open space
> For her to move about in, uncontrol'd. (Wordsworth 1991: ll. 10.632–5)

Wordsworth criticises revolutionary social institutions for failing to establish cohesion. Whereas he had previously echoed Rousseau's disdain for 'the regal Sceptre, and the pomp / Of Orders and Degrees', he now determines that the 'interregnum' has left a moral void (Wordsworth 1991: ll. 9.219–20). Wordsworth now associates revolutionary society with violence and coerciveness. He parts ways through a metaphorical act of surgery, whereby the poet dissects his own body from the body politic:

> . . . I took the knife in hand,
> And, stopping not at parts less sensitive,
> Endeavoured with my best of skill to probe
> The living body of society
> Even to the heart. (Wordsworth 1991: ll. 10.872–6)

Wordsworth penetrates the core of the social body to separate himself from the social contract, echoing Gillray's visual iconography of bodily fragmentation as a type for social breakdown. Simpson reads such 'mutilated, misfitting or ill-coordinated body parts . . . [as] the visible signatures of a new world order, one of commodity labour and abstract ghostly social ties' rather than the robust embodiment of bygone times (Simpson 2009: 162). Even at the height of his revolutionary euphoria, Wordsworth identifies a strain in the new model of government. The individual citizens fail to conform to the one collective body of a general will. This difficulty soon has urgent and practical ramifications as the social body starts disintegrating into conflicting factions all vying for power. With the onset of the Reign of Terror, Wordsworth comes to recognise that although individualism may offer a fertile ground for change, it cannot produce a new version of community. Rousseau's general will violates its originary values of personal freedom, and is deployed to justify murder and force in France.

Wordsworth backtracks, turning his attention to distinguishing between rightful and abusive kings. His monarchism is apparent even in the radical 'Letter to the Bishop of Llandaff'. He now targets Napoleon's hypocritical coronation:

> . . . a Pope
> Is summon'd in, to crown an Emperor;
> This last opprobrium when we see the dog
> Returning to his vomit, when the sun
> That rose in splendour, was alive, and moved
> In exultation among living clouds
> Hath put his function and his glory off,
> And (turn'd into a gewgaw, a machine)
> Sets like an opera phantom. (Wordsworth 1991: ll. 10.969–77)

Napoleon's return to the regurgitated despotic model generates a complex reflection on the relations between nature and society that gave rise to the revolution. The 'dog / Returning to his vomit' suggests a natural depravity which is the opposite of the sun that 'moved / In exultation among living clouds', implying a dark side of nature that the revolution unveils. The 'sun / That rose in splendour', the sense of organically intertwined natural and social rejuvenation effected by the revolution, is inverted into a *deus ex machina*: 'a gewgaw, a machine . . . / . . . an opera phantom'. Deborah Jenson comments on the theatricality of revolutionary violence, which involved dramatically staged public executions and carnage (Jenson 2001: 14). Utopian revolutionary nature emerges as a cheap theatrical imitation. Wordsworth's initial vision of a society born from nature, which combines private individuals into a collective social body, collapses into its antithesis, into artifice and violence.

Wordsworth's disgust with the French Revolution temporarily leads him to shun social institutions and to blame ideological forces:

> ... When a taunt
> Was taken up by scoffers in their pride,
> Saying, 'Behold the harvest which we reap
> From popular Government and Equality',
> I saw that it was neither these, nor aught
> Of wild belief engrafted on their names
> By false philosophy, that caused the woe,
> But that it was a reservoir of guilt
> And ignorance, fill'd up from age to age,
> That could no longer hold its loathsome charge;
> And burst, and spread in deluge through the Land. (Wordsworth 1991:
>   10.459–69)

Wordsworth distinguishes himself from anti-Jacobin scoffers, who accuse 'popular Government and Equality' of being a false philosophy. He criticises the counterrevolutionary reaction in England:

> Our Shepherds (this say merely) at that time
> Thirsted to make the guardian Crook of Law
> A tool of murder. (Wordsworth 1991: ll.10.665–9)

Alluding to the treason trials of 1794 in which radicals faced death on charges of sedition, he ascribes the failure of the French Revolution to a tradition of 'false philosophy' which motivates the 'wild belief' which has taken revolutionary France by storm. This current failure extends beyond the French Revolution towards a broader theoretical difficulty uniting private individuals into a larger social entity; a weakness that Wordsworth had first associated with his own lack of theoretical grounding is now recognised as a more general problem characterising political theories, which likewise prove to be poorly informed.

Wordsworth's criticism of theory clearly echoes Edmund Burke's attack on 'people ... so taken up with theories about the rights of man that they have totally forgotten his nature' (Burke 1987: 56).[12] Burke argues that society cannot be conducted according to abstract principles of equality (ibid. 153). For the same reason, legislation is 'too arduous to be accomplished with no better apparatus than the metaphysics of an undergraduate, and the mathematics and arithmetic of an exerciseman' (ibid. 162). In his 1850 *Prelude*, Wordsworth appends an apostrophe to the 'Genius of Burke', begging his forgiveness for not having acknowledged his 'eloquent tongue' when he first heard him in London (Wordsworth 1985: l. 7.517). Chandler argues that Wordsworth came to regard Burke as a kind of prophet, who already knew in 1790 what Wordsworth would only learn from painful experience (Chandler 1984: 29). In 'A Letter to the Bishop of Llandaff' Wordsworth had termed Burke an 'infatuated moralist' and attacked his concept of constitution (Wordsworth 1974b: 36). He argues that

> Mr. Burke rous'd the indignation of all ranks of men, when by a refinement in cruelty superior to that which in the East yokes the living to the dead he strove to persuade us that we and our posterity to the end of time were riveted to a constitution by the indissoluble compact of a dead parchment, and were bound to cherish a corse at the bosom. (Wordsworth 1974b: 48)

Wordsworth's allusion to the practice of suttee to describe Burke's necrophilic adherence to the constitution suggests his anxiety about the prospect of a dead social body in which the vital friction between individuals reaches a standstill. Simpson observes that in poems such as 'Resolution and Independence' and 'Simon Lee' 'Wordsworth both performs and resists reproducing the deadening forces of the modern world around 1800 in a cycle of energy and entropy' (Simpson 2009: 187). The idea of the social body as driven by internal energies which threaten to die out returns, we will see, in Wordsworth's *Excursion* and later writings. In the 1850 *Prelude* Wordsworth conceives of Burke as part of the lifecycle of the social body; Burke is

> . . . old, but vigorous of age,–
> Stand[ing] like an oak whose stag-horn branches start
> Out of its leafy brow. (Wordsworth 1985: ll. 7.519–21)

The oak, an emblem of British monarchy and of the Restoration, symbolises organic cohesion and a Burkean privileging of the endurance of traditions 'old, but vigorous in age'.

Wordsworth now rejects individualism:

> What there is best in individual man,
> Of wise in passion and sublime in power,
> What there is strong and pure in household love,
> Benevolent in small societies,
> And great in large ones also . . .
> . . .
> . . . these momentous objects
> Had exercised my mind, yet had they not
> Though deeply felt been thoroughly understood
> By Reason; nay far from it. (Wordsworth 1991: ll.10.685–92)

Wordsworth's portrayals of his childhood and of his sojourns in London and post-revolutionary Europe describe a movement from nature to a society founded on the rights of the private individual. Wordsworth does have a 'deeply felt' intuition of how this new model of community should work. But he remains troubled by the fact that communal values are not 'thoroughly understood / By Reason' and seeks a stronger rationale for uniting private individuals into a coherent whole while retaining their sovereignty, the 'best in individual good'.

Repeatedly, following the revolution, Wordsworth emphasises the desire to ground happiness in a universal reality: 'Not favor'd spots alone, but the whole earth / The beauty wore of promise' (Wordsworth 1991: ll.10.719–20). This ideal is to be fulfilled in the here and now:

> Not in Utopia, subterraneous fields,
> Or some secreted Island Heaven knows where;
> But in the very world which is the world
> Of all of us, the place where, in the end
> We reap our happiness, or not at all. (Wordsworth 1991: ll.10.741–5)

Secreted islands and utopias cannot offer a broad social vision. When revolution fails, Wordsworth resorts to the private individual, the sole positive fragment that he is able to extract from Rousseau's theory. In this post-Revolutionary chapter Wordsworth consoles himself that

> As the desert hath green spots, the sea
> Small islands planted amid stormy waves,
> So that disastrous period did not want
> Bright sprinklings of all human excellence. (Wordsworth 1991: ll. 10.470–3)

Wordsworth finds 'human excellence' in the specific and the individual. He describes this new value through the simile of natural oases – Edenic 'green spots' and 'small islands' – which may recall Rousseau's interest in botany and the Elysium of Clarens, an oasis of idealised pseudo-natural serenity. Margery Sabin discusses Rousseau's image of the island as a metaphor for a self that is 'circumscribed and separate from the causes of discord outside' (Sabin 1976: 115). She connects Wordsworthian memory to Rousseau's description of self-isolation in *The Confessions* (ibid. 96–7). Following Rousseau's precedent of a self-reflexive withdrawal into memory, Wordsworth famously proffers

> There are in our existence spots of time,
> Which with distinct preeminence retain
> A renovating Virtue, whence, depress'd
> By false opinion and contentious thought
> Or aught of heavier or more deadly weight
> In trivial occupations, and the round
> Of ordinary intercourse, our minds
> Are nourish'd, and invisibly repair'd. (Wordsworth 1991: ll.11.243–50)

These spots of time represent a turning point in *The Prelude*, whereby Wordsworth resists the French Revolution and its attendant theories of contract, and moves to the sovereignty of the individual mind. Simpson notes that these spots 'protest against . . . the mechanics of commodity form' by developing an alternative, spasmodic approach to time (Simpson 2009: 138). Liberated from communal standards, Wordsworth acquires the

> . . . deepest feeling that the mind
> Is lord and master, and that outward sense
> Is but the obedient servant of her will. (Wordsworth 1991: ll. 11.256–8)

By privileging private individuality, he can now guarantee order and cohesion, at least within his own mind. As a result, he is able to impose his vision on the world in a new manner:

> I seem'd about this period to have sight
> Of a new world, a world, too, that was fit
> To be transmitted and made visible
> To other eyes. (Wordsworth 1991: ll.12.380–3)

Through poetry, Wordsworth transmits his own visionary experience 'to other[s]'. On the summit of Snowdon, he reflects on the supremacy of the individual mind, which has weathered revolution and crisis:

> . . . the mind of man becomes
> A thousand times more beautiful than the earth
> On which he dwells, above this Frame of things
> (Which 'mid all revolutions in the hopes
> And fears of men doth still remain unchanged). (Wordsworth 1991:
>   ll.13.452–6)

If social and natural values had previously formed the individual, the mind now both literally and figuratively rises above revolutions and the earth. Wordsworth places 'revolutions in the hopes / And fears of men' in parentheses, syntactically subordinating the social to the private and emphasising personal experience in the place of social institutions or historical processes. The famous Simplon Pass episode of *The Prelude* anticipates this focus on individual sovereignty. Wordsworth describes the realisation that he has unwittingly crossed the Alps as a moment of jarring dissonance which paradoxically yields insight into his vocation as a poet. Here he finds proof that

> Our destiny, our nature, and our home
> Is with infinitude, and only there,
> With hope it is, hope that can never die,
> Effort, and expectation, and desire,
> And something evermore about to be. (Wordsworth 1991: ll. 6.529–42)

Completion is no longer an objective criteria, but becomes a property of the individual will.

This Pisgah vision atop of Mont Blanc – parallel to the concluding ascent of Mount Snowdon – is often seen as marking a new phase in which Wordsworth ceased writing great works of poetry, and also stopped engaging significantly with politics.[13] Critics have contrasted the young Wordsworth with a conservative, older alter ego, who represents Wordsworth's 'own earliest and dullest critic, unsure of the ardor, belief, and assertion of his younger self' (Onorato 1971: 16). As a result, the afterlife of the 1805 *Prelude* – its 1850 version and *The Excursion* – is often dismissed as infelicitous to the modern literary and political sensibility. Expressing a self-professed preference for the final version of *The Prelude*, Wordsworth himself sought to legitimise multiple versions of this work by prescribing '[to follow] strictly the last copy of the text of an Author' (Wordsworth 2000a: 5.236). Yet surprisingly, despite significant differences of perspective and Wordsworth's attempt to supersede the 1805 version, he makes sparse narrative changes to his poem. Wordsworth maintains the viewpoint of events as they unfolded at the time and as they refract his later perspective, aiming to represent 'two consciousnesses, conscious of myself / And of some other Being', his earlier self (Wordsworth 1991: ll. 2.32–3).What changes rather than the story, especially after publishing *Poems in Two Volumes* in 1807, is Wordsworth's use of language as a reflection his changing ideology. This is tangible in his re-drafting of the 1805 *Prelude* into its 1850 version. Discussing his post-revolutionary despair in 1805, Wordsworth remarks:

> So that disastrous period did not want
> Such sprinklings of all human excellence
> As were a joy to hear of. (Wordsworth 1991: ll.10. 442–4)

In 1850, the comfort of 'human excellence' becomes subordinate to divine authority:

> So *that* disastrous period did not want
> Bright sprinklings of all human excellence
> To which the silver wands of saints in heaven
> Might point with rapturous joy. (Wordsworth 1985: ll. 10.483–6)

Human interlocutors, who are 'a joy to hear' in 1805, become the 'silver wands of saints in heaven' in the later version. For twentieth- and twenty-first-century readers, Wordsworth's Christian embellishment seems to eclipse the individual sovereignty which Wordsworth celebrates in the 1805 *Prelude*.

Nonetheless, in this later development, Wordsworth retains his model of ongoing reciprocal tensions between notions of individuality and society. As Steven Affeldt argues apropos of the general will in *The Social Contract*, society needs to retain friction between its individual members in order remain a collective entity, and not a unitary will that finally excludes its members (Affeldt 2000: 556). Wordsworth becomes preoccupied with this dialectic tension, and anxious about its possible collapse. His comments on terminating the thirteen-book *Prelude* suggest his anxiety about the fragility of the individual will:

> I finished my Poem about a fortnight ago, I had looked forward to the day as a most happy one . . . but it was not a happy day for me – I was dejected on many accounts; when I looked back upon the performance it seemed to have a dead weight about it, the reality so far short of the expectation. (Wordsworth 1988: 1.594)

Wordsworth had already used the phrase 'dead weight' in his metaphor of 'cruelty, superior to that which in the East yokes the living to the dead' in the 'Letter to the Bishop of Llandaff' (Wordsworth 1974b: 48). This collocation is initially associated with Burke's constitution. Here it becomes connected to a kind of writerly postpartum depression. In the 'Essay, Supplementary to the Preface of *Lyrical Ballads* (1800)' of 1815, Wordsworth critiques literature that does not actively engage the individual agency of the reader using similar terms:

> Is it to be supposed that the reader can make progress of this kind, like an Indian prince or general – stretched on his palanquin, and borne by his slaves? No; he is invigorated and inspirited by his Leader, in order that he may exert himself; for he cannot proceed in quiescence, he cannot be carried like a *dead weight*. Therefore to create taste is to call forth and bestow power. (Wordsworth 1974a: 82, emphasis added)

Wordsworth invokes the colonial register of oriental despotism to propose a redeployment of power whereby the private reader becomes an agent in social and semantic formation, rather than a despotic 'dead weight' for whom the author must cater. Wordsworth's language in this passage shapes Coleridge's assertion, in the *Biographia Literaria* (1818), that 'the reader should be carried forward' by the aesthetic pleasure of the text alone (Coleridge 1983: 2.14). Through these three very different examples – Wordsworth's early critique of Burke, his disappointment with his (temporarily) completed *Prelude* and his reflections on relations between authors and their readers – Wordsworth demonstrates a pervasive concern with the collapse of freedom. Like Coleridge, he regards literature as a means of encouraging individual freedom. The writer should not be a drudge, carrying his readers, but their leader, invigorating and empowering his audience. If a reader who unquestioningly adopts a ready-made system is 'carried like a dead weight' by its author, Wordsworth suggests that his own arrival at a conclusive version of his poem renders him a passive nonentity (Wordsworth 1974a: 82).

Coleridge singles out the departure from fixed forms as Wordsworth's foremost contribution to their common *Lyrical Ballads* enterprise: 'Mr. Wordsworth . . . give[s] the charm of novelty to things of every day, and . . . excite[s] a feeling analogous to the supernatural, by awakening the mind's lethargy from the familiarity of custom' (Coleridge 1983: 2.7). Wordsworth promotes radical freedom in his dynamic style: 'had I met these lines running wild in the deserts of Arabia, I should have instantly screamed out "Wordsworth!"' (Coleridge 2002: 1.453) With the freedom from fixed categories comes the ability to question social structures and retain ambivalences, suggested in Coleridge's assessment that Wordsworth's 'language [in *Descriptive Sketches*] was not only peculiar and strong, but at times knotty and contorted, as by its own impatient strength' (Coleridge 1983: 1.77). Coleridge imagines Wordsworth's language as a complex body with its own internal life and conflicts, using imagery parallel to that of Rousseau to suggest the ability to tolerate conflict, alluding to the thickets that Rousseau's forest-like discourse creates in *Rousseau, Judge of Jean-Jacques*.

For Wordsworth, formal closure eliminates agency and the freedom to exercise one's own will. His notion of his poem as a disappointing performance solicits new versions, as his subsequent thirty years of revision of *The Prelude* inevitably suggest.[14] Therefore, more than being a source of frustration, Wordsworth's dejection and sense that his poem has failed to match his expectations opens up new possibilities and the solace provided by the possibility to continually develop the self. Ambiguity and lack of closure characterise Wordsworth's approach to poetry throughout his career. Francis Jeffrey condones Wordsworth's equivocal diction and accuses him of being 'more obscure than a Pindaric poet of the seventeenth century' (Jeffrey 1860: 459).[15] As a result, 'the doctrine which . . . [*The Excursion*] is intended to enforce, we are by no means certain that we have discovered' (ibid. 460). Later generations of critics have been similarly disturbed by Wordsworth's equivocation, so that new historicist scholarship reads the ending of the 1805 *Prelude* as Wordsworth's ultimate act of socio-historical evasion, where Wordsworth obscures the social contexts of his poem through recourse to obscure diction.[16] Wordsworth draws this obscurity in part from Rousseau's own complex approach to literature as less committed to standards of consistency than other forms of discourse and as a site for redefining the individual. Wordsworth departs from other aspects of

Rousseau's thought, rejecting his agonistic relationship between nature and society, which are separated by a sharp dividing line. In this regard Coleridge is far closer to Rousseau than Wordsworth as his mariner crosses the line separating civilisation from nature, a transgression that Wordsworth criticises for having many 'great defects' (Wordsworth and Coleridge 2008: 289). By contrast, Wordsworth emphasises that his own character always maintains a balance between self and environment.

Wordsworth expresses concern about a lack of balance between the individual and society through his criticisms of Adam Smith and William Godwin in *The Prelude*, otherwise dissimilar thinkers whom he charges with a similar excessive individualism. These negative comparisons foreground the ongoing importance of community to Wordsworth's poetic vision in terms that depart from the social contract and return to a neo-Aristotelian communitarianism. Wordsworth quarrels with Smith's perceived failure to reconcile individuals within a broader system and with his weak account of sociability. In *The Wealth of Nations*, Smith suggests that by pursuing private sentiments and interests people also inevitably promote the wellbeing of others. Smith's *Theory of Moral Sentiments*, which had entered the popular imagination in the 1790s and was published in a sixth and final edition in 1790, presents the more complex model of sociability through sympathy and alienation. Smith is troubled by the problem that people 'feel so little for another, with whom they have no particular connexion, in comparison of what they feel for themselves' (Smith 2002: 101). He questions his assertion that a regard for individuals will entail a regard for the multitude, and formulates a theory of sympathy through impartial spectatorship. Following Smith's own doubts about his theory of sociability, Wordsworth complains of 'the utter hollowness of what is named / The wealth of Nations' (Wordsworth 1991: ll. 12.77–8). His 1850 *Prelude* continues this attack on 'theories / Vague and unsound' and 'the Books / Of modern Statists' for doing injustice to 'life, human life, with all its sacred claims / Of sex and age, and heaven-descended rights' (Wordsworth 1985: ll. 13.69–70, 13.71–2, 13.73–4). Connell argues that Wordsworth is not only addressing Smith himself, but more generally a post-Smithian tradition within political economy, represented by such diverse figures as Thomas Malthus, David Ricardo and Godwin (Connell 2001: 16). Wordsworth criticises the exclusion of meaningful social identities of gender, age and locality from political economy which the Smithian impartial spectator (and the Malthusian urban planner and Godwinian necessitarian, to boot) must set aside in order to form moral judgments. Instead of these abstract, deracinated models of sympathy, Wordsworth strives to reintegrate 'a more judicious knowledge of the worth / And dignity of individual man' into the 'laws, and fashion of the State' (Wordsworth 1991: ll.13.80–1, 13.104). Wordsworth suggests that these models of political economy are founded on the elision of private identities.

In his 'Essay, Supplementary to the Preface of *Lyrical Ballads* (1800)', Wordsworth critiques a prevalent view of literature as having 'no fixed principles in human nature . . . to rest upon' (Wordsworth 1974a: 71). Wordsworth ascribes this misapprehension to Smith, whom he dismisses as 'the worst critic, David Hume not excepted, that Scotland, a soil to which this sort of weed seems natural, has produced' (ibid. 71, note). Hume and Smith base their respective social theories on the notion of self-interest. Hume argues that '*self-interest is the original motive of the establishment of justice*', and therefore also of society (Hume 1978: 499). Smith similarly asserts self-interest as the main principle of socialisation (Smith 2002: 23). By using a derogatory natural metaphor to critique Hume and Smith, Wordsworth suggests that their individualistic accounts of human nature are pre-human in the Hobbesian sense, devoid of the principle of fellow feeling privileged in Scottish Enlightenment thought. Their respective defences of self-interest are repugnant to Wordsworth's collectivist sensibilities, representing what he perceives to be a violent and lawless social vision. In his *Tract on the Convention of Cintra* (1808), Wordsworth uses the metaphor of bad weeds to critique the Rousseauvian philosophical tradition rather than that of Hume and Smith, echoing Coleridge's association of Rousseau with theories of natural semination in his anecdote about his Nether Stowey garden. Wordsworth's indictment of Scottish political economy and Rousseau through the shared image of weeds reinforces his view of both as similarly individualistic. To justify the English and Spanish as well-matched allies against Napoleon's army, Wordsworth asserts that 'the paradoxical reveries of Rousseau, and the flippancies of Voltaire, are plants which will not naturalise in the country of Calderon and Cervantes' (Wordsworth 1915: 177). The *philosophes* represent a negative form of nature, like the Convention of Cintra itself – a controversial peace treaty between British and French forces that allowed the defeated French to evacuate Portugal – which Wordsworth describes as 'a solitary straggler out of the circumference of nature's law – a monster which could not propagate and had no birthright in futurity' (ibid. 97). Wordsworth suggests that Rousseau's 'paradoxical reveries' are a threat to the social order, alluding to the characteristically Rousseauvian conflict between social and individual needs which motivates Wordsworth's knotty poetics.

Whereas Wordsworth sets aside his subsequent disappointment with Rousseau, the same can certainly not be said of his attitude to Godwin.

He presents Godwin as inherently unsound and finds himself unable to provide a diachronic account of his initial attraction, counter to his usual practice of maintaining 'two consciousnesses' of past and present perspectives, a double vision which allows him to remember why he initially admired the revolution and also to recall his love for Coleridge at the point when the two were no longer on speaking terms (Wordsworth 1991: l. 2.32). Wordsworth admits to temporarily succumbing to Godwin's view of 'human Reason's naked self [as] / The object of its fervour' (ibid. ll. 10.817–18). He ascribes his admiration of Godwin to a 'time when all things tended fast / To depravation' (ibid. ll. 10.805–6). Wordsworth disdains Godwin's model of 'self-knowledge and self-rule', preferring actual political institutions to the coercive internalisation of social control (ibid. l. 10.819). He criticises 'build[ing] social freedom on its only basis: / The freedom of the individual mind' (ibid. ll. 10.824–5). This approach deprives individuals of their autonomy and subjects them to 'the blind restraint of general laws' (ibid. l. 10.826). In response, Wordsworth suggests reintroducing a consideration of specific 'accidents of nature, time, and place', which constitute the private individual (ibid. l. 10.822). His apostrophe to Dorothy and Coleridge at the end of *The Prelude* is a synecdoche for the turn to more local social relations (ibid. ll. 13.211–68). Sarah Zimmerman classifies these addressees as types for broader society, so that even at his most withdrawn and conservative, Wordsworth always involves his readers in shared social concerns and contexts (Zimmerman 2000: 102).[17]

Wordsworth's criticisms of Godwin are really exaggerated versions of those directed at Rousseau, who influenced Godwin's attempt to combine radical individualism with social arrangements in his 1793 *Political Justice*. Godwin develops Rousseau's criticism of social institutions, openly positing all forms of government as bondage: 'man is in a state of perpetual progress. He must grow either better or worse. . . . By its very nature, political institution has a tendency to suspend the elasticity, and put an end to the advancement of mind' (Godwin 1993a: 106). At some future point, because differences among individuals 'are accidental varieties' and 'there is but one perfection to man', Godwin anticipates 'the dissolution of government' (ibid. 48). He departs from Rousseau's account of individuals originating in a pre-social state of nature by returning to a view of sociability as an innate property. Godwin suggests that natural sociability will ultimately guarantee political conformity without the need for external institutions:

If, as Rousseau has somewhere asserted, 'the great duty of man be to do no injury to his neighbour', then this negative sincerity may be of considerable account: but, if it be the highest and most indispensible business of man to study and promote his neighbour's welfare, a virtue of this sort will contribute little to so honourable an undertaking. (Godwin 1993a: 464–5)

In the next chapter we will see that deep within the private Godwinian individual is an inherently sociable consciousness struggling to break free, so that Godwinian individualism proves to be an oxymoron, as its pursuit leads to radical conformity. Wordsworth's disdain for Godwin arises from his insight into Godwin's articulation of a fundamentally Rousseauvian paradox.

Utopia in *The Excursion*

The Excursion continues Wordsworth's critique of abstract political theory and his quest for a more significant basis of sociability which now takes on neo-Aristotelian overtones. The story of *The Excursion* continues where *The Prelude* left off, repeating the narrative of revolution and reaction, but with a twist. This time, Wordsworth recasts his autobiography in far less ambiguous terms through the character of the Solitary, an allegorical representation of the poet. Like Wordsworth, the Solitary is led astray by the French Revolution and by Godwinism, the latter of which drives him to the brink of suicide;[18] unlike the Wordsworth of *The Prelude*, the Solitary eventually subordinates his individuality to social institutions represented by Christianity, and thus redresses the balance between the individual and society in favour of the latter. *The Excursion*'s resolution of *The Prelude*'s more open-ended social dilemmas renders it an explicitly didactic text. The various characters – the speaker, the Wanderer, the Solitary and the pastor – affirm one another's perspectives, rather than engaging in the ambivalent, dialectical ideologies which characterise *The Prelude*. The utopian communitarianism that emerges is incompatible with the trajectory of self-alienation and conflict, the knots that characterise *The Prelude* across its various versions. Wordsworth's writing suffers the 'dead weight' ensuing from the loss of individual volition that he so feared would happen.

Through the character of the Wanderer, Wordsworth clearly rejects individualism and comes to celebrate

Creatures, that in communities exist,
Less, as might seem, for general guardianship
Or through dependence upon mutual aid,
Than by participation of delight
And a strict love of fellowship, combined. (Wordsworth 2007: ll. 4.443–6)

A 'strict love of fellowship', identified with the church, is contrasted with individualistic rationales for forming societies – the 'general guardianship' and 'dependence upon mutual aid' for private benefit argued by Rousseau in his *Social Contract*, and the 'participation by delight' that Wordsworth had encountered in Europe immediately after the revolution. Wordsworth rules out individualism as a rationale for community. His speaker observes that states and kingdoms have failed to represent justice:

> . . . Earth is sick,
> And Heaven is weary of the hollow words
> Which States and Kingdoms utter when they talk. (Wordsworth 2007:
>   ll. 5.378–80)

Smaller communities have modestly more success in reconciling sociability with individualism. But even here only an elect 'few . . . mingle with their fellow-men / And still remain self-governed' (Wordsworth 2007: ll. 5.385–6). Nature is similarly unable to balance personal integrity with social cohesion. In spite of their misleadingly peaceful demeanour, the country villagers living close to nature 'partake man's general lot / With little mitigation', facing disappointment and the squandering of their potential like everyone else (ibid. ll. 5.427–8). The catastrophic results of Rousseau's social theory are demonstrated by the Solitary, who is driven to suicidal despair by radical rhetoric. The pastor consoles him:

> We may not doubt that who can best subject
> The will to Reason's law, and strictliest live
> And act in that obedience, he shall gain
> The clearest apprehension of those truths,
> Which unassisted reason's utmost power
> Is too infirm to reach. (Wordsworth 2007: ll. 5.513–17)

The Solitary, who personifies the private will, overcomes individualistic revolutionary theory and submits to a more general authority. The enjambment of 'the will' to the verb 'subject' syntactically enacts a new model, whereby individuality is relegated to broader systems.

Elsewhere, Wordsworth clearly criticises the ills of individualism and advocates communitarianism. Like Rousseau who asserts that dissident elements in the social body must be 'forced to be free', the Wanderer suggests that a surfeit of freedom paradoxically produces enslavement, and so must be curtailed. Here Wordsworth has departed from Affeldt's vitalist model of friction between individual and general wills, and towards a more deterministic reading of the social contract

as prescribing the complete absorption of the individual will within
the general will, closer to Rousseau than to Kantian interpretations of
contract. Describing an aging couple, the Wanderer exclaims:

> O happy! yielding to the law
> Of these privations, richer in the main! –
> While thankless thousands are opprest and clogged
> By ease and leisure; by the very wealth
> And pride of opportunity made poor. (Wordsworth 2007: ll. 5.828–32)

Through the oxymoron of privations that make one richer, or of
being 'opprest and clogged / By ease', Wordsworth suggests that individual agency is incompatible with the greater good, and eventually also
harmful to the individual. Instead Wordsworth prescribes total submission to collective laws as optimal to personal and political freedom.
This total submission cancels the dialectic between individual and social
being, producing a state of entropic inertia that translates into a loss of
rhetorical force in Wordsworth's poetry.

In a scene that symbolises this shift from individual sovereignty to
social coercion, Wordsworth's characters chance upon a mildewed copy
of *Candide*, which is being used to prop up a dilapidated children's
playhouse. They deem *Candide* the 'dull product of a scoffer's pen' and
blame it for leading the Solitary astray (Wordsworth 2007: l. 2.510).
Its location indicates Wordsworth's critique of individualistic values.
As Kenneth Johnston argues, 'the allegory is obvious: a ruined "petty"
civilization founded on no better stay than ... [Voltaire's] caustic
rationalism' (Johnston 1984: 268). The book's compost-like condition
of decomposition indicates Wordsworth's rejection of Voltaire's
argument that social wellbeing starts with private happiness in his call
to 'cultivate our gardens' (Voltaire 2005: 130). By categorising *Candide*
as refuse, Wordsworth suggests that 'cultivat[ing] our gardens' leads
to the Solitary's solipsistic demise and to social breakdown through
the French Revolution, which Wordsworth associates with Rousseau,
who is grouped with Voltaire in the *Tract on the Convention of Cintra*
(Wordsworth 1915: 177).

The state of nature, the post-Enlightenment garden of individuality,
does not foster social harmony and cohesion, but strews ruin in
Wordsworth's final reckoning. Here Wordsworth moves away from
his own postulation of an easy transition between the state of nature
and the state of society in *The Prelude*. He also turns from Rousseau's
vital friction between private and general wills. More than two hundred
years later, Wordsworth's account of the inception of this modern
dilemma in *The Prelude* fascinates readers far more than its utopian

resolution in *The Excursion*. Questions of what unites individuals and whether cultivating one's garden benefits others, which emerge from Rousseau's writings, shape Wordsworth's unprecedentedly involved and introspective *Prelude*. They have remained at the foreground of modern culture, eclipsing Wordsworth's final collapse into utopianism and vacancy.

Notes

1. Existing studies of *The Prelude* and Rousseau mainly focus on Wordsworth's relationship to *The Confessions*. See Gregory Dart, who suggests that the interpretation of Rousseau's first-person narration as a politically radical form in the aftermath of the French Revolution shaped Wordsworth's subjectivism (Dart 1999: 180). Margery Sabin contrasts Rousseau's characteristic conflict between imagination and social constraints in *The Confessions* with Wordsworth's redemptive account of imagination (Sabin 1970: 339–40). Nancy Yousef compares Rousseau's sense of himself as an outcast in *The Reveries of the Solitary Walker* with the humanistic vision that Wordsworth produces from his solitude in *The Prelude* (Yousef 2004: 129–32).
2. Major discussions include works by Marilyn Butler (1982), David Bromwich (1998), Nicolas Roe (2002), and John Bugg (2013).
3. Susan Wolfson describes Wordsworth's practice of editing as 'a devolutionary tale: the revisions seem less to signify improvement than a hardening of sensibility, the story of decline, default, and anticlimax that gets told about the career as a whole' (Wolfson 1997: 101). A similar view is offered by many others, notably Stephen Parrish, the general editor of *The Cornell Wordsworth*, who explains that the series aims 'to bring the early Wordsworth into view. Wordsworth's . . . lifelong habit of revision . . . [has] obscured the original, often the best, versions of his work' (Wordsworth 1991: v). An interesting exception to this consensus is argued by Alan Liu, who entertains 'the possibility that Wordsworth was his own critic' in his later work (Liu 1989: 456). Liu thus reverses Richard Onorato's evaluation that in his later years Wordsworth was an acerbic critic of his younger self (Onorato 1971: 16).
4. For this 1980s account of Wordsworth's flight from imagination, see Marjorie Levinson's foundational argument:

    > Wordsworth is most distinctly Wordsworth, most Romantic and most successful in those poems where the conflicts embedded in his materials, motives, and methods are most expertly displaced, and where, as a result, the poetry looks most removed from anything so banal as a polemic or a position. (Levinson 1986: 4)

    Liu describes Wordsworth's 1805 *Prelude* as 'a mimetic denial of history so vigorous, full, and detailed that denial, the shaped negation, becomes itself the positive fact' (Liu 1989: 48). And Jerome McGann proposes that *The*

Prelude 'annihilates its history, biographical and socio-historical alike, and replaces these particulars with a record of pure consciousness' (McGann 1983: 90).

5. Martha Woodmansee and Mark Osteen identify the emergence of a new economic school of literary criticism that has developed from new historicism and cultural studies (Woodmansee and Osteen 1999: 4).

6. Philip Connell defines British Romanticism as a reaction against post-Enlightenment concepts of market value (Connell 2001: 119). Similarly, Matthew Rowlinson considers Romanticism 'as a historically specific response to the newly abstract commodity-form assumed by writing in the period and to the exceptional indeterminacy of the forms of money for which it was exchanged' (Rowlinson 2010: 192).

7. For discussions of Romanticism and Enlightenment epistemology, see Cathy Caruth's argument that Wordsworth's concern with states of self-disruption derives from John Locke's narrative of sensation as an uncontrolled aspect of the self (Caruth 1991: 14–15). Nancy Yousef argues that British Romantic literature criticises Enlightenment political theory for presenting the individual as developing independently of social interactions (Yousef 2004: 118). Alan Bewell analyses Wordsworth's fascination with social outcasts as providing a means of understanding consciousness through conjectural social histories (Bewell 1989: 28).

8. Monique Morgan notes this prospective pattern of development in *The Prelude*, where the narrative is known from the beginning and the emphasis is on how the associations converge (Morgan 2009: 308).

9. To some extent, the Cambridge episode in book three anticipates Wordsworth's account of London. Wordsworth arrives at Cambridge with similar expectations. These are disappointed by an alienating 'gaudy Congress, framed / Of things, by nature, most unneighbourly' (Wordsworth 1991: ll. 3.662–3).

10. In his *The Life of Napoleon Buonaparte* (1830), William Hazlitt describes the optimism and national pride that the French Revolution inspired in the English prior to 1793, as they saw France following in their footsteps:

> The Revolution of 1688 gave the death's wound to the doctrine of hereditary right . . . This example, set by the English people and confirmed by English philosophers, was the glass in which France (if she knew her own dignity and interest) was to dress herself. There was an honest simplicity and severity in our style of our civil architecture . . . that acted as a foil to the Gothic redundancy and disproportioned frippery of our continental neighbors. (Hazlitt 1830: 1.99)

Stripped of artifice, France enters a joyous state of nature very similar to that described by Wordsworth in his account of his initial visit of 1790:

> The difference [was] not between the old and new philosophy, but between the natural dictates of the heart and the artificial and oppressive distinctions of society . . . From Nature's bastards, they had become her sons, children of one common parent; in all their towns and villages you were met with songs of triumph, with the festive dance and garlands of flowers, as in a time of jubilee and rejoicing. (Hazlitt 1830: 1.191)

11. Wordsworth cites these lines in the original French (Wordsworth 1974b: 36).
12. David Simpson points out the longevity of Burke's idea that theory is a dangerous force (Simpson 1993: 151–2).
13. Jonathan Wordsworth assesses Wordsworth as less interesting as 'he lives in less interesting times' from this point onwards (Wordsworth 1992: 38). Charles Rzepka argues that Wordsworth's genius was fundamentally solipsistic; when he became an established family man and bureaucrat after the revolution he no longer needed to withdraw, and his poetry lost its salience (Rzepka 1986: 99). In his biography of Wordsworth Stephen Gill argues that Wordsworth's changing politics detracted from his poetry (Gill 1989: 320). John Bugg explains that Wordsworth's poetics were written strategically to evade repressive governmental practices and the threat of prosecution in the 1790s and was defined by this specific political context (Bugg 2013: 149).
14. In his biography of Wordsworth, Stephen Gill notes that his habitual revision was always accompanied by 'illness, fatigue, and sleepless nights' (Gill 1989: 192). Wordsworth links confrontation with the finality of form to notions of death and disease, which he counteracts with a poetics of indeterminacy and with revision.
15. Francis Jeffrey lists the sheer length of Wordsworth's poetry, its didacticism – involving 'a series of long sermons and harangues' – and Wordsworth's predilection for 'eminently fantastic, obscure, and affected' diction as the major factors inhibiting its clarity (Jeffrey 1860: 458, 459, 460).
16. See for example Alan Liu, who asserts: '[the imagination] crosses its mountain pass, climbs its cloud-veiled peak, to enter a new land where collective loss can be imagined the gain of the individual' (Liu 1989: 455).
17. Richard Eldridge similarly notes the value that Wordsworth places on context:

> Wordsworthian Romanticism is marked by a continuous awareness of the local and temporal situatedness of human thought, so much so that human thought is typically represented as occasioned by specific places and as including an awareness of its own temporal development. (Eldridge 2001: 105–6)

18. Sally Bushell also relates Wordsworth's 1812 composition of the Solitary's narrative describing the deaths of his wife and two children to Wordsworth's loss of his own two children, Catherine and Thomas, earlier that year (Bushell 2003: 11).

Part III

Novels

Chapter 5

Empiricism's Secret History: *Fleetwood* and Rousseau

The perfection of the human character consists in approaching as nearly as possible to the perfectly voluntary state. We ought to be upon all occasions prepared to render a reason for our actions. We should remove ourselves to the farthest distance from the state of mere inanimate machines. (Godwin 1993b: 34)

The Romantic poems and novels discussed in this book all criticise the social contract tradition for failing to integrate the social body into a totality.[1] But Romantic poetry also maintains a critical distance from philosophical discourse, as suggested by Samuel Taylor Coleridge's sceptical representation of Jean-Jacques Rousseau and by Wordsworth's shifting viewpoints in *The Prelude*. By contrast narrative fiction has always been an integral aspect of philosophical argumentation, and particularly of empiricism. For this reason, the Romantic novel is more closely aligned with social contract theory than is Romantic poetry. Whereas Coleridge and Wordsworth can propose reorganising society in lieu of contract (along sceptical and neo-Aristotelian lines respectively), William Godwin, Mary Shelley and Thomas Carlyle all focus their works on dissident individuals that are excluded from social construction, and explore their predicaments through the techniques of fiction. Wordsworth associates Godwin with an inexcusable position of extreme individualism. But this is a partial reading of Godwin's 1793 *Enquiry Concerning Political Justice*, which does not engage with its radically communitarian politics. And Wordsworth also ignores Godwin's rendering of private perspectives of malaise and discontent in his novels. In anatomising the ills of individualism, Godwin's novel *Fleetwood: Or, The New Man of Feeling* (1805) features Rousseau the philosopher as a fictional character. In *Mandeville, A Tale of the Seventeenth Century in England* (1817) Godwin fictionalizes the first Earl of Shaftesbury, Anthony Ashley Cooper, grandfather of the third Earl of Shaftesbury Anthony Ashley Cooper, patron of John Locke and founder of the

Whig party, as a character in his novel. In this chapter, I shall show how Godwin forms these characters and presents their ideologies as disruptive forces. In *Fleetwood* and in *Mandeville*, Godwin reduces Rousseau and Shaftesbury respectively, towering figures in their times, to a relatively minor scale, enacting their focus on the small individual instead of the big social picture, and thus also displacing their philosophical systems from the centre to the margins. In Rousseau's case this involves casting him posthumously as a dead character whose legacy still haunts the living. *Things as They Are; or, The Adventures of Caleb Williams* (1794) is perhaps a more obvious case for my argument, with its frequently cited treatment of the underhand workings of power and its destructive effects on individual lives. However the relationship to philosophy and to actual figures in that novel, while important, remains indirect and allusive.[2] By contrast, *Fleetwood* and *Mandeville* establish a direct line with the empiricist tradition.

Godwin's characterisations of Rousseau and the first Earl of Shaftesbury have been largely overlooked due to the critical tendency to separate Godwin's career into an initial radical phase and a relatively moderate later one, following the more general tendency to organise Romanticism by genre and discrete political positions.[3] So great is this divide that Percy Shelley's poetry is sometimes cited as 'more Godwinian than Godwin', a more faithful adaptation of the *Enquiry Concerning Political Justice* (1793) than any of Godwin's novels, which actually formulate a discrete and critical perspective on his political writings (St. Clair 1989: 341).[4] But much like Coleridge, Wordsworth or Rousseau himself, Godwin is less affected by discrete chronological phases and genres than by inherently conflicting positions.[5] A view of his writings as divided between a non-Rousseauvian political phase and a sentimental literary one obscures the conflict between society at large and the private individual in his works. In his advertisement to the 1798 version of *Political Justice*, Godwin classifies his 'alterations . . . though numerous . . . [as] not of a fundamental nature' (Godwin 1993b: 8). Godwin further maintains that he has not 'change[d] . . . the principle of justice, or any thing else fundamental to the system' (Godwin 2006: 52). Instead, he justifies *Political Justice*'s ongoing development in terms of his progressivist thesis that all intellectual endeavour participates in an inevitable trajectory of perfectibility (Godwin 1993b: 7). Godwin's main positions and conflicts therefore remain stable. Although critics have suggested that his relationship with Mary Wollstonecraft in 1796 altered his opinions on domesticity, he consistently retains his rejections of marriage and biological parentage throughout all versions of *Political Justice* as well as in his novels (ibid. 337, 340).[6]

Godwin suggests that reading David Hume's *Treatise of Human*

Nature after writing the 1793 *Political Justice* led him to attribute greater agency to the individual (Godwin 2007b: 54). He argues that the original *Political Justice* overlooks individual feeling and the 'private affections' (ibid. 53).[7] Most critics accept Godwin's explanation that this earlier version of *Political Justice* neglects 'the humbler part of our nature' and the condition of man as 'a fluctuating and variable animal' (Godwin 1993b: 419). In the preface to *St. Leon*, Godwin declares that after completing the 1793 *Political Justice* he came '[to] apprehend domestic and private affections as inseparable from the nature of man' (Godwin 2006: 52). However, Godwin's developing emphasis on sentiment does not stand in opposition to his earlier focus on politics. James Chandler's and Hina Nazar's politicised accounts of sentimentalism allow for a reading of Godwin's sentimental novels within his political theory that follows the precedent set by Rousseau's career.[8] Following these arguments I propose to read Godwin's novels as expressions of the underlying tensions of his political theory, and to locate these tensions, along with Godwin's deployment of literature as philosophy's 'judge', broadly within the empiricist tradition. Social contract theory, which unites political philosophy with Rousseauvian sentimental literature, is not usually considered as a context for Godwin's works because of the tendency to separate the two. Moreover, like Coleridge, Godwin mainly had bad things to say about the social contract. But, as with Coleridge, Godwin's complaints warrant close attention as expressions of an investment in this tradition, rather than articulations of dismissal.

Godwin and the Social Contract

Godwin's main bone of contention with contract theory is its postulation of the individual as a potentially pre-social entity. In an autobiographical note Godwin explains that this dislike of radical individualism was determined by his education. He recalls being taught 'ineffable contempt, of Rousseau, and other chicken-hearted doctrinists' by his rational dissenting instructors (Godwin 2007b: 34). Instead of timorous Rousseauvian individualism, Godwin follows his tutor's neo-Aristotelian view that individuals have a robust natural regard for one another:

> If, as Rousseau has somewhere asserted, 'the great duty of man be to do no injury to his neighbour', then this negative sincerity may be of considerable account: but, if it be the highest and most indispensable business of man to study and promote his neighbour's welfare, a virtue of this sort will contribute little to so honourable an undertaking. (Godwin 1993b: 165–6)

Godwin reacts to Rousseau's thin social model by developing a counter-theory of innate sociability.[9] He proposes that 'Man is a social animal. How far he is necessarily so will appear, if we consider the sum of advantages resulting from the social, and of which he would be deprived in the solitary state' (Godwin 1993a: 404). According to Godwin, individuals participate in a larger system of necessity, whereby 'all the parts . . . are strictly connected with each other, and exhibit a sympathy and unison by means of which the whole is rendered intelligible' (ibid. 272). You must defer to this unison 'with the same unalterable firmness of judgment and the same tranquillity as [to] . . . the truths of geometry' (ibid. 173). Godwin further deems personal differences 'accidental varieties. There is but one perfection to man' (Godwin 1993b: 118).

In social contract theory individuals precede society; for Godwin society precedes the individual, a neo-Aristotelian axiology which he calls 'necessity'. To describe necessity as a relationship of deep interconnection, Godwin uses the metaphor of chains, an image which he draws from Rousseau's suggestion that 'Man was / is born free, and everywhere he is in chains' (Rousseau 1994c: 131). Like Adam Ferguson's notion of society as an arch, Godwin imagines individuals as united by a benign natural bond. Necessity guarantees that all are woven together into one fabric: 'human affairs, through every link of the great chain of necessity, are admirably harmonised and adapted to each other' (Godwin 1993a: 118). William St. Clair comments on Godwin's repeated use of the chain as a metaphor of causation, which 'with suitable poetic ambiguity . . . was now successfully linked to the other chains'; notably, the 'Great Chain of Being' with its implications of natural sociability, and the less benign 'icy chains of custom' with their connotations of coercion (St. Clair 1989: 89). Alluding to the latter, Godwin uses the notion of society as a great chain to explain why Caleb Williams feels coerced into forgiving Ferdinando Falkland:

> I thought with unspeakable loathing of those errors, in consequence of which every man is fated to be, more or less, the tyrant or the slave. I was astonished at the folly of my species, that they did not rise up as one man, and shake off chains so ignominious, and misery so insupportable. (Godwin 2000: 238)

These chains bind individuals to each other, but also bind them into a system of necessity, a position that Mary Shelley later develops in her use of this Godwinian / Rousseauvian trope.

Through its imagery of chains *Political Justice* pushes Rousseau's forced freedom to its logical extreme. Here, individuals are left with no choice about their participation in social structures. Whereas Rousseau had tried to reduce the costs of conformity for the individual will, Godwin abnegates volition to maximise cooperation. He suggests that morality in a rational and designing mind is not essentially different from morality in an inanimate substance. A man of certain intellectual habits is fitted to be an assassin, a dagger of a certain form is fitted to be his instrument. (Godwin 1993a: 368)[10]

The subject is a phenomenal element rather than a rational agent, and has no real grasp of causality. Godwin compares the mind to a billiard ball, acted upon by other balls, 'a vehicle through which certain causes operate' (Godwin 1993a: 168). Through this metaphor of random causation, Godwin alludes to Hume's influential critique of a priori assumptions of cause and effect in the *Enquiry Concerning Human Understanding*: 'We fancy, that were we brought, on a sudden, into this world, we could at first have inferred, that one Billiard-ball would communicate motion to another upon impulse' (Hume 2000: 28). Through this example Godwin suggests that causes are beyond human comprehension, and that individual actions provide a false impression of inner causality, which is in fact externally motivated. Godwin reiterates Thomas Hobbes's influential notion of freedom as the mere absence of impediment. You cannot actually master why things work the way they do, but can only attempt to recognise them through empirical observation, perceiving them, however fleetingly, as they are. Caleb's pursuit of Falkland's secret and his subsequent persecution illustrate the dangers of seeking to know the cause. Godwin's concept of necessity hence guarantees sociability, but in doing so takes the form of an extreme determinism whereby the mind becomes a mechanism acted upon by greater forces. Peter Howell suggests that Godwin's ambivalence toward individualism distinguishes him from individualistic social contract writers, as Godwin both privileges and rejects individuality: 'to be an individual . . . at the extreme of the Godwinian sense, is to empty oneself of individuality' (Howell 2004: 78). I read this extreme ambivalence towards individualism as a direct outcome of empiricist political theory's age-old chicken-and-egg argument about whether natural sociability or the individual constitute the origins of society. Godwin explains that he has arrived at his concept of the individual from reading 'Locke on Human Understanding . . . and those respecting education from the Emile of J.-J. Rousseau' (Godwin 1993a: 13). These treatises empower the individual as the site of perception and experience, but also endow the environment with ontological priority.

In *Julie* Rousseau examines the point where the individual and general wills meet and fracture one another. Godwin's example of this clash is *Political Justice*'s 'fire cause' episode. In this passage Godwin constructs a thought experiment whereby he deems François Fénelon 'of more worth than his chambermaid, and there are few of us that would hesitate to pronounce, if his palace were in flames, and the life of only one of them could be preserved, which of the two ought to be preferred' (Godwin 1993a: 50). Godwin suggests that 'it would have been just in the chambermaid to have preferred the archbishop to herself. To have done otherwise would have been a breach of justice' (ibid. 50). In revising *Political Justice*, Godwin repeats this argument by applying this sacrifice to oneself, one's spouse, one's benefactor, one's parent, and one's sibling (Godwin 1993b: 63). The outcome is always the same: moral duty overcomes personal affection to reflect broad social utility and the contingent worth of the individual in terms of social utility, represented by the inevitable preference for Fénelon.[11] Godwin's radical displacement of personal ties led Elizabeth Hamilton and other anti-Jacobins, Charles Lloyd included, to argue that his philosophy incurred 'a dereliction of all the principles of natural affection . . . annihilating the sweet bonds of domestic attachment' (Hamilton 2000: 271). Yet Godwin's language in the fire cause emphasises the ongoing importance of private, domestic relations to his panoramic socio-theological perspective, despite his insistence that they do not always reflect political justice. In choosing Fénelon over his maid, Godwin suggests that

> we are not connected with one or two percipient beings, but with a society, a nation, and in some sense with the whole family of mankind. Of consequence that life ought to be preferred which will be most conducive to the general good. (Godwin 1993a: 50)

Godwin's metaphor of the 'family of mankind' foregrounds the importance of domestic values in social hierarchies. In *Political Justice*'s initial and most radical iteration, Godwin prophesies that humans aspiring to perfectibility will eventually overcome the inconveniences of government and the indignities of sleep and death. His concepts of necessity and perfectibility, through the example of the fire cause and the 1793 *Political Justice*'s utopian vision of human development, assume a proto-utilitarian perspective that derives from social contract theory's concept of a general will which seeks to arrive at the greatest good for the greatest number of individuals under the necessarily flawed conditions of a social contract that unites asocial individuals. For Godwin, the individual remains the primary telos of sociability, but this individual's ties to the general good become mandatory rather than voluntary. I demonstrate that Godwin's novels explore the non-utopian reality that the will encounters in its internal struggle to conform to these chains. This is the dark underside that motivates the intensely hyperbolic fanfare with which Godwin proclaims the coming of future harmony in *Political Justice*.

An Individualist Education

Fleetwood is the cautionary tale of a misanthrope and his painful path of socialisation as he becomes a reformed 'man of feeling', an ironic type for a regenerated society. Casimir Fleetwood is Godwin's Everyman, and his case points to the many fissures and inconsistencies among individuals within Godwin's theory of necessity. In what follows, I lay out a reading of Fleetwood as a profoundly Rousseauvian character, through an analysis of his individualist epistemology and education, his subsequent isolation and paranoia, and his attempt to find companionship in friendship and marriage. Through the character of Fleetwood, Godwin repeats Coleridge's ambivalent identification with 'the crazy ROUSSEAU' whose madness Coleridge ascribes to his cultural milieu (Coleridge 1969a: 132). But while Coleridge is unable to distinguish Rousseau from the society that produces him, Godwin identifies more closely with the Rousseauvian position and can distinguish the individual will from the cultural conditions that produce it. Whereas Rousseau marks an alienated nothingness for Coleridge, infecting others with his porous lack of social identity, Godwin recognises Rousseau as a formative omnipresence, albeit a troublesome one, in modern culture and explores his limits in terms of gender, as rights of contract cannot be extended to women.

Fleetwood's father adheres to Rousseau's model, raising his son in radical seclusion in Romantic Merionethshire to love 'my own immediate ancestors', but '[to] hate ... mankind' (Godwin 2001a: 216). In *Emile* Rousseau asks, 'to form this rare man, what have we to do? Very much, doubtless. What must be done is to prevent anything from being done' (Rousseau 2010: 166). Rousseau proposes sheltering children from society and allowing them to learn through their senses:

> Arrange all things so that the child has knowledge of . . . all those within his reach and finds others by induction. But I would prefer a hundred times over his being ignorant of them than you having to tell them to him. (Rousseau 2010: 291)

Rousseau suggests that direct instruction will form a corrupting 'dependence on men, which is from society . . . Dependence on men, since it is without order, engenders all the vices' (Rousseau 2010: 216). Because he is raised in the spirit of *Emile* and is not trained to conform to external standards or social codes, Fleetwood develops a misanthropic bent, a latent aspect within Rousseau's educational treatise that Godwin (and Mary Shelley in his wake) render manifest. Fleetwood recalls being 'a spoiled child. I had been little used to contradiction, and felt like a tender flower of the garden, which the blast of the east wind nips' (Godwin 2001a: 54). He blames his later loneliness on this 'early solitude in Wales. I came into the world prepared to be a severe and unsparing judge' (ibid. 215).

In *Mandeville, A Tale of Seventeenth Century England*, the parallel asociability of the protagonist's environment has an added historical dimension. *Mandeville* opens with James VI's occupation of Ireland. The English endeavour 'to reclaim the wild Irish from what might almost be called their savage state' (Godwin 1992b: 9). In this Hobbesian state of nature, Charles Mandeville reflects

> the Papist and the Protestant . . . were to my thoughts like two great classes of animal nature, the one, the law of whose being it was to devour, while it was the unfortunate destiny of the other to be mangled and torn to pieces by him. (Godwin 1992b: 44–5)

Mandeville transposes this violence into the English Civil War, where he is defeated in battle by his childhood friend turned Parliamentarian. Mandeville comes to recognise that 'every man thrives by the ruin of another', as in Hobbes's war-like state of nature where individuals fight one another claw and tooth (Godwin 1992b: 87). After Mandeville's parents are murdered by Catholics, he is raised by his reclusive uncle in the manner 'less . . . of an animal, than a vegetable', a version of Hobbes's initial asocial state of nature (ibid. 189). Godwin suggests that works of philosophy think very little of the outcome of antisocial values which leaves their readers defenceless: 'the books are always written by those who are the professors of teaching, never by the subjects' (ibid. 61). Mandeville is irrevocably maimed by his early loss and by the politics of this miseducation: 'human nature is so constituted, that, till the propensity is cured, as mine had been, man naturally seeks the society of his like' (ibid. 127). As an adult, Mandeville dreams of establishing 'a misanthropic club, where the knot that bound the members together, and the features that they held in common, should be a disappointed and embittered spirit' (ibid. 132). The oxymoron of a misanthropic club darkly parodies social contract sociability, where the only tie uniting individuals is their distaste for social interaction, Hobbes's weak rationale for forming a society. Mandeville earns Shaftesbury's patronage, but eventually recognises that his mentor's primary motivations are an antisocial disposition of Rousseauvian *amour propre*:[12]

> In Sir Anthony I traced a character compounded by strange and discordant elements. Ambition was the ruling passion of his soul. But his mind was

fluctuating and unstable, and unresolved . . . He had set out in life a royalist: offended by some transaction which he conceived his merits to be undervalued he turned parliamentarian. (Godwin 1992b: 112)

As a result of Shaftesbury's inconstancy, weakness and political factionalism, catalysed by Mandeville's inadequate socialisation, Mandeville is defeated in battle and branded like a slave (Godwin 1992b: 325). His name alludes to Bernard Mandeville, adding *The Fable of the Bees'* justification of greed as a social virtue to Godwin's broader charges against the individualist tradition in recent political theory. Through the character of Mandeville, Godwin reflects: 'philosophy, how specious is they name . . . The passions of the human mind laugh at philosophy', which cannot undertake a positive account of sociability and merely reflects destructive dependencies and *amour propre* (ibid. 173–4).

Through Fleetwood's and Mandeville's miseducations Godwin rejects Rousseauvian educational models based on excessive freedom and with them *Political Justice's* utopian vision of a perfectible society of individuals. Godwin formulates an indictment of related empiricist theories of education, epistemology and government. In adulthood, Fleetwood comes to a partial realisation of the shortcomings of this upbringing. He recalls his youth as 'a nonage, the infancy of man. It was visionary, and idle, and unsubstantial' (Godwin 2001a: 93). Fleetwood does not become the exemplary subject of *Emile*, but follows a mundane course of adventures 'as for the most part have occurred to at least one half of the Englishmen now existing, who are of the same rank of life as my hero' (ibid. 47–8). Neither does he become the utopian self-governing individual of *Political Justice*, whose superior judgment precludes the need for organised society. Godwin's criticism of individualism incorporates Scottish Enlightenment theories of natural sociability, which come into play to form a psychomachia-like agon between conflicting perspectives of liberalism and benevolence (the Adam Smith problem). Through the standoff between these positions, Godwin explores the viability of a *tertium quid* of reformed sociability, which – if successful – would mediate between the two poles of individualism and benevolence.

In *Fleetwood* Godwin pursues this possibility through the subplot of Ruffigny, who advocates benevolence as an alternative to empiricism's weak account of sociability. To counterbalance his lonely upbringing Fleetwood seeks out his adopted relative in 'the district in which the Swiss Liberty was engendered', an overdetermined landscape imbued with allusions to *Julie's* more utopian moments and to Romantic poetry (Godwin 2001a: 123). But beneath this fantasy lurk other aspects of

Rousseau's legacy. The orphaned Ruffigny was sent as a child by his uncle M. Vaublanc to a Lyons silk mill, which Vaublanc presents as a 'pure and exemplary a society' (ibid. 147). Behind this utopian exterior hides the dystopian drudgery of Charles Dickens's *Hard Times* or of Thomas Malthus's *Essay on Population*. The labouring child becomes 'a sort of machine; his limbs and articulations are converted, as it were, into wood and wires' (ibid. 161). Fleetwood's grandfather Ambrose rescues Ruffigny and explains that this act redeploys 'the great distribution of human society' in more equitable terms (ibid. 195). Through Ruffigny's intercession, Godwin introduces an alternative rationale for sociability which displaces power relations with local kinship and benevolence.[13] Inspired by Ruffigny and these values, Fleetwood seeks to overcome his lonely upbringing and to become a member of society: 'I felt what I was, and I pined for the society of my like. It was with inexpressible sorrow that I believed I was alone in the world' (ibid. 116). He desires,

> to consider myself as part only of a whole. If that which produces sensation in me, produces sensation no where else, I am subsequently alone . . . But if there is a being who feels the blow under which I flinch . . . that being is a part of myself. (Godwin 2001a: 231–2)

Through Ruffigny's story, Godwin evokes a Scottish Enlightenment postulation of the universality of sensory perception (echoing Francis Hutcheson). This principle motivates Fleetwood's grandfather to adopt this child as his own. Seeking to balance his own misanthropic ways with principles of benevolence, Fleetwood seeks out and befriends the Humean Mr Macneil. Godwin introduces Macneil as 'a Scotchman' (Godwin 2001a: 242). Like Hume, Macneil presents himself as 'no humourist, nor misanthrope', an antidote to the Romantic tendency to use the imagination to displace human relations (ibid. 243). Hume's own view of the imagination as a necessary aspect of social relations, articulated through Macneil, offers an alternative to Fleetwood's Romantic model. Hume suggests that fiction imposes coherence on the fragmented chaos of human interactions. Because it is necessary, fiction qualifies as a quasi-natural human invention.

Rousseau's Ghost

In addition to personifying Humean benevolence, Macneil also carries the added prestige of having a former connection to the deceased Rousseau: 'Macneil . . . had resided much in foreign countries, and was supposed particularly to have possessed the confidence of the celebrated

Jean Jacques Rousseau, who had been some years an inhabitant of the banks of the Windermere' (Godwin 2001a: 234). The details of the Macneil–Rousseau friendship loosely repeat the history of Rousseau's exile to England, where he was cared for by Hume, who arranged for his lodgings in Staffordshire (Damrosch 2005: 432). During this visit Rousseau's mental health is reported to have declined, leading Hume to assess: 'he is plainly mad, having long been maddish' (quoted in ibid. 432). Like Hume, Macneil rebukes Rousseau's paranoid existence 'in a world of his own, [in which he] saw nothing as it really was' (Godwin 2001a: 244). He reports 'I was convinced, from a multitude of indications, that Rousseau was not in his sober mind' (ibid. 244). Macneil ascribes Rousseau's paranoia to 'the displeasing events that had befallen him, or . . . any seeds of disease kneaded up in his original constitution' (ibid. 244). As a result, Rousseau's ties to reality are tenuous:

> When he was induced to dwell for a time upon the universal combination which he believed to be formed against him, he then undoubtedly suffered. But he had such resources in his own mind! He could so wholly abstract himself from this painful contemplation. (Godwin 2001a: 244)

In writing *Fleetwood* Godwin fictionalises Rousseau as a dead character whose legacy affects the living and migrates into the character of Fleetwood, as well as into Godwin's discussions of his own character. In analysing himself in an autobiographical fragment, Godwin determines that 'the two leading features of my character are sensibility and insensibility', a tendency to paradox resulting from hypersensitivity toward the self and an attendant lack of sensitivity toward the environment, qualities that he associates with the characters of Rousseau and Fleetwood (Godwin 2007a: 59).[14] In the preface to *Fleetwood*, Godwin criticises 'certain persons, who condescend to make my inconsistency the favourite object of their research', alluding to the deluge of anti-Jacobin attacks on his perceived Rousseauvian predilection for paradox that include Charles Lloyd's advertisement to *Edmund Oliver* and Francis Jeffrey's attack on Robert Southey's *Thalaba the Destroyer* in *The Edinburgh Review* (Godwin 2001a: 48). At the turn of the nineteenth century this tendency to paradox was often associated, especially by the conservative press, with radicalism and with an individualistic assault on the institutions of society. Through the character of Fleetwood, Godwin suggests that this inconsistent temper targeted by his critics is culturally constructed, impacted by an excessively individualistic value system. Ruffigny's comments on Rousseau reinforce Godwin's view that Rousseau is not to blame for his derangement: 'if men of powerful and vigorous minds, as Rousseau and others, have surrendered themselves to the chimeras of a disturbed imagination . . . what wonder that I, a boy of eight years, should be subject to a similar alarm?' (ibid. 154). Rousseau's paranoia marks an absence of nurture which undermines his naturally vigorous nature. Rousseau's underlying good nature also explains Macneil's attitude of 'veneration and a tenderness toward this extraordinary man' despite all of his flaws (ibid. 243). As Rousseau's double, Fleetwood sympathises with his 'constitutional temperament which was saturnine and sensitive', exacerbated by a solipsistic environment (ibid. 215). He describes himself in Rousseauvian fashion as 'the most capricious and wayward being that ever existed. I never remained permanently in one state of mind' (ibid. 320). Repeatedly Godwin presents misanthropy (and subsequently misogyny) as an inevitable response to a larger culture of individualism, and not the personal failing of the individual, so that his early distaste for Rousseau is produced by his cultural environment. Rousseau's paranoia during his visit to England is similarly presented as an inevitable response to his persecutions in Switzerland and France.

Catherine Gallagher suggests that by incorporating real figures into novels and altering the details in subtle ways, novelists are able to isolate the point of contact between individuals and broader philosophical systems. If large-scale historical revisions can sometimes obscure the specific causes governing events, which are lost in a maze of possibilities, 'the Enlightenment search for small causes with large results' is motivated by the need to pinpoint history's local determining factors (Gallagher 2010: 18). This way novelists can draw attention to 'the "*petites causes*" preference: the focus on individual personality . . . and a predilection for non-rational motives, mistakes and anomalies' (ibid. 18). *Petites causes* both demonstrate how individuals precede and shape history, and also underscore the precarious quality of their actions and ideologies, which often work against the broader interests of society. These observations help frame two of Godwin's significant narrative alterations in writing about Rousseau and Hume in *Fleetwood*. The first is his relocation of Rousseau's visit to England from Staffordshire to the Romantic Lake District. In his account of Fleetwood's childhood, Godwin echoes 'Lines, Written above Tintern Abbey', in which Wordsworth compares himself to

> a roe
> [bounding] o'er the mountains, by the sides
> Of the deep rivers, and the lonely streams. (Wordsworth and Coleridge
> 2008: ll. 68–70)

Fleetwood explains: 'My earliest years were spent on mountains and precipices, amidst the roaring of the ocean and the dashing of waterfalls. A constant familiarity with these objects gave a wildness to my ideas, and an uncommon seriousness to my temper' (Godwin 2001a: 53). He recalls feeling like 'a wild roe among the mountains of Wales' (ibid. 241). Fleetwood lives in North Wales, the Lake District and the Swiss Alps, settings that are all associated with Wordsworth's poetry. By bringing Rousseau to the Lake District, Godwin compares Rousseau's legacy with Wordsworth's, pinpointing the solitary Romantic sensibility as the cause of Rousseau's and Fleetwood's painful uncouplings from society.

A second important revision that works to underscore the gap between Rousseauvian individualism and Scottish Enlightenment benevolence is Godwin's representation of Hume, historically a solitary and eccentric character, as a family man and pillar of his community.[15] Macneil, a domesticated rewriting of Hume, endeavours to reform Fleetwood's sympathetic bonds and integrate him into society. He criticises the intense visionary compensations which Romantic misanthropy and isolation activate in Rousseau:

> People talk of the raptures of solitude; or with what tenderness they can love a tree, a rivulet, or a mountain. Believe me . . . they deceive themselves . . . There is a principle in the heart of man which demands the society of his like. He that has no such society, is in a state but one degree removed from insanity. (Godwin 2001a: 251)

Instead of Romantic escapism, Macneil draws Fleetwood's attention to

> how much good neighbourhood there is in the world! what readiness in every man to assist every stranger that comes his way . . . I am a philanthropist, in the plain sense of the word. Whenever I see a man I see something to love. (Godwin 2001a: 249)

He explains: 'in every man that lives . . . there is much to commend. Every man has in him the seeds of a good husband, a good father, and a sincere friend' (Godwin 2001a: 248). Fleetwood is attracted to Macneil's Scottish Enlightenment postulation of sociability as a natural propensity. He praises Macneil's own family as a model for this ideal sociability, admiring their 'concord of affection without any jarring passions; so much harmony of interests, yet each member of the family having a different pursuit' (ibid. 246–7).[16] Macneil proposes marriage to Fleetwood as an expression of natural sociability: 'beget yourself a family of children! . . . call about your distant relations! Sit down every day at table with a circle of five or six persons, constituting your own domestic group' (ibid. 252). Fleetwood's subsequent request to marry Macneil's youngest daughter Mary initially leads Macneil to question his principle of universal feeling and consider 'how difficult is it to put one's self exactly in the place of another', pointing to an underlying fissure between political ideals and social realities (ibid. 257). But finally, and mistakenly, Macneil stakes his family's destiny on the conjunction of theory and practice, and accedes to the marriage as an affirmation of his ideology of natural sociability. Fleetwood looks back on this marriage and his subsequent quest for kinship with deep regret: 'every one of his advices had fallen out unhappily on me' (ibid. 383). Through these ruminations, Godwin emphasises that sociability cannot be fostered *ex nihilo* from a condition of radical withdrawal, as in Rousseau's *Confessions*. Raised in a culture which values the solitary, male individual and a deterministic branch of epistemology, and supported by an education which places minimal checks on the individual will, Fleetwood is justly wary of forming connections with others.

Wollstonecraft and Marriage's Secret Contracts

To cure Fleetwood of his misanthropy, Macneil constructs a social contract allegory in miniature, following Hume's view of fiction as a necessary component of socialisation. He considers

> composing a little novel or tale in illustration of my position. I would take such a man as my friend Fleetwood . . . I would put him on board a ship; he will, of course, be sufficiently disgusted with every one of his companions . . . I would cause him to be shipwrecked on a desert island, with no companion but one man, the most gross, perverse, and stupid of the crew. (Godwin 2001a: 249)

Inevitably, Macneil suggests that this crew member would reconcile Fleetwood to the entire human community, serving as a synecdoche for broader society. Macneil's allegory employs the social contract register of return to 'a desert island' state of nature as an imagined social origin. In *Caleb Williams* Godwin alludes to Prospero's island to describe Caleb's retreat to rural Wales, suggesting the frustrated desire to revert from persecution in England to a state of nature, an alternative space where social values can be defined (Godwin 2000: 393). But as with Prospero's exile from Milan to the Mediterranean island, or with Rousseau's withdrawal to the Ile St. Pierre in the *Reveries of the Solitary Walker*, Macneil's imagined island represents a highly politicised social position that remains embattled by the forces which generated this need for retreat. After dispensing his advice to Fleetwood, replete with the allegory of shipwreck and reform, Macneil himself is shipwrecked and perishes together with all of his family but Mary. Hume uses the figure of near-shipwreck to reflect on the epistemological crisis of meaning that his theory has produced:

> Methinks I am like a man, who having struck on many shoals, and having narrowly escap'd ship-wreck in passing a small frith, has yet the temerity to put out to sea in the same leaky weather-beaten vessel, and even carries his ambition so far as to think of compassing the globe under these disadvantageous circumstances. (Hume 1978: 263–4)

Shipwreck is a metaphor for the nihilistic risks that scepticism poses – the possibility of the breakdown of meaning that Hume's 'leaky weather-beaten vessel' encounters in its departure from 'the most usual conjunctions of cause and effect' (Hume 1978: 267). Macneil's shipwreck – following this allusion to Hume – points to the breakdown of cohering values. In Godwin's terms (which significantly depart from Hume's own narrative) these cohering values are family and community. The shipwreck incurs the loss of the Macneil family's wealth, Fleetwood's abuse of Mary, and the shattering of Macneil's interrelated myths of marriage, benevolence, and sociability through habit and empiricist social regeneration, as well as the legacies of Ruffigny and of Fleetwood's paternal grandfather Ambrose to boot, representing a severe crisis in patriarchal ideals of a 'kindred of love'.

Fleetwood and Mary later express guilt about the Macneils' deaths, sensing that they have been sacrificed to darker, antisocial values played out within their subsequent marriage. They subsequently learn that the Macneils refused the ship captain's offer to rescue two of the four family members: 'this kindred of love refused to be separated; they could not endure to pass lots on their lives ... father, mother, and daughters preferred to perish together' (Godwin 2001a: 267–8). This demonstration of the Macneils' extreme altruism, echoing the dilemma of *Political Justice*'s famous fire cause, contradicts Godwin's argument about the potential contribution of an individual to society, whereby drawing lots would have taken precedence over the loss of all (Godwin 1993a: 50). Godwin suggests that had two of the four Macneils survived, Fleetwood's decline into spousal abuse would have been averted. As Mary later accosts Fleetwood, 'if I had patrons and protectors still living, if I had not come dowerless to your bed, you could not have used me thus ungenerously' (Godwin 2001a: 419). Even before the shipwreck, Fleetwood has a strong premonition that Macneil and family are already dead, casting doubt on the values that Macneil presents (ibid. 264). He later imagines them 'as so many victims, robed in white, and crowned with chaplets, marching along the beach, as to be sacrificed', imagery conveying punishment and ritual atonement (ibid. 268). The Macneils' tragic deaths mark a turning point in *Fleetwood*. Through this episode Godwin reveals the underpinnings of utopian values of natural sociability, Scottish Enlightenment sympathy, and the theological-utilitarian reasoning of the famous fire cause in excessive individualism, misanthropy and extreme misogyny.

Mary echoes Wollstonecraft in her name, character and desire to extend Rousseau's egalitarianism to women. Carole Pateman observes that the marital contract and the civil sphere of patriarchy rely on the subordination of women, who are excluded from political subjecthood and have a legally inferior part in the marriage contract (Pateman 1988: 8, 11).[17] In *Julie* and *The Rime of the Ancient Mariner* marriage represents a conservative value system, which Rousseau's and Coleridge's fictions both finally reject. Julie recognises that she is an object of barter between men, and the wedding guest is detained from stepping over the marital threshold to celebrate the marriage of his next of kin. Mary Lyndon Shanley argues that the marital contract naturalises contingent bonds, and ascribes them an irrevocable, permanent status (Shanley 1979: 82). In *Political Justice*, Godwin argues that 'human beings, who enter into the engagements of domestic life, should remember, that however man and wife may in interests and affections be one, yet no interests and affections can prevent them from being in many respects distinct' (Godwin 1993a: 303). Therefore, 'it is absurd to expect the inclinations and wishes of two human beings to coincide through any long period of time' (Godwin 1993b: 337). Godwin emphasises that contrary to popular opinion, 'promises and compacts are in no sense the foundation of morality', and often stand in direct opposition to it (ibid. 91). In this context, Godwin suggests that 'marriage is a system of fraud' (Godwin 1993a: 453). Marriage sours the best intentions: 'it really happens in this as in other cases, that the positive laws which are made to restrain our vices, irritate and multiply them' (ibid. 454). Like government or the social contract, marriage is formed to protect individuals by committing them to ties which are only contingently favourable.[18] When circumstances inevitably change, the commitment becomes pernicious. Godwin emphasises that 'truth and virtue . . . will flourish most, when least subjected to the mistaken guardianship of authority and law' (ibid. 323).

Godwin embraces Wollstonecraft's criticism that 'the private or public virtue of women is very problematical for Rousseau', who excluded women from political subjecthood in *Emile* (Wollstonecraft 2007b: 176). Wollstonecraft rejects Rousseau's constraining notion of women as objects of male possession:

'educate women like men,' says Rousseau, 'and the more they resemble our sex the less power they have over us.' This is the very point I aim at. I do not wish them to have power over men; but over themselves. (Godwin 2007b: 85)

In his *Memoirs of the Author of A Vindication of the Rights of Woman*, Godwin repeats Wollstonecraft's view that women are equal to men. He praises 'the strength and firmness with which the author repels the opinions of Rousseau . . . respecting the condition of woman' (Godwin 2001b: 75). But Godwin also seeks to accommodate Wollstonecraft to the gender norms of late eighteenth-century England.[19] He acknowledges a 'class of men who believe they could not exist without such pretty, soft creatures to resort to, [who] were in arms against the author of so heretical and blasphemous a doctrine' (ibid. 75). Among this 'class of men' are Godwin's intended readers to whom Godwin apologises for his wife's 'somewhat amazonian temper', which obscures 'a woman lovely in her person, and, in the best and most engaging sense, feminine in her manners' (ibid. 75, 76).

These conflicted attitudes materialise in the character of Mary, who both asserts her right to sovereignty, and finally defers to patriarchal authority. In the preface to *Caleb Williams*, Godwin discusses his decision to construct the character of Caleb in the first person. He suggests that first-person narration voices the 'private and internal operations of the mind', as opposed to the more distancing effect of third person narration (Godwin 2000: 448). Significantly, although Wollstonecraft's novels are narrated by first-person female characters, adapting Samuel Richardson's epistolary female narrators, Godwin's novels enact the silencing of women.[20] While his male characters are focalised as complex individuals, his female characters are observed and described by men. Macneil expresses the opinion that 'man marries because he desires a lovely and soothing companion for his vacant hours; woman marries, because she feels the want of a protector, a guardian, a guide, and an oracle' (Godwin 2001a: 254). Because men and women are not on equal footing, their interaction is fraught with difficulties and misunderstandings. By contrast, male characters intuitively understand one another. Fleetwood passionately courts Macneil and admires his 'manly appearance' (ibid. 242). Macneil reciprocates by complimenting Fleetwood as a handsome man, capable of winning a 'beauteous bride' (ibid. 254).[21] Fleetwood's self-professed 'favourite theory about the female sex' postulates that 'however it might in certain instances be glossed over, all women were in the main alike, selfish, frivolous, inconstant, and deceitful' (ibid. 317). Fleetwood affirms this distinction, emphasising that women and men occupy separate spheres: 'till the softer sex has produced a Bacon, a Newton, a Homer, or a Shakespeare, I will never believe it' (ibid. 252). Thus, Fleetwood and Macneil view Mary as an object of exchange. By contrast, Mary asserts her independence.

Fleetwood's plot of marital abuse erupts when Mary requests Fleetwood's private closet, his sanctuary 'from almost prattling infancy . . . In an unlucky moment my wife pronounced the decree, "It shall never be yours again!"' (Godwin 2001a: 292). This closet connects the drawing room to Fleetwood's bedroom, representing a middle space between public and private zones (ibid. 291–2). It privileges Fleetwood with complete secrecy in the passage between these two spheres: 'if I might not resort to my favourite haunts at perfect liberty, if I could not reach them unseen to any human eye, they were nothing to me' (ibid. 294). This closet, like Falkland's trunk in *Caleb Williams*, is a *mise en abyme* for the double impulses of exposure and concealment that motivate the genre of the seventeenth- and eighteenth-century secret history. Secret histories expose the private stories of public figures, giving their readers access to the true stories and backstage corruptions of power. Eve Tavor Bannet suggests that these secret histories were loosely based on the disclosure of courtly confidentialities. By the eighteenth century, the secret history had emerged from the confines of the royal court to focus on the clandestine operations of arbitrary government (Bannet 2005: 378). Courtly and domestic closets belonged to different kinds of architectural spaces, including studies for men (like Fleetwood's) and the more intimate female boudoir. The privileged space of the study, and sometimes of the boudoir, was increasingly exposed to public surveillance over the course of the eighteenth century.[22] Julie Carlson argues that Godwin's marriage to Wollstonecraft 'shifts the valence of the authority, autonomy, and authenticity' away from the solitary Romantic writer and – by extension – his closet, indicating a changing gendering of authority (Carlson 2007: 3). Drawing on these works, I suggest that Godwin extends the genre of the secret history to bear on the gender politics that underlie political theory.

Initially Fleetwood and Mary share the closet, where they read the seventeenth-century drama of a husband who submits to execution after one month of marriage, John Fletcher's *A Wife for a Moneth* (Godwin 2001a: 300, note 2, 303). Godwin emphasises Fleetwood's momentary impression of triumph over the gender divide:

> We communicate with instantaneous flashes, in one glance of the eye, and have no need of words . . . I see how my companion feels the passages as they succeed; I learn new decrees of taste and am confirmed in the old. Male and female tastes are in some respects different natures; and no decision upon

a work of art can be consummate, till it has been pronounced on by both. (Godwin 2001a: 299)

But Mary finally frustrates this expectation. Godwin emphasises that Fleetwood delights in seeing Mary in his closet, but cannot validate the independent point of view that this space allows her (Godwin 2001a: 293). Fletcher's book, like the closet, becomes an object of contention and uncoupling as Mary demands autonomy in marriage and refuses to confirm Fleetwood's perspectives and tastes. She prefers the Rousseauvian hobby of botanising to reading Fletcher's misogynistic drama of marital subordination (ibid. 300–1). Although Mary is so exceptionally candid, 'that it was scarcely possible to believe that a thought could pass in her heart, which might not be read in her face', Fleetwood reads her desire for autonomy as infidelity, the undoing of his own prerogatives (ibid. 246). Because Mary occupies his closet (ibid. 292) Fleetwood worries about his own position, which threatens to become that of 'a passive machine' (ibid. 281): 'her smiles drew me from my most steadfast purposes, and made me as ductile as wax to the aims she proposed' (ibid. 317). He suspects Mary of exercising 'art' and making him 'her dupe' (ibid. 307). Mary voices similar concerns about her own autonomy:

> Mistake me not, my dear Fleetwood. I am not idle and thoughtless enough, to promise to sink my being and individuality in yours. I shall have my distinct propensities and preferences . . . I hope you will not require me to disclaim them. In me you will have a wife, and not a passive machine. (Godwin 2001a: 281)

Fleetwood fears that asking for his closet back will disclose his secret *amour propre* and lack of sociability (Godwin 2001a: 294). By means of an inversion, reinforced by her newly established metonymic connection to this secret space, he projects this flaw back onto Mary: '"Mary, Mary", said I sometimes to myself, as I recurred to the circumstance, "I am afraid you are selfish! and what character can be less promising in social life, than hers who thinks of no one's pleasure but her own"' (ibid. 295). This desire to 'be something' and Mary's concomitant fear of becoming 'a passive machine' suggests the volatile gender politics that render autonomy the exclusive province either of men or of women in Godwin's analysis, and points to empiricist political theory's underlying exclusions of gender.

Fiction

Fleetwood seeks to overcome his sense of subjection, whereby he imagines that Mary manipulates him like 'ductile ... wax' (Godwin 2001a: 317). He procures the clothes of Mary and her imagined lover Kenrick and orders a wax modeller to form their likeness (ibid. 386–7). Fleetwood's customary marital feast on the date of his wedding anniversary, and arrangement of the dummies of Mary and Kenrick in intimate postures, reflects a decline into a Rousseauvian position of paranoia, a condition whereby fiction takes precedence over reality: 'my mind underwent a strange revolution. I no longer directly knew where I was, or could distinguish fiction from reality' (ibid. 387). The realistic tableau formed by these grotesque wax effigies expresses Godwin's deep-seated suspicion of fiction. In the preface to *Caleb Williams*, Godwin addresses his novel to 'persons whom books of philosophy and science are never likely to reach' echoing *Julie*'s anti-literary editor persona (Godwin 2000: 55). Mark Philp speculates that Godwin probably turned to novel-writing as an alternative source of income when his political theory was rejected (Godwin 1993a: 10).[23] Godwin also discusses the novel as a steady but unambitious source of profit, which caters to an inferior 'class of readers; consisting of women and boys' distinct from the gentleman readers of theoretical texts to whom Godwin apologised for Wollstonecraft's Amazonian rhetoric (ibid. 463). Relating these anti-literary values to misogyny, Godwin praises Locke as 'a man of uncommonly clear and masculine understanding' who focuses on 'facts and phenomena' instead of 'the invention of fanciful theories' (Godwin 1797: 345, 347). He applies these principles to his own writings, arguing that

> the true effect of a good style is to enable us to apprehend the ideas of our author without adulteration. We . . . are conscious of no impediment . . . Our first sensation from his writings, is that of his thoughts, and nothing else. (Godwin 1797: 387)

But Godwin also repeats Locke's covert ambivalence toward language by contradicting his anti-literary position with an antithetical literary praxis. In the *Essay Concerning Human Understanding*, Locke argues that 'the signification of words' can become 'like a mist before people's eyes' when used obscurely (Locke 1993a: 276). Locke is concerned that an infelicitous, subjective use of words can lead readers astray 'in the great wood of words' (ibid. 322). Godwin recognises that Locke's use of figurative language flagrantly subverts his semantic content.

Accordingly, he criticises Locke's language for being 'defective' and of 'depraved taste' (Godwin 1797: 347). He suggests that Locke's 'fine-spun, mystical and fruitless complexity, might have been better and more clearly expressed in two lines' (ibid. 312). However, Godwin formulates these abundant hyperboles criticising Locke in the same rich literary style which he takes pains to dismiss, employing the metaphor of 'fine-spun . . . complexity' to undermine the use of figurative language.

Godwin extends this criticism of theoretical language to Rousseau. He privileges Rousseau's philosophical achievements over his rhetoric, which Godwin deems eloquent and flawed: 'to his [Rousseau's] merits as a reasoner we should not forget to add, that the term eloquence is perhaps more precisely descriptive of his mode of composition, than that of any other writer that ever existed' (Godwin 1993a: 273, note). Godwin's use of the double negative 'not forget' and tentative 'perhaps' forge a gap between his explicit praise of Rousseau's eloquence and an underlying scepticism towards Rousseau's views, which Godwin develops in his novels through the concept of character. While classifying rhetoric as embellishment which is worthy of appendix but not of any major commentary, Godwin also implies a constructivist view, borrowed from Hobbes, that language really does form reality and needs to be taken seriously and treated with great caution. In *Political Justice* Godwin asserts moral character as the result of impression rather than any inherent predisposition: 'we bring into the world with us no innate principles: consequently we can be neither virtuous nor vicious as we first come into existence' (ibid. 10). Reflecting the deterministic dynamics of this formulation of character, Godwin asserts: 'man in society is variously influenced by the characters of his fellow men; he is an imitative animal, and, like the camelion, owes the colour he assumes, to the colour of the surrounding objects' (Godwin 1797: 288). Capitalising on character's double literary and print denotations, Godwin argues that the advent of moveable type produces an important change in social structures (Godwin 1993a: 107). Print provides a major step in 'improv[ing] the social institutions of man' (as Godwin says of the value of truth in a related passage), as literary characters now become imminently reproducible through their readers' perceptions, much as texts are through their typesets (ibid. 115).[24]

Following empiricist epistemological models which prioritise the environment in the formation of perceptions, Godwin assumes a characteristic eighteenth-century view of novel reading as a potentially dangerous activity. He describes his own character during the act of reading as that of 'a sort of intellectual camelion, assuming the colour of the substances on which I rest', enacting this permeable quality of textual reproduction on the subject (Godwin 1797: 27). Like the marks on a *tabula rasa*, literary characters impact their impressionable readers and change them, generally for the worse, as suggested by Fleetwood's predilection for Fletcher's play and his subsequent decline into spousal abuse. Caleb connects his own destructive quest for knowledge to the ill effects of reading,

> I could not rest till I had acquainted myself with the solutions that had been invented for the phenomena of the universe. In fine, this produced in me an invincible attachment to books of narrative and romance. I panted for the unravelling of an adventure with an anxiety. (Godwin 2000: 60)

Godwin thus refers to the novel as a vehicle for disseminating an inferior version of his political theory to a wide audience. Yet, at the same time, he also privileges fiction with insight into political theory's underlying difficulties, and suggests that it has a visceral, tangible impact on the lives of its readers.

Godwin's ambivalent attitude to fiction and language is an important step in understanding his broader anxiety about sociability as a deterministic mechanism that paralyses the will – the underside of *Political Justice*'s optimistic doctrine of necessity. Godwin ascribes his own dislike of Rousseau to the ductility of his mind, which was formed in youth by rational dissent values to reject individualism. He employs mummies and wax effigies as metaphors that express a gendered condition of permeability, which leads to the loss of self-ownership.[25] Thus, Godwin describes Fleetwood's humiliation at having to adapt himself to his new environment at Oxford by using this register of subjection: 'I no longer gave free scope to the workings of my own mind, but became an artificial personage, formed after a wretched and contemptible model' (Godwin 2001a: 73). Ruffigny warns Fleetwood to beware of books: 'a book is a dead man, a sort of mummy, embowelled and embalmed', voicing Godwin's empiricist anxiety that books may take supernatural possession of their readers (ibid. 122). In turn, Mary speaks of resisting being the wax doll of Fleetwood's paranoid fantasies, which 'grinned and chattered' to his will (ibid. 387). Empiricist automaton imagery of mummies, dummies and wax imprints marks an extreme position of servility that undermines sovereignty, the painful reality behind *Political Justice*'s assertion of the individual as a veritable billiard ball pushed by circumstances beyond her understanding.

Mary resists the gendered Gothic matrices of automaton subjection. She helps Fleetwood overcome his misanthropy and his excessive individualism, bears him an heir and guides him back to sociability after his decline into paranoia. At the end of *Fleetwood*, a lost generation is replaced by a regenerated society, figured through the birth of their son and the re-establishment of primogeniture as a conservative guarantor of social cohesion. Unlike *Julie*, which explores an alternative narrative of life outside the social contract through the breakdown of the utopian community in Clarens, *Fleetwood* concludes with conformity, as the Fleetwood lineage is secured and Ambrose's principles of benevolence finally take the upper hand. The false descendent, Fleetwood's nephew Gifford, is deposed, and the true one, Fleetwood's infant son, is acknowledged. Like Rousseau in *Julie* or Coleridge in *The Rime of the Ancient Mariner*, Godwin gestures toward individuals that are excluded from social contract theory's culture of individualism. Yet finally, he points to the predominance of a deep-set gender hierarchy, in which women serve as auxiliaries to a social contract founded on inherent inequalities that privilege conformity. Even Mary's dissidence is based on her patriarchal status: she admonishes Fleetwood that 'the daughter of Macneil shall never forgive this!' (Godwin 2001a: 409).

Godwin's final novel *Deloraine* (1833) sheds light on the gender politics that motivate conformity. Deloraine, the protagonist, marries the much younger Margaret Borrodale, whose lover William is reported to have been shipwrecked, a metaphorical predicament of epistemological and social crisis in the terms suggested by Hume's *Treatise*, Macneil's shipwreck in *Fleetwood*, and the mariner's in Coleridge's *Rime*. Following William's presumed loss, Deloraine courts Margaret, while suggesting that William is his real object of desire: 'in my adherence to Margaret I was a very woman' (Godwin 1992a: 139). Deloraine is able safely to realise his homosocial fascination with William through Margaret's 'body [which] was a corpse, void of every thing offending and repulsive, but which on the contrary was more beautiful, more ravishing, more celestial, than any living mortal could ever be' (ibid. 91). His fascination with William and Margaret is necrophilic in its celebration of Margaret's subaltern status as a vacant conduit for relations between men and in its postulation of William as dead, a melancholy object of repressed desire.[26] Margaret is 'what a favourite toy or plaything is to an affectionate child . . . She was like the fetiche of an Arabian devotee' (ibid. 103). The simile of the 'fetiche' joins the register of wax effigies and mummies, expressing an extreme vision of empiricist subjectivity which denies individual agency, and subsumes the private will into a patriarchal social body. The fetiche represents a fantasy of radical submission, whereby Godwin imagines Deloraine as an oriental subordinate controlled by his fetish object, an automaton in a social economy that abnegates individual volition. Like Rousseau's paranoia in *Fleetwood*, this is a socially determined reaction to a system that promotes cultural determinism and fixed gender identities. When William unexpectedly returns and threatens to become a genuine and direct object of same-sex desire, Deloraine murders him, seeking to return him to his former melancholic status. This act is driven by homophobic panic and by William's fear of losing Margaret. At this point Margaret's lost vitality momentarily returns, 'driving away from her all preceding weakness, and substituting instead an energy that seemed to exceed human energy. Volumes were comprised in that instance' (ibid. 144). Margaret discovers her lost voice: 'my life has been all submission, submission to my father, submission to my husband. But it shall be so no longer' (ibid. 144). This realisation provokes Margaret's death from a ruptured vessel in her heart. As Ranita Chattarjee explains, in this scene of momentary self-realisation, 'Margaret sacrifices herself on the altar of patriarchal homoerotic exchange' (Chattarjee 2007: 33). Godwin inscribes Margaret's voice within male authority. It is viable only inasmuch as it expresses a patriarchal social contract. When William dies, she is necessarily silenced. The dead William, like Rousseau in *Fleetwood*, becomes a melancholic object of desire, a Gothic ghost that must remain dead and cannot assume a tangible cultural presence

Aristotle's ghost, which had haunted the empiricist tradition, migrates and evolves into the uncanny figure of Rousseau in Godwin's texts. Rousseau's constricting notion of individuality in general, and of the gender politics of social contract theory in particular, live on in Godwin's writings. Godwin's rewriting of political philosophy in the feminised form of the novel suggests that gender becomes an increasingly important category in understanding why the newly theorised society of individuals of social contract theory fails to cohere.

Notes

1. Mary Poovey argues that the concept of a social body emerged in the late eighteenth century in response to the demise of centralised power and the transition to modern industrial capitalism (Poovey 1995: 7). The Hobbesian idea that individuals are 'functional equivalents within the state was closely tied to the notion that value is a function of quantity', a capitalist concept of the social body (ibid. 29). Mass culture required self-rule that was maintained by moral philosophy and – potentially – also by fiction (Poovey 1998: 147).
2. In readings of *Caleb Williams* Ferdinando Falkland is often interpreted as a representative of Burkean views. See for example James T. Boulton (1963) and David McCracken (1970). Gregory Dart suggests that through the registers of Caleb's and Falkland's respective discourses Godwin critiques

Rousseau and the third Earl of Shaftesbury (Dart 1999: 95). Penny Fielding argues that *Caleb Williams* explores the epistemological underpinnings of *Political Justice*'s utopian concept of the general good, a future condition that therefore always remains unknown (Fielding 2009: 385).

3. Mona Scheuermann distinguishes between earlier themes of political radicalism in *Political Justice* and *Caleb Williams* and the subsequent psychological preoccupations of *Fleetwood* and *Deloraine* (Scheuermann 1983: 16–17). Evan Radcliffe classifies *Political Justice* as an anti-narrative text, contrasting it with a subsequent emphasis on subjective narratives in *Caleb Williams* and in Godwin's other novels (Radcliffe 2000: 532). William St. Clair maintains that Godwin pursued the rationalism of 'Locke and Hartley through Hume and the French *philosophes* to its culmination in *Political Justice*', only turning to Rousseau's confessional mode in the late 1790s (St. Clair 1989: 184). See also Mark Philp (Philp 1986: 38), Gary Kelly (Kelly 1976: 192), Paul Hamilton (Hamilton 1990: 43), John Bender (Bender 1994: 125) and Pamela Clemit (Clemit 2005: 167) for the argument that Godwin's career consisted of diachronically sequenced radical and sentimental phases.

4. Percy Shelley adheres to Godwin's manifest position in *Political Justice* which emphasises individual volition and imagines free love as a radical liberal alternative to marriage. By contrast, Godwin's novels are less concerned with utopian ideals than with analysing the problems created by social institutions. On the Godwinian politics of Shelley's free love see Anahid Nercessian (Nercessian 2012: 131).

5. Hamilton counteracts critics that accuse Coleridge and Godwin of political apostasy by suggesting that their later works continue engaging with politicised models through symbolic and allegorical modes respectively (Hamilton 1990: 43, 56).

6. Mitzi Myers and Hamilton both argue that Godwin becomes more sentimental after his marriage to Wollstonecraft (Myers 1983: 310–11; Hamilton 1990: 43).

7. Frank B. Evans traces Godwin's self-professed focus on individual perception instead of 'actions in the material world' to Hume (Evans 1940: 633–4).

8. Chandler analyses the late eighteenth-century culture of sentiment through Smith's concept of 'distributed feeling. It is an emotion that results from social circulation' (Chandler 2013: 11–12). Hina Nazar classifies sentimentalism within a liberal discourse of autonomy which prioritises individual deliberation, in contrast to the older model of obedience to a suprasensible authority (Nazar 2012: 1–3). G. A. Starr argues that, typically, sentimental novels focus on an individual character who 'cannot grow up and find an active place in society' (Starr 1994: 181). These characters are synecdoches for fissures in the broader social fabric.

9. Godwin's argument that 'man is a social being. In society the interests of individuals are intertwined with each other, and cannot be separated' also repeats Adam Ferguson's argument of natural sociability (Godwin 1797: 1). Godwin restates Ferguson's assertion that 'mankind are to be taken in groups, as they have always subsisted. The history of the individual is but a detail of the sentiments and thoughts he has entertained in the view of

his species' (Ferguson 1995: 10). The Godwin diary shows no entries on Ferguson. However, Daniel O'Neill demonstrates that Mary Wollstonecraft read discussions and extracts from Ferguson's *Essay on the History of Civil Society* which she probably shared with Godwin (O'Neill 2008: 110).

10. In *Memoirs of Modern Philosophers*, Elizabeth Hamilton parodies Godwin's radical determinism, suggesting that it is a manipulative pretext for avoiding familial and social duties. Bridgetina Botherim replies to her mother's request to entertain their guests, 'and do you think I am now *at liberty* to remain here? Have I not told you again and again that I am under *the necessity* of preferring the motive that is most preferable?' (Hamilton 2000: 46).

11. Robert Lamb identifies complementary strains of eighteenth-century utilitarianism and rational dissent theology in this process of deliberation; desert is based on qualities of merit and virtue evaluated by an omniscient and rational deity (Lamb 2006: 148).

12. Dart identifies the character of Falkland in *Caleb Williams* with the third Earl of Shaftesbury's patrician values and reads the novel as an exposé of 'the secret complicity between "primitive" Jacobinism and feudal despotism, between the metaphysic of conscience developed by Rousseau and Robespierre and the ideology of chivalry espoused by Burke and Shaftesbury' (Dart 1999: 95).

13. Julie Carlson suggests that for Godwin the figure of male friendship becomes a synecdoche for broader questions 'on how best to befriend humanity' under the pressure of post-revolutionary disappointment (Carlson 2011: 133).

14. The character of Rousseau also closely echoes Godwin's negative portrait of 'the man of taste and liberal accomplishments' in *Political Justice* (Godwin 1993b: 211). This man 'knows the pleasures of solitude, when man holds commerce alone with the tranquil solemnity of nature . . . He partakes in the grandeur and enthusiasm of poetry. He is perhaps himself a poet' (ibid. 211). In contrast to this involuted sensibility, Macneil resembles Godwin's 'man of benevolence', who counterbalances the antisocial man of taste: 'study is cold, if it be not enlivened with the idea of the happiness to arise to mankind' (ibid. 211).

15. In the *Treatise of Human Nature*, Hume describes his domestic isolation: 'I fancy myself some strange uncouth monster, who not being able to mingle and unite in society, has been expell'd from all human commerce, and left utterly abandoned and disconsolate' (Hume 1978: 264). Hume describes a bachelor lifestyle of solitary walks by the riverside and philosophical reverie interposed by interludes of conversation and backgammon (ibid. 269–70).

16. Edward Duffy suggests that Macneil's household is modelled on the utopian domestic community of *Julie*'s Clarens (Duffy 1979: 50).

17. See also Michael McKeon's discussion of the gender politics of contract theory and marriage (McKeon 2005: 124, 154).

18. Lamb notes that Godwin's view of promises as immoral extends to his rejection of social contract theory (Lamb 2009: 124).

19. Despite this desire to accommodate Wollstonecraft, Godwin also advocates 'plain dealing, truth spoken with kindness, but spoken with sincerity . . . the most wholesome of all disciplines' (Godwin 1993b: 162). This produced

the bluntly candid *Memoirs of the Author of A Vindication of the Rights of Woman*, in which, according to Robert Southey, Godwin expressed 'the want of all feeling in stripping his dead wife naked', and exposing Wollstonecraft's own carefully concealed secret history (quoted in Carlson 2007: 41). Godwin concedes, 'I have a singular want of foresight on some occasions, as to the effect what I shall say will have on the person to whom it is addressed' (Godwin 2007a: 58).

20. Marguerite in *St. Leon* and Henrietta in *Mandeville* both challenge St. Leon and Mandeville, but ultimately submit to their pessimism and misanthropy.

21. Eve Kosofsky Sedgwick observes that the Gothic novel – a genre Godwin engaged with in *Caleb Williams* – is motivated by the unsettling realisation that 'for a man to be a man's man is separated only by an invisible, carefully blurred always-already-crossed line from being interested in men' (Sedgwick 1985: 89). Much has been written on homosocial elements, homoerotic desire and its attendant anxiety in Godwin's novels, especially *Caleb Williams*. See William D. Brewer (Brewer 2000), Robert J. Corber (Corber 1990), Alex Gold Jr. (Gold 1977), A. A. Markley (Markley 2004: para. 1) and Sedgwick (Sedgwick 1985: 91–2).

22. In *Pamela*, Mr B cross dresses and invades Pamela's closet, suggesting the anxieties about gender identity associated with the eighteenth-century closet (Richardson 2008: 199).

23. See also Angela Esterhammer (Esterhammer 2000: 289) and A. A. Markley for the similar argument that Godwin's novels popularise his political theory for a general audience (Markley 2004: para. 1).

24. See Deidre Shauna Lynch who traces this mimetic concept of character to the empiricist thesis that individuals are formed by their perceptions (Lynch 1998: 34).

25. Mary Jacobus points to Mary Shelley's use of 'mummy' as a pun referring to the dead Wollstonecraft (Jacobus 1995: 79).

26. See Judith Butler, who argues that 'the melancholic answer to the loss of the same-sexed object is to incorporate and, indeed, *to become* that object' (Butler 1999: 81).

Chapter 6

Gendering the General Will: *Frankenstein*'s Breaches of Contract

It is true, we shall be monsters, cut off from all the world; but on that account we shall be more attached to one another. (Shelley 1996a: 109)

Mary Shelley's criticism of the foundations of a society that forges different routes for men and women is often noted as one of *Frankenstein*'s most powerful statements.[1] What has perhaps been less obvious, and which I lay out in this chapter, is its relationship to social contract theory. *Frankenstein* presents a sustained engagement with the central problem of this book – social contract theory's question of whether individualism is compatible with sociability. In the creation stories of the creature and of his planned but unrealisable female mate, Shelley points to the social contract's underlying dilemmas. All readers of *Frankenstein* agree with Victor that his creation of the monster was a terrible mistake, and yet few are certain about how it should be resolved. Shelley offers two vexed solutions to one of Romanticism's most haunting problems – the creature's dilemma. The first, explored in the plot of *Frankenstein*, unfolds with an air of tragic inevitability; Victor destroys his creature and – by extension – himself. But the second solution that Shelley raises, through the creature's earnest behest that Victor make him a partner, presents a different set of obstacles. Shelley invites her readers to sympathise with the monster's predicament, but not with its resolution in the nightmarish prospect of a 'race of devils . . . propagated upon the earth, who might make the very existence of the species of man a condition precarious and full of terror' (Shelley 1996a: 128). Shelley devises her own critique of social contract theory by bringing William Godwin's wax effigies, texts and fetishes from his novels *Fleetwood* and *Deloraine* together with Mary Wollstonecraft's reflections on gender politics. She transforms Godwin's automatons into Victor's male creature and his envisioned female counterpart, examining their separate paths in a culture that excludes women from the social contract. Shelley criticises

Godwin's and Wollstonecraft's assumption that women may have a potential place within the social contract, and emphasises their silencing within her own radically gendered reading of the general will.

The influence of Rousseau's literary writings on *Frankenstein*, a profoundly intertextual novel, is well established; but Shelley's dialogue with his works of political theory is not.[2] The main thrust of scholarship on Shelley's relation to Rousseau's political philosophy focuses on his concept of natural man, the most detailed discussion being James O'Rourke's analysis of the creature's development through a reading of Rousseau's *Discourse on the Origins of Inequality* (O'Rourke 1989: 547–50).[3] O'Rourke suggests that the creature responds to Victor's rejection by gradually changing from innocence to civilised corruption, following the trajectory of human history from an individualistic state of nature to social being. O'Rourke bases his reading of *Frankenstein* on Shelley's much later 1836 encyclopaedia entry on Rousseau, where her outrage over Rousseau's abandonment of his children eclipses her attention to his political theory. In order to draw parallelisms between *Frankenstein* and this entry, O'Rourke emphasises similarities between *Frankenstein*'s 1818 and 1831 versions, the latter of which is broadly cotemporaneous with the encyclopaedia article.[4] But this comparison elides some important changes in Shelley's perspective. Hence, whereas critics tend to overemphasise shifts in Coleridge's, Wordsworth's and Godwin's positions, Shelley's own significant alterations and her contextual approach to authorship are often overlooked, as are the different cultural contexts of her early and later phases.

These differences are apparent in the discrete historical settings of the 1818 and 1831 versions of *Frankenstein*. In 1818, Shelley provides a detailed itinerary of Victor's travels through post-revolutionary France, the period in which *Frankenstein* is set: 'we arrived at Havre on the 8th of May, and instantly proceeded to Paris, where my father had some business which detained us a few weeks' (Shelley 1996a: 143). By contrast, in 1831 Shelley contracts this journey into a much briefer account: 'we left Paris on our way to Switzerland' (Shelley 2000: 153). In this later version, Shelley also relocates Henry Clerval's interest in Anglo-French culture to colonial India. In the 1818 *Frankenstein* Victor receives word from 'Clerval, entreating me to join him. He said that nearly a year had elapsed since we had quitted Switzerland and France was as yet unvisited' (Shelley 1996a: 131). In 1831 Clerval's focus shifts: 'he said he was wearing away his time fruitlessly where he was; that letters from the friends he had formed in London desired for his return to complete the negotiation they had entered into for his Indian enterprise' (Shelley 2000: 148). Here Clerval is guided by the goal of 'materially assisting the progress of European colonisation and trade' in India (ibid. 139). Whereas the 1818 *Frankenstein* emphasises the political tensions of Rousseau's social theory and the attendant background of the French Revolution and the Reign of Terror, reflecting the novel's historical setting in the mid-1790s, the 1831 version relates to later political concerns. This change of focus has made the 1831 version a less popular choice for contemporary readers who often regard the 1830s as a post-Romantic period, exemplified by the consensus that Wordsworth's 1805 *Prelude* is superior to its 1850 version.[5]

If the 1830s represent a discrete historical phase in literary periodisation, and also in Shelley's career, and her encyclopaedia entry is focused on Rousseau's parental neglect more than on his social philosophy, then thematic engagements within the 1818 version offer an alternative approach to Shelley's complex treatment of Rousseau's political theory.[6] In this early period, Shelley considers Rousseau primarily within a political context. In a letter to Fanny Imlay of 1816, she describes her visit to Geneva:

> a small obelisk is erected in the glory of Rousseau, and here (such is the mutability of human life) the magistrates, the successors of those who exiled him from his native country, were shot by the populace during that revolution, which his writings mainly contributed to mature, and which, not withstanding the temporary bloodshed and injustice with which it was polluted, has produced enduring benefits to mankind. (Shelley 1980: 1.20)

Shelley connects Rousseau's social theory to her own political context, which was still absorbing the impact of his works on the French Revolution in 1816. The Shelleys conceive of Rousseau as a household presence, an immediate part of their reality. Accordingly Shelley's *History of a Six Weeks' Tour* (1817) recounts their travels where the dust seems only recently to have settled on Rousseau's footprints. Her journal entries of 1815 to 1818 record reading Rousseau's *Reveries of a Solitary Walker*, *Emile*, *La Nouvelle Heloise* and *The Confessions*. As a crucial volume of Shelley's journal from May 1815 to July 1816 is missing, her chronicles remain incomplete (Shelley 1987: xxxi–xxxii). Yet even if Shelley never read Rousseau's political writings directly, Percy Shelley's readings and their preoccupation with the works of Godwin and Wollstonecraft, both of whom responded extensively to Rousseau's social contract philosophy make Rousseau an important influence.[7]

In *Frankenstein* Shelley focuses her critique of Rousseau's political theory through the character of the creature, who from his inception is a social being planned to establish 'a new species' (Shelley 1996a:

37).[8] Diana Reese comments on the creature's relation to Rousseau's general will, suggesting that he represents 'female nonsubjects, slaves and servants', all of whom are excluded from Rousseau's concept of sociability (Reese 2006: 58). In a similar vein, Susan Lanser identifies the creature with the eighteenth-century novel's vocation of enfranchising marginalised social groups (Lanser 2005: 486). Discussing Malthus, Clara Tuite reads the monster as an embodiment of elements excluded from the body politic, representing 'the abjected product of the bourgeois Malthusian creature of "moral restraint"' (Tuite 1998: 141). These critics all point to the dynamic of exclusion in their various readings of monstrosity. However, exclusion turns out to be an inherent aspect of the creature's constitution, as well as of his planned mate's. Through her creation stories of the creatures' respective bodies, Shelley forms a detailed critique of social contract theory. The creatures expose the elements of society that are left out of the social contract, and – more importantly – they question and refract the concept of social coherence altogether.[9]

Social Withdrawal

Scholars have long noted Victor's excessive individualism as the tragic flaw which leads him to produce the creature. Comparisons of Victor and Rousseau usually emphasise the causal relationship between social withdrawal and the neglect of duty. But Shelley also points to a constructive relationship between these shortcomings and a new model of sociability, connecting withdrawal to social vocation. By introducing Victor as 'by birth a Genevan' she alludes to Rousseau's self-identification on the title page of *The Social Contract*, which Rousseau signs as '*J.-J. Rousseau Citizen of Geneva*' (Shelley 1996a: 21; Rousseau 1994c: 127).[10] By the same token, Shelley draws an analogy between the creature and Rousseau's treatise – both produced by Genevan citizens. Victor plans his creature to realise a grandiose social vision: 'a new species would bless me as its creator and source; many happy and excellent natures would owe their being to me' (Shelley 1996a: 37). He imagines the creature as an expression of his hopes for social amelioration and the recognition that this would bring: 'I had begun life with benevolent intentions, and thirsted for the moment when I should put them in practice, and make myself useful to my fellow-beings' (ibid. 67). These aspirations echo Rousseau's goal of social reform, expressed in his famous assertion that 'man was born free and everywhere he is in chains . . . How did this change occur? I do not know. What can make it legitimate? I believe I can answer this question' (Rousseau 1994c: 131). Shelley articulates a critique of these chains in her novel *Matilda*, written shortly after *Frankenstein*, in 1819. When Matilda's neglectful aunt dies, she reflects, 'the chains of habit are so strong that even when affection does not link them the heart must be agonized when they break' (Shelley 1996b: 17). Shelley develops Godwin's metaphor of chains which connect people, suggesting that chains often also bind us to bad relationships. By using her father's imagery, Shelley further demonstrates the formative impact of innate connections. Matilda's father confesses his incestuous love for Matilda by quoting from *A Wife for a Moneth*, a text that Shelley associates with *Fleetwood* and connects to the thematics of extreme patriarchal oppression, represented by father–daughter rape (ibid. 35). Chains become a figure for a vision of society as fundamentally coercive.

Victor evades the negative aspect of social ties. He approaches his project of forming a creature by entering a state of profound isolation which draws on Rousseau's *Reveries of the Solitary Walker* and *The Confessions*. In the *Reveries of the Solitary Walker*, Rousseau recounts his retreat from persecution in Geneva and Paris to the Ile St. Pierre. Although ecstatically immersed in nature on the island, Rousseau emphasises that withdrawal always remains a social disposition that – like Fleetwood's states of Romantic retreat – responds to political tensions: 'I clamber up rocks and mountains, I go deep into vales and woods in order to slip away, as much as possible, from the memory of men and from the attacks of the wicked' (Rousseau 2000: 65). Victor's retreat also responds to Rousseau's account of his withdrawal to a solitary cottage in *The Confessions*. By closely reflecting this account Shelley emphasises that no good can come of a social theory hatched in isolation from social relations. Following the bad example set by Rousseau, Victor exiles himself from his family and his native Geneva: 'two years passed in this manner, during which I paid no visit to Geneva, but was engaged, heart and soul, in the pursuit of the same discoveries which I hoped to make' (Shelley 1996a: 34). These discoveries involve a Rousseauvian state of abstinence, so that Victor abandons his family and friends, and even forgoes food and sleep. Repeating Rousseau's language in *The Confessions*, Shelley draws an ironic contrast between Victor's introspection and his burgeoning environment:

> the summer months passed while I was thus engaged, heart and soul, in one pursuit. It was the most beautiful season; never did the fields bestow a more plentiful harvest, or the vines yield a more luxuriant vintage: but my eyes were insensible to the charms of nature. (Shelley 1996a: 38)[11]

Through her account of Victor's making of the creature, Shelley juxtaposes a private experience of withdrawal on the one hand with the formation of a new social model on the other. She critiques Victor's approach to sociability by emphasising that it derives from introspection rather than direct social involvement. Frankenstein's creature, produced through his creator's splicing of withdrawal with political ambition, points to a weakness in Victor's approach which Shelley relates to Rousseau's own account of his political philosophy as a fantasy that responds to states of extreme isolation in *The Confessions*.

Shelley's approach to Rousseauvian literary withdrawal is shaped by David Hume's view of literature as a legitimate outlet for fantasies, which would otherwise threaten to contaminate reality.[12] In her journals, Shelley complains of being 'neither independent, alone or settled – . . . I cannot live as I do – without a metaphor I cannot live' (Shelley 1987: 2.456). She implies that the function of metaphor is to provide stability to identity. But *Frankenstein* repeats Hume's warning that such metaphors must not cross the lines separating fiction from reality, and must remain firmly within the bounds of the literary text.[13] To fortify the boundaries of her own novel, she distances and encases the creature's narrative in *Frankenstein*'s box-like epistolary form.[14] Shelley focuses her critique of this transgression through allusions to Coleridge's *Rime of the Ancient Mariner*. Arctic voyager Robert Walton and solitary entrepreneur Victor Frankenstein are both modelled on the prototype of the mariner, as well as on the figure of Rousseau – the idiosyncratic social theorist who paradoxically courts social improvement through retreat. Walton writes to his sister of his travels, 'I am going to unexplored regions, to "the land of mist and / snow;" but I shall kill no albatross, therefore do not be alarmed for my safety' (Shelley 1996a: 14). The figure of the albatross recurs later on, when Victor realises that he must form a partner for his creature before he can marry Elizabeth: 'could I enter into a festival with this deadly weight yet hanging round my neck, and bowing me to the ground' (ibid. 117).[15] Like the mariner, Victor has sinned against nature and is barred from the marriage ceremony, which becomes a type for a broader predicament of social exclusion.

Coleridge's hybrid form, combining lyric with ballad elements, dictates *The Rime of the Ancient Mariner*'s appearance in *Frankenstein*. It is at the points of formal interruption and heightened experience, when Coleridge digresses from the ballad stanza, that Shelley quotes from his *Ancient Mariner*. Drawing on this formal tension between the ballad quatrain and its lyrical digressions in Coleridge's *Rime*, she evokes Victor's fear of his monster by citing the mariner's simile expressing his horror on waking to see his dead shipmates still on board beside him:

> Like one, that on a lonely road,
> Doth walk in fear and dread,
> And having once turn'd round, walks on
> And turns no more his head:
> Because he knows, a frightful fiend
> Doth close behind him tread. (Coleridge 2001: ll. 446–51)

Shelley's citation draws a direct analogy between the mariner's punishment for killing the albatross and Victor's rejection of his supernatural creature and subsequent persecution by the monster. In quoting this stanza almost verbatim (Shelley merely changes 'that' to 'who') and opening and closing her novel in Coleridge's polar landscape (albeit Arctic rather than Antarctic), emphasising to her readers that this is the mariner's 'land of mist and / snow', Shelley draws an analogy between her novel and the poem (Shelley 1996a: 14). Beth Lau suggests that the critical tendency to classify Romantic writers by gender has led to an overlooking of *Frankenstein*'s affinity with the *Ancient Mariner* (Lau 2009: 92); while Michelle Levy emphasises 'the ways in which Coleridge and Shelley sought to eradicate, or at least to mitigate, the damage caused by reckless discovery' (Levy 2004: 694). This affinity cuts across gender boundaries, as Lau and Levy suggest, and also across the borders of literary genre. Maureen McLane's analysis of the eighteenth-century ballad revival emphasises the political stakes of this choice. The ballad revival foregrounds values of nationalism and domestic stability (McLane 2008: 132). The archaic spellings of the 1798 *Rime*, the version available to Shelley at this time, and the thematic emphasis on oral history through the mariner's retelling of his tale anchor the poem in a nationalist ideal of historical continuity.[16]

Crook dates the fictional correspondence that constitutes *Frankenstein* to 1796, two years before the 1798 *Rime of the Ancyent Marinere* was initially published, indicating a proleptic timescale. She notes that at the time that Shelley was writing *Frankenstein* Coleridge's 1798 version had already gained popularity and would have been recognisable to her intended readers, but not to the fictional characters or to Victor or Walton, who nonetheless quote from it with apparent familiarity (Shelley 1996a: note 14).[17] McGann identifies two temporal frameworks in this 1798 iteration of Coleridge's *Rime*: '*(a)* an original mariner's tale; *(b)* the ballad narrative of the story', which he dates to the seventeenth century (McGann 1981: 50). If the *Rime* is read within the temporal framework of a seventeenth-century ballad narrative of a medieval mariner's tale, then its anachronistic appearance in *Frankenstein* makes sense, given the broad circulation that such ballads had in the late eighteenth century, and Walton's own fascination with travel tales.

Coleridge's *Rime* is misread by the characters of Walton and Victor in *Frankenstein*, not as the lyrical ballad which Shelley and her readers knew it to be, but as a true history. In misconstruing the *Rime* in these crucial terms, Shelley critiques Coleridge's advice in the *Biographia Literaria* to suspend readerly disbelief (Coleridge 1983: 2.6). Walton and Victor regard the mariner's tale as a reflection on a social modus vivendi rather than a work of imaginative fiction. Shelley's account of the creature as a precocious but undiscerning reader who misreads *Paradise Lost* 'as a true history', points to the same fallacy, whereby fiction is mistaken for truth (Shelley 1996a: 97). In the creature's case, this results from his insufficient guidance and the faulty empiricist logic of self-induction, which stands in for direct nurturance and natural sociability (echoing Godwin's criticisms of Rousseau and Hobbes in *Fleetwood* and *Mandeville*). In Walton's and Victor's cases, their errors result from a similar lack of parental guidance and faulty empiricist educations. Shelley criticises Coleridge for failing to account for the importance of social context in his theory of poetic faith, and points to a parallel difficulty in Rousseau.

In *Frankenstein* Shelley rewrites the mariner's tale from a yet bleaker standpoint than does Coleridge, who is able to deliver his protagonist to an alternative, albeit unhappy, existence on the margins of society as a hermit or a wandering Jew. By contrast, Shelley rejects Walton's planned career as an Arctic explorer and the creature's as a social outcast and émigré. From her perspective, informed by the difference of gender, exclusion from the wedding and thus from society translates into death. Although getting somewhat ahead of my argument here, it is worth noticing the crucial centrality of coverture in Shelley's thinking, informed by Wollstonecraft's observation that 'females, in fact, denied all political privileges, and not allowed, as married women, excepting in criminal cases, a civil existence, have their attention naturally drawn from the interest of the whole community to that of the minute parts', a view which profoundly influenced Shelley (Wollstonecraft 2007b: 220). Wollstonecraft argues that the centre of society, represented by patriarchy and its marriage contracts, is oppressed by what Gayatri Chakravorty Spivak calls 'acts of epistemic violence', the marginalisation of social groups 'as other and subject to domination' (Spivak 1995: 76). Shelley suggests that this predicament also applies to Victor and his male creature, so that a social contract founded on exclusions ultimately compromises all members of society, leaving them solitary. Where Coleridge accepts large parts of Rousseau's political rhetoric, albeit ambivalently, and imitates his ostracised status, Shelley, by contrast, rejects him.

In her 1836 encyclopaedia entry for Lardner's *French Lives* Shelley develops an extended critique of Rousseau's paternal deficiencies from the broad perspective of gender.[18] Her account repeats the domesticated narrative of Hume that Godwin had formulated through the character of Macneil in *Fleetwood*. Shelley criticises Rousseau's view 'that entire independence, even of natural duties, was the state congenial to man', an ideology which Rousseau developed, in her view, to sanction his abandonment of his children (Shelley 2002a: 366).[19] She proposes, instead, the counterfactual fantasy that 'these children might have clustered around him in his days of desertion, have cheered his house with smiles, and been a help and support in his age. He would not have felt friendless' (ibid. 335). Rousseau's individualism abnegates these vital ties, which Shelley seeks to resurrect through the image of a domesticated Rousseau in her later works. To similar effect, she constructs a conjectural narrative of the character of Sophie d'Houdetot from *The Confessions*. Shelley admits,

> although she has left little behind her by which we may trace her life, yet we are touched and pleased, and finish by declaring her worthy for her own sake of that attention, which we first bestowed on her for another's. (Shelley 1823: 68)

Shelley's writing focuses on the suppressed narratives behind the empiricist master discourses of individualism, bringing to life the stories of women and children excluded from the social contract as an alternative to the ideology of isolation she associates with Coleridge and Rousseau.

Making Empiricist Monsters

Frankenstein extends Godwin's criticism of empiricist models of education in *Fleetwood* and *Mandeville*. In contrast to the predicament of Godwin's characters, who become what they read, Shelley suggests that intertextual relations produce unpredictable results in readers who may form new positions, instead of merely reproducing familiar older ones. Fiction does not create automatons, but monsters with wills of their own. This insight is heavily informed by the social contract's ambiguous construction of women as non-political subjects, who nonetheless have independent wills and thus the potential for political aspirations. Women may read political theory and demand that the same rights be extended to them. Wollstonecraft here is a point in case. Shelley's unconventional perspective on Rousseau's social theory reflects her status as a woman writer in a philosophical tradition dominated by men, and in a literary tradition in which her absent mother is the sole female precedent. In *Thoughts on the Education of Daughters*, Wollstonecraft asserts that 'children very early contract the manners of those about them' (Wollstonecraft 1994: 5). Following Shelley's view that reading produces unpredictable results, I contend that in *Frankenstein* she was thinking through Rousseau's social contract in her own terms, and not just through her mother's works.[20] Wollstonecraft suggests that women are often unable to find a place in a society which discriminates against them. She attempts to resolve the inherent conflicts of Rousseau's social theory by endeavouring to read him as a champion of progress, a perspective that she borrows from the Scottish Enlightenment.[21] Espousing values of natural sociability, Wollstonecraft regards gender as a local problem which her *Vindication of the Rights of Woman* then undertakes to correct.[22] By contrast, Shelley ascribes both her talents and her ethical sensibility to the epistemic violence of gender politics, suggesting that with very few exceptions gender privilege corrupts the social body: 'I . . . hate a sex who are strong only to oppress – moral only to insult' (Shelley 1987: 2.488). She turns to Wollstonecraft, whom she often represents as an absence.[23] Hence, Shelley '*respectfully inscribe*[s]' *Frankenstein* to 'William Godwin, Author of Political Justice, Caleb Williams &c' on the novel's title page (Shelley 1996a: 5); in contrast, she never directly mentions Wollstonecraft. But *Frankenstein*'s subtitle, 'The Modern Prometheus', invokes Henry Darnford's manipulative praise of Rousseau as 'the true Prometheus of sentiment' in *The Wrongs of Woman, or Maria* (Wollstonecraft 2007a: 262). Darnford pens this reference to Rousseau in the margins of his copy of *Julie* as a billet-doux to seduce Maria. In *Frankenstein* Shelley moves Rousseau's errors from the figurative margins of Wollstonecraft's *mise en abyme* text to the foreground of her novel, demonstrating that Rousseau's shortcomings (and thereby also Wollstonecraft's reading of them) are not marginal flaws or secondary texts, but symptomatic of problems central to the body politic.

To appreciate this rewriting, we need briefly to look at the parallelism that Shelley forms between the character of Jemima in *The Wrongs of Woman, or Maria* and Victor's creature. Supernaturalism is figurative in Wollstonecraft's account of Jemima 'as a creature of another species', which becomes 'cut off from human converse . . . a ghost among the living' (Wollstonecraft 2007a: 278, 283). Wollstonecraft's metaphor is literalised in Shelley's portrayal of the creature as a genuine monster: 'concealed by long locks of ragged hair; but one vast hand was extended, in colour and apparent texture like that of a mummy' (Shelley

1996a: 166–7). Mary Jacobus notes that 'mummy', which describes the creature's body, is also a pun on 'mother' – in an allusion to the dead Wollstonecraft (Jacobus 1995: 79). The creature's mummified, desiccated flesh echoes the hag-like 'shrivel[ed]' and 'furrow[ed]' skin of Jemima (Wollstonecraft 2007a: 274–5). The mummy also recalls the gendered automatons of Godwin's novels *Fleetwood* and *Deloraine*. Beneath Rousseau's account of originary individuality, Shelley elicits a concurrent narrative of dependence, loss and subjection. In Rousseau's theory, humans do not instinctively care for each other, and only value their self-preservation. They reproduce through 'blind inclination . . . This need satisfied, the two sexes no longer recognized each other, and even the child no longer meant anything to his mother as soon as he could do without her' (Rousseau 1992a: 43). *Frankenstein* enacts the absence of mothers in Rousseau's theory by turning to the inadequacies of Wollstonecraft's reading of Rousseau and her excuse that 'the weaknesses of character that he himself depicts . . . never appear to have arisen from depravity of heart' (Wollstonecraft 1989: 409).

Responding to Wollstonecraft, Shelley undertakes her own revision of Rousseau's *Emile*. Rousseau advocates an indirect approach to education. He argues that children develop best when left to learn independently and cites lightning as an exemplary object for exercises in self-induction:

> The distance from which thunder is coming can be judged by the time which passes from the lightning to the clap. Arrange things so that the child has knowledge of all these experiments, that he makes all those within his reach, and that he finds the others by induction. But I prefer a hundred times over his being ignorant of them to you having to tell them to him. (Rousseau 2010: 291)

Rousseau emphasises that direct instruction cannot foster the independent thought necessary for good citizenship. Still, children need supervision if they are to be protected from their corrupting environments. Supervision must therefore be provided indirectly, in this passage by a hidden hand arranging things for the child's knowledge. In *Frankenstein* Shelley repeats Rousseau's pedagogical exercise with lightning, which is a symbol for Enlightenment insight. Left by his parents to his own devices, Victor becomes enraptured by 'natural phenomena that take place every day before our eyes', singling out the influence of 'a most violent and terrible thunder-storm' as producing his passion for electricity – the vital force that film versions of *Frankenstein* have since adopted in the creature's birth scenes (Shelley 1996a: 27). Victor's education is entirely unsupervised, with no benign tutor arranging things behind the scenes. He complains that his father never took the time to explain why Cornelius Agrippa is 'sad trash' (ibid. 25). This renders him an unorthodox thinker, insufficiently prepared for Rousseauvian citizenship, which requires a quantum of supervision necessary for forming moral evaluations.

Thus considered, Rousseau's theory of education leaves the need for socialisation represented by the hidden presence of the instructor too vague. When Victor arrives at university, M. Krempe notes his eclectic background: 'I little expected in this enlightened and scientific age to find a disciple of Albertus Magnus and Paracelsus. My dear Sir, you must begin your studies entirely anew' (Shelley 1996a: 31). Victor admits 'it may appear very strange, that a disciple of Albertus Magnus should arise in the eighteenth century' (ibid. 26). He is initially suspicious of Krempe's empiricist approach, accusing him of 'exchang[ing] chimeras of boundless grandeur for realities of little worth' (ibid. 32). But Victor later acknowledges Krempe's 'sound sense and real information' (ibid. 34). Whereas Krempe encourages Victor to study the natural world around him, Victor is intuitively more inclined to M. Waldman, who posits an Idealistic faith in '[natural] philosophers, whose hands seem only to dabble in dirt' but who have 'indeed performed miracles' (ibid. 32). Shelley exposes a gap between Rousseau's criticism of guidance in *Emile* and his disparate emphasis on the need strictly to supervise children's reading. Rousseau connects Emile's liberty to explore his environment free from instruction to an abstinence from books, and limits his fictional pupil to a single book in childhood – *Robinson Crusoe* (Rousseau 2010: 332). Rousseau explains that 'there is often nothing which is more deceptive than books, and which renders less faithfully the sentiments of those who wrote them' (ibid. 468). Only when Emile reaches late adolescence does Rousseau contemplate exposing him to other works of literature and science (ibid. 516–17). Rousseau's model of reading echoes Wolmar's Elysium: instead of genuine freedom, it produces a forced and contrived quasi-natural environment.

Shelley's criticism of Rousseau's theory of education extends to the creature. The creature's inability to distinguish between Milton and Constantin de Volney becomes a point in case for Victor's parental neglect, a reminder of his abandonment. Shelley also prefaces Victor's narrative with the story of Walton's precocious and unsupervised reading. Walton betrays his father's dying wish because he has been led astray by books that he reads when alone in his uncle's library: 'my education was neglected, yet I was passionately fond of reading. These volumes were my study day and night' (Shelley 1996a: 11). His lack of guidance creates a voracious hunger for literature. Walton's early exposure to travel romance leads him to undertake his treacherous journey to the North Pole: 'I try in vain to be persuaded that the pole is the seat of frost and desolation, it ever presents itself to my imagination as the region of beauty and delight' (ibid. 9–10). In *Frankenstein* books fail to substitute for direct relations of nurturing, guidance and socialisation. This deep suspicion of books, based on Thomas Hobbes's conception of language as artificial and not founded in natural sociability, is demonstrated most clearly in the case of the creature. Like Shelley's own text, composed of allusions to myriad literary sources including *The Rime of the Ancient Mariner* and *Paradise Lost*, the creature's body has a palimpsestic quality. His 'wrinkled' and 'yellow skin' has the texture of parchment (ibid. 39). He is even produced as a textual entity, assembled from the writings of Cornelius Agrippa, Albertus Magnus and Paracelsus. And as a textual being, he is an uncannily prolific reader, assimilating Plutarch's *Lives*, Goethe's *The Sorrows of Werter* and de Volney's *Ruins* with apparent ease and without any direct formal education (ibid. 95, 89). The creature soon perceives an arbitrary relationship between signifier and signified, reflecting Hobbes's empiricist view of language as a secondary property which does not express a primary tie between people: 'the words they uttered, not having any apparent connexion with visible objects, I was unable to discover any clue by which I could unravel the mystery of their reference' (ibid. 83). When the creature does manage to acquire language by eavesdropping on Felix De Lacey teaching Safie, he finds that it condemns him to a fragmented existence, from which death is the only reprieve. Here Shelley casts judgment on Rousseau's model of indirect education, suggesting that it does not guarantee adequate supervision and socialisation; no one orchestrates the creature's education. The creature reflects,

> of what a strange nature is knowledge! It clings to the mind, when it has once seized on it, like a lichen on the rock. I wished sometimes to shake off all thought and feeling; but I learned that there was but one means . . . and that was death. (Shelley 1996a: 90)

He takes revenge in textual form, leaving his 'mark' on the bodies of Clerval and Elizabeth, and also providing Victor with 'marks in writing on the barks of the trees, or cut in stone, that guided me, and instigated my fury', in the final chase (Shelley 1996a: 135, 150, 156). The creature shows Victor the power of language by bringing him Felix and Safie's letters to confirm the truth of his tale (ibid. 92). Victor in turn shows these letters to Walton as evidence of his own narrative (ibid. 160). Victor requests to see Walton's notes 'and then himself corrected and augmented them in many places . . . "Since you have preserved my narration," he said, "I would not that a mutilated one should go down to posterity"' (ibid. 160).

Expressing Shelley's profound suspicion of naive and unsupervised uses of discourse, the creature evolves as a poorly edited patchwork of texts. This hybrid composition provokes his rejection from social communities, as their members find the visible contrast between his different elements disturbing. Shelley draws attention to the creature's individually fine parts, sensibility and persuasive rhetoric; but these cannot assuage the effect of his ghastly overall appearance. The blind De Lacey easily befriends the creature, but Felix beholds him with horror. Similarly, Victor's love turns to loathing when he finishes making the creature and views him in his entirety. Shelley provides a detailed account of the development of the creature's ugliness and the impediment it constitutes to his participation in the model of sociability for which he was destined. During the creation process, Victor struggles to contain the creature's parts within a unified whole: 'although I possessed the capacity of bestowing animation, yet to prepare a frame for the reception of it, with its intricacies of fibres, muscles, and veins, still remained a work of inconceivable difficulty and labour' (Shelley 1996a: 36–7). In attempt to solve the problem, Victor enlarges the creature: 'as the minuteness of the parts formed a great hindrance to my speed, I resolved, contrary to my first intention, to make the being of a gigantic stature' (ibid. 37). This enlargement renders the creature's composite nature glaringly visible: 'his yellow skin scarcely covered the work of muscles and arteries beneath; his hair was of a lustrous black, and flowing; his teeth of a pearly whiteness; but these luxuriances only formed a more horrid contrast with his watery eyes' (ibid. 39–40). The effect of horror is produced by the contrast among the creature's diverse parts, which have no prior relationship to each other and apparently belong to several different species. Victor explains that in forming the creature, 'the dissecting room *and the slaughter-house* furnished many of my materials', as did 'bones from charnel houses' (ibid. 38, emphasis added). In their natural proportions, in their designated stations and in isolation, the creature's parts are beautiful. Their translation to a large scale and their piecemeal juxtaposition within one body as a 'filthy mass' of organs accentuates their fissures and points of incompatibility (ibid. 110).

The aesthetic effect of failed totality points to an underlying problem in the language of the body politic as a 'cybernetic organism, struggling to survive in its environment. It possessed no fully autonomous sovereign mind, only a complex brain and nervous system that would work to produce a unity of perception and feeling from the diverse "tissues" and "organs" that constituted the organism' (Bates 2012: 177). Without a centralised principle of sovereignty this body politic cannot regulate itself and lacks coherence. Drawing on eighteenth-century developments in the field of chemistry, Rousseau figured the transformation from individuals to a unitary body politic as a chemical process (ibid. 190). Although the body politic conceives of itself as a structural unity, it lacks concrete experience and internal coordination (ibid. 195). Later, the creature recalls his emergence into consciousness as one of disparate parts and organs converging into a whole: 'before, dark and opaque bodies had surrounded me . . . but I now found that I could wander at liberty' (Shelley 1996a: 76). The creature does not come into being as a *tabula rasa* or solitary individual, but is formed of diverse bodies and past experiences. His first impulse is to try to classify himself from his chaotic origins:

> no distinct ideas occupied my mind; all was confused. I felt light, and hunger, and thirst, and darkness; innumerable sounds rang in my ears . . . the only object that I could distinguish was the bright moon, and I fixed my eyes on that with pleasure. (Shelley 1996a: 77)

The creature's composition from manifold bodies establishes his alienation in terms that are not merely affective, but also constitutional.

The creature experiences rejection because he is himself a figure of social anomaly – formed of individual parts which share no common background and which are discordant and disturbing to all who see him. He transcends individual proportions to become – as his xenograft quality suggests – an embodiment of a broader, corporate social body that fails to cohere. In this regard, he grotesquely allegorises Rousseau's general will and its predecessor, the older model of the body politic. The creature echoes the frontispiece of Hobbes's *Leviathan*, which represents a body of superhuman proportions composed of singular elements, a similarity noted by Chris Baldick who reads both the monster and the Leviathan as types for the dismemberment of the body politic (Baldick 1990: 16). In her journal entries of 1818 and 1820, Shelley records reading Hobbes's *On Man* and also notes that Percy Shelley read *Leviathan* (Shelley 1987: 1.287, 311–13). Her attention to the *Leviathan*'s presence in their household suggests her possible previous familiarity with its iconic title-page illustration of the composite sovereign body, re-visualised in *Frankenstein* through the monster's genesis as a conglomerate social body.

Having been formed to fulfil a social vision, the creature aspires to leave his solitary state and realise Victor's original plan of founding 'a new species' (Shelley 1996a: 37). Responding to his rejection by

Victor and others, the creature determines that he will need a partner to become sociable: 'it is true, we shall be monsters, cut off from all the world; but on that account we shall be more attached to one another' (ibid. 109). Their solitude will be that of a new race. The creature uses the contractual language of conditions and being 'bound by ties', presenting the creation of this partner as a prerequisite for Victor's own forthcoming marriage:

> you, my creator, detest and spurn me, thy creature, to whom thou art bound by ties only dissoluble by the annihilation of one of us. You purpose to kill me. How dare you sport thus with life? Do your duty towards me, and I will do mine towards you and the rest of mankind. If you comply with my conditions, I will leave them and you at peace; but if you refuse, I will glut the maw of death until it be satiated with the blood of your remaining friends. (Shelley 1996a: 74)

The creature warns Victor against his one-sided behaviour, invoking a rhetoric of mutual responsibility and appealing to Victor's private interests – to his concern for his own well being and for his loved ones. Initially Victor concedes 'what the duties of a creator towards his creatures were, and that I ought to render him happy' (Shelley 1996a: 76). But, disillusioned by the values of community that the creature invokes, Victor finally turns his back on him, asserting that they are not 'bound by ties' (ibid. 74). Through the creature's language of private needs and Victor's final indifference towards him, Shelley forms a criticism of the self-interested rhetoric of social contract theory, which does not provide a sufficient ground for sociability. Ultimately, both Victor and the creature remain on the same side of the argument, expressing an individualism which forecloses the possibility of any community between them.

In addition to Rousseau's social contract, Shelley alludes to other prominent eighteenth-century accounts of society in the construction of the creature. She cites de Volney's *Ruins* as a major influence on the creature's course of education, and alludes to Smith's invisible hand in configuring the creature's relationship with the De Lacey family. Shelley was probably exposed to de Volney's *Ruins* via Percy, who read it to Harriet in 1811 (Nablow 1989: 172). Like Harriet, and possibly like Shelley herself, the creature becomes acquainted with de Volney orally. He overhears Felix reading *The Ruins* to Safie, and intuitively agrees with de Volney's critique of 'the strange system of human society' with its 'immense wealth and squalid poverty' (Shelley 1996a: 89). Like Wollstonecraft, de Volney expresses an Enlightenment faith that individual and social wellbeing are causally related. De Volney argues that 'the sum of individual felicities has constituted the general felicity' (de Volney 1828: 43). He also criticises 'whimsical geniuses, who from moroseness, from wounded vanity, or from a disgust to the vice of society, have conceived chimerical ideas of the savage state', alluding to the notoriously misanthropic Rousseau of *The Confessions* (ibid. 193).[24] Instead, de Volney suggests that the pre-social state is an exhausting battle for survival, in which people are originally isolated but finally become sociable by necessity:

> At first formed naked both in body and in mind, man found himself thrown, as it were by chance, on a confused and savage land . . . Like other animals, without experience of the past, without foresight of the future, he wandered in the depth of the forest, guided only and governed by the affections of his nature; by the pain of hunger, he was to seek food and provide for his subsistence; by the inclemency of the air, he was urged to cover his body. (de Volney 1828: 37)

De Volney imagines that natural man was impelled by a socially constructive variety of egotism to flee his predicament of isolation and form a society. He presents egotism as conducive to progress, as a disposition distinct from what he terms as the 'propensity to hurt our neighbor' (de Volney 1828: 37). The creature's disappointment, which follows hard on the heels of his exposure to the aptly named *Ruins*, is bitter and sharp. Inspired by de Volney's Enlightenment faith in sociability and driven by loneliness to desperation, the creature reveals himself to the De Laceys, hoping to find friendship. His subsequent rejection by the proponents of natural sociability explodes the illusion that individual and collective needs can converge.

Shelley extends her critique of Enlightenment sociability by invoking Smith's invisible hand theory to describe the creature's attempts to befriend the De Laceys.[25] We may recall Smith's use of the invisible hand as a highly influential metaphor for sympathy among the different parts of the social body (Smith 2002: 215). Eleanor Courtemarche notes the

> great deal of magic in invisible hand social theory. The transformation of vice into virtue is amazing enough, but there is also the market's apparent self-organization, and the mysterious distance between cause and effect. (Courtemanche 2011: 195)

Shelley questions Smith's optimistic, semi-mystical model through the creature's attempts to form a community with the De Laceys. On discovering the identity of their benefactor, the De Laceys figuratively bite the 'invisible hand' that feeds them. They first beat the creature and then rapidly decamp from his neighbourhood. They abandon their home and destroy their garden, their sole meagre source of livelihood, which is left in ruin. Nora Crook notes Shelley's reference to *Candide*, which defines social wellbeing as each individual cultivating their own garden (Crook 2000: 85, note a; Voltaire 2005: 130). After helping Felix, the creature 'observe[s], with pleasure, that he did not go to the forest that day, but spent it repairing the cottage and cultivating the garden' (Shelley 1996a: 85). The De Lacey's subsequent rejection of the creature and the abandonment of their garden painfully expose the broader failure of the Enlightenment vision of social cohesiveness as propounded by Smith, de Volney and Voltaire. Shelley emphasises that no model of community can hold individuals together, not even Rousseau's theory of a general will, which acknowledges and negotiates among individual differences, indicating that the needs of individuals are not mutually reconcilable within a broader social body.

The Female Creature

Victor's failure to form the female creature is Shelley's test case for the failure of contract theory. Victor justifies this pivotal decision by invoking his allegiance to his fellow humans, which exceeds both his duty towards his creature and his concern for his own wellbeing. He reflects,

> Had I a right, for my own benefit, to inflict this curse upon everlasting generations? . . . I shuddered to think that future ages might curse me as their pest, whose selfishness had not hesitated to buy its own peace at the price perhaps of the existence of the whole human race. (Shelley 1996a: 128–9)

Here Victor's reasoning is complicated by a pervasive identification with the creature which motivates his crucial decision. It is Victor's fear that the female creature will refuse to submit to a masculine ordering of her destiny that prevents him from keeping his contract with the creature. This second time around Victor is understandably reluctant to make another creature. He recalls having been too excited to record his method the first time, explaining that 'this discovery was so great and overwhelming, that all the steps by which I had been progressively led to it were obliterated' (Shelley 1996a: 36). But his terror of the female creature is also gender specific. Victor requires a special study trip to Britain in order to form her because he cannot find the information readily available in Switzerland or its environs: 'I had heard of some discoveries having been made by an English philosopher, the knowledge of which was material to my success' (ibid. 115). These comments and Shelley's pun on material emphasise the female creature's bodily difference from the male creature. Whereas Victor intuitively knows how to assemble the male creature, and produces him in a flurry of activity generated by readings in a patriarchal tradition that began at home and continued at university, this female challenges his expertise and requires a new body of knowledge. The details of Victor's research in England remain vague. Eventually Victor continues to Scotland to finish his project. This journey to the outreaches of the Scottish Enlightenment, with its revision of empiricist individualism to encompass sociability, implies the female creature's planned destiny as a sociable companion for the male creature and the values of benevolence ('sympathies' which the monster speaks of sharing). To create a female version of the monster Victor needs to travel from Rousseauvian individualism, represented by Switzerland, towards a Hutchesonian model of natural sociability. But as Wollstonecraft observes, women are excluded from both of these theories, leading to Victor's final resolution to destroy the female creature (Wollstonecraft 2007b: 116). Unlike Wollstonecraft, who had hoped to revise Enlightenment theory to accommodate women, Shelley criticises its various discourses for all being founded on an inherent structure of gender exclusion that overlooks core values of common humanity.

The female creature raises a series of questions about her status which Shelley leaves unanswered. If the creature's body is a mini-society, then would she represent a separate mini-society? David William Bates suggests that Rousseau's account 'of these fictional cybernetic political bodies creates a wholly new state of nature, one that exists between individual states as they confront one another in the effort to maintain life' (Bates 2012: 177–8). Given this logic, would the male and female creature then be separate states that would go to war with one another? Rousseau never explicitly excludes women from citizenship in *The Social Contract* and does not discuss gender. He uses the default '*homme*' in an apparently universal sense. Carole Pateman argues that the social contract pertains to male individuals and does not explain differences of gender. It purports to be universal but within it only men qualify as individuals. Contract theory's 'patriarchal construction of the difference between masculinity and femininity is the political difference between freedom and subjection . . . sexual mastery is the major means through which men affirm their manhood' (Pateman 1988: 207). As Pateman observes, 'women have no natural freedom. The classic pictures of the state of nature also contain an order of subjection – between men and women' (ibid. 206). Shelley suggests that Rousseau's general will does not represent a broader community that includes its female members, but merely reflects the perspective of a single male individual. Rousseau himself emphasises that although individuals retain private wills and dispositions, for the sake of social stability it is nonetheless necessary that every 'citizen consents to all laws, even those passed in spite of him' (Rousseau 1994c: 200). This leaves women, who are not clearly defined as political subjects, but whom Rousseau does perceive as having wills of their own, in a precarious situation as possible threats to society – potentially resistant to its control. Shelley's view that reading produces alarmingly unpredictable results means that neither Victor nor the creature would have any control over this female creature were she to gain cultural literacy, as she would be necessarily independent. In *Emile* the subordination of women becomes more explicit. Rousseau explains his decision to restrict education to boys because if women were to gain power, 'men would finally be their victims and would see themselves dragged to death without ever being able to defend themselves' (Rousseau 2010: 533). Such a reversal of roles 'would soon incur the ruin of both, and mankind would perish by the means established for preserving it' (ibid. 533). In *Frankenstein* the social values which produce the monster are not extended to women. Yet women may nonetheless demand them, hence Victor's concern that the female creature might resist her mate's authority.

Once Victor has crossed the Channel and begins work, he worries that the female creature may not cooperate with his demand for exile or might refuse to enter into a social contract with her male counterpart. He imagines that she 'in all probability was to become a thinking and reasoning animal' and might therefore 'rebel against a compact made before her creation' (Shelley 1996a: 128). In a singular moment of gender-based solidarity with his creature, Victor imagines, 'she might also turn with disgust from him to the superior beauty of man; she might quit him, and he be again alone' (ibid. 128). Even her possible cooperation with Victor and his creature still would not preclude the problem of potential offspring and his plan to establish a new society with her in 'the vast wilds of South America' (ibid. 109). In his *Discourse on the Origins of Inequality*, Rousseau illustrates his account of natural man with references to travel narratives of the peoples of North and South America (Rousseau 1992a: 72–3). Shelley's allusion to 'the vast wilds of South America' draws on Rousseau's collocation of the state of nature with the new world, a fabled 'second state of nature', and on the attendant colonial myth of an empty land which is gendered as feminine. The creature reports overhearing Felix read from de Volney's *Ruins* about the European colonisation of the indigenous peoples in the Americas to Safie. He 'heard of the discovery of the American hemisphere, and wept with Safie over the hapless fate of its original inhabitants' (Shelley 1996a: 89).[26] The creature's identification with the plight of the Native Americans suggests the subversive potential of his plan of immigration, which would be the first step on the way to producing a new society.

Returning to the state of nature could eventually challenge the politics of gender and colonisation which sustain patriarchy. The creature's final departure into 'darkness and distance' at the end of *Frankenstein* leaves his destiny ambiguous (ibid. 170). But as a solitary entity who is unable to reproduce, even were he to survive, he could not pose an existential threat to the human race.

Victor destroys the female creature to guarantee social stability and explains that this act pre-empts a possible revolution in sexual politics and undermining of patriarchal sovereignty. Shelley imagines the female creature's destruction through the language of rape: 'I thought with a sensation of madness on my promise of creating another like him, and, trembling with passion, tore to pieces the thing on which I was engaged' (Shelley 1996a: 129). The register of sensation, passion and engagement suggests that Victor is motivated in this act by gender politics. Spivak notes Victor's convoluted understanding of the female creature, whereby 'the (il)logic of the metaphor bestows on her a prior existence which Frankenstein aborts, rather than an anterior death which he reembodies' (Spivak 1985: 255). Shelley juxtaposes the female creature's powerless status and silenced voice with Victor's privileged position, and also with the charismatic and articulate male creature, whose narrative occupies a third of Shelley's text and has had the effect for many readers of stealing the show.[27] By contrast, the female creature's voice can only be accessed by 'measuring silences', which Spivak proposes as the sole means of representing subaltern perspectives (Spivak 1995: 82). When Victor discards her remains into the ocean, he hears the 'gurgling sound' of escaping oxygen (Shelley 1996a: 132). Shelley leaves the source of this sound evocatively vague; the gurgling may simply be air trapped in the folds of the female creature's body, but is also the closest that her voice comes to articulation.

Thinking of *Frankenstein* in terms of a subaltern female perspective calls on a strategy of reading that dwells on absences. Shelley reflects on Godwin's difficulties constructing a female perspective within social contract theory. Instead she figures female agency indirectly, via the figure of antimetabole. In her account of Victor's creation of the male monster, she draws attention to the moment when antithetical categories of life and death, work and loss, and desire and revulsion cross paths:

> I beheld the corruption of death succeed to the blooming cheek of life; I saw how the worm inherited the wonders of the eye and brain. I paused, examining and analysing all the minutiae of causation, as exemplified in the change from life to death, and death to life. (Shelley 1996a: 35–6)

In the charnel-houses, Victor becomes fixated with 'how the worm inherited the wonders of the eye and brain', using these worm-eaten organs to construct his creature. The figure of antimetabole in 'the change from life to death, and death to life' pinpoints Victor's fascination with the actual moment of chiastic transition between the two states. But when the creature finally coalesces, Victor's vision shifts to squeamish revulsion: 'I had worked hard for nearly two years, for the sole purpose of infusing life into an inanimate body . . . Now that I had finished, the beauty of the dream vanished, and breathless horror and disgust filled my heart' (Shelley 1996a: 40). Victor's creation inspires horror because it is unable to hide its origins in death and loss. The female creature works through a parallel inverse logic whereby death and loss threaten – like the fetiche in Godwin's *Deloraine* – to come to life again and make demands upon the political domain. Shelley figures the possibility of a female will through its absence.

Like the aborted female monster, the voices of her female counterparts in the novel are similarly difficult to discern. Safie speaks a foreign language, and Justine Moritz's testimony is trampled on by the court of law. Crook notes that Margaret Walton Saville, Walton's sister, shares Shelley's initials, suggesting her identification with this silent addressee (Shelley 1996a: 10, note a). Elizabeth, the main female character of the novel, often classified as 'one of the earliest of the Angels in the House, the staple of Victorian woman worship to come', does emerge from within the patriarchal narrative at several key points (Joseph 1993: 27). When Victor leaves for England, postponing their marriage, she writes that her 'only regret is that she had not the same opportunities of enlarging her experience, and cultivating her understanding' as does Victor (Shelley 1996a: 118). She also cites her uncle's view that although her brother Ernest is better suited to farming than being a judge, 'I ought to be an advocate myself' (ibid. 45). Victor contrasts his own love of natural science with Elizabeth's passion for fiction. Through this analogy Shelley points to Elizabeth's possible literary ambitions: 'the world was to me a secret, which I desired to discover; to her it was a vacancy, which she sought to people with imaginations of her own' (ibid. 24). Introducing the 1831 *Frankenstein*, Shelley reflects on her own voice as one of assemblage from the existing forms of society rather than of invention *ex nihilo* (ibid. 178).[28] This comment expresses the gendered reticence about authority which is often noted in discussions of *Frankenstein*. But more importantly it suggests that reticence is a political strategy, like antimetabole. Shelley contends that texts and political theories, albeit formed in isolation and at times by groups excluded from the body politic – in this case women – nonetheless aspire to become collective entities and to compete for a status within the general will. In the 1831 introduction she comes to view herself as a kind of general will which embodies the manifold sources that went into her making. As Spivak suggests, marginalisation means that the disempowered cannot speak their way into the public domain (Spivak 1995: 93). To recover 'the woman's voice-consciousness' you have to look beyond patriarchal discourse, or turn it inside out through strategies of reticence, absence or inverse repetition (ibid. 93). By reworking Godwin's and Wollstonecraft's texts, as well as Coleridge's and Rousseau's, Shelley carves out her place within a greater literary general will, and also demonstrates the fundamental and formative power that social ties have in creating the individual perspective.

Kevin Cope notes the impact of social contract theory on the form of the novel at the turn of the nineteenth century. He suggests that eighteenth-century sentimental fiction is modelled on the general will in its attempts at 'absorbing variant individuals into the fiction of the totality' (Cope 1989: 937). Like *Fleetwood*, *Frankenstein* explores these concerns from a different viewpoint than Cope's idea of fiction as a unifying genre which tests the proposal that individuals of varying interests and identities may nevertheless assent to a common social order. Rather than aspiring to cohesion, Shelley considers the individual units of society and their difficulty assimilating with one another, which produces the alienation of Victor and his creature. The diverse narratives of Walton, Victor, the creature and Shelley herself do not form a whole, but compete for the reader's sympathies, creating a space that reflects on values of both literary and social cohesion. Shelley leaves her readers unable to side with either Victor or the creature – characters with whom it is difficult to sympathise – sceptical of the various forms of solidarity (of gender, kinship, aesthetic totality and humanity retrospectively) that each invokes in his defence, and haunted by the repressed narratives of the female creature, of Margaret Walton Saville and of Elizabeth, positions which *Frankenstein* tacitly raises alongside the more dominant voices of Walton, Victor and the creature. Shelley develops Rousseau's approach to the literary as a form which questions the costs of sociability for the individual. *Frankenstein*'s two creatures embody the fissures and doubts underlying changing models in political theory which Shelley examines through the estranged perspective of the gendering of this tradition.

Notes

1. For readings of *Frankenstein* as a proto-feminist text, see Barbara Johnson (Johnson 2014: 23), Anne K. Mellor (Mellor 1989: 40) and Jacques Khalip (Khalip 2009: 139).
2. In her foreword to a recent collection of Barbara Johnson's writings, *A Life with Mary Shelley*, Cathy Caruth argues that Johnson reclaimed Romanticism from its prior focus on great male poets by drawing together Mary Shelley's and Rousseau's concerns with autobiographical writing and literary theory (Johnson 2014: xii).
3. On *Frankenstein*'s relation to Rousseau's sentimental works, see David Marshall (1988). For discussions of the creature as a representation of Rousseau's natural man, see Mellor (Mellor 1989: 45–7) and Nancy Yousef (Yousef 2004: 155–7).
4. See also James O'Rourke's subsequent article, which reads the 1831 *Frankenstein* as an interpretation of the 1818 version (O'Rourke 1999: 366).
5. In her Introduction to the second edition of *Frankenstein*, Johanna M. Smith notes the influence of the Reform Bill on the 1831 version of *Frankenstein* (Shelley 2000: 14–15); Nora Crook discusses the theme of Italian liberation (Crook 2000: 5).
6. Another possible context for Shelley's growing distaste for Rousseau may have been difficulties with Percy Shelley. Donald H. Reiman and Neil Fraistat suggest that Percy drew a parallelism between his own love for Jane Williams and estrangement from Mary Shelley in 1822, and Rousseau's account of his unrequited love for the Countess d'Houdetot in *The Confessions*, and subsequent story of the tragic love of Julie and Saint Preux, all of which Percy Shelley expressed in *The Triumph of Life* (Percy Shelley 2002: 482).
7. On Percy Shelley's familiarity with Rousseau's political theory, see Edward Duffy (Duffy 1979: 91). See also Percy's records of his readings of Rousseau in his letters, which includes *Emile*, *Julie*, *Discourse on the Arts and Sciences* and the *Reveries of a Solitary Walker* (Shelley 1964: 483).
8. See O'Rourke's analysis of the creature's direct relationship to Rousseau's political theory (O'Rourke 1989: 547–50).
9. Anna E. Clark makes a similar point about discussions of the monster and Adam Smith. She suggests that 'it is not only the novel's thematic content but also its formal structure' that reflects Shelley's response to Smith's theory of sympathy and impartial spectatorship (Clark 2014: 259).
10. See Gregory Dart who observes that this simple gesture effectively unites Victor with Rousseau (Dart 1999: 2).
11. Compare the passage from book nine of *The Confessions*, discussed in Chapter 2: 'I made these meditations in the finest season of the year, in the month of June, under fresh groves, to the song of the nightingale, to the murmuring of streams' (Rousseau 1995: 358).
12. Mary Shelley read Hume's *History of England*, his 'Treatise on the Passions', and his *Essays and Treatises on Several Topics*, in which Hume posits the state as an extension of the family (Shelley 1987: 2.654; Hume 1800: 35). She is influenced by his values, by his style, and by his theory of induction. Monique Morgan finds references to Humean induction

in the creature's narrative. She argues that Shelley appears familiar with Hume's *Treatise of Human Nature*, and notes that the creature applies Hume's methodology in his manner of learning (Morgan 2006: para. 4). Sarah Tindal Kareem suggests that Shelley defamiliarises Hume's empiricist account of experience through the creature's narrative (Kareem 2014: 211). David Womersley conjectures that Percy probably read the *Treatise of Human Nature*, which would have thus become accessible to Shelley (Womersley 1986: 165). It seems plausible that Shelley may also have been influenced by Hume's account of himself as a 'strange uncouth monster, who not able to mingle and unite in society, has been expell'd [from] all human commerce, and left utterly abandon'd and disconsolate' in her construction of the creature (Hume 1978: 264).

13. In this idea, Shelley also echoes Edmund Burke's assertion that the French Revolution is a monstrous theory that should never have been put into practice. In 1815, Shelley read Burke's argument that 'the more deeply we penetrate into the Labyrinth of Art, the further we finds ourselves from those ends for which we entered it' (Shelley 1987: 2.639; Burke 1982: 76).

14. See Janis McLarren Caldwell's observation on the contrast between the creature's story and the novel's narratorial voice: 'the famous "frame" or "box-within-a box" surrounding Frankenstein's narration, surrounding the monster's autobiography, gives this novel about monstrosity a perverse neatness' (Caldwell 1999: 266).

15. In the 1831 version Shelley alludes to Coleridge even more explicitly. Walton writes to his sister that he will not return home 'as worn and woeful as the "Ancient Mariner?" You will smile at my allusion; but I will disclose a secret. I have attributed my attachment to, my passionate enthusiasm for, the dangerous mysteries of ocean, to the production of the most imaginative of modern poets', namely Coleridge, from whom Walton derives 'a love for the marvellous, a belief in the marvellous, intertwined in all my projects, which hurries me out of the common pathways of men, even to the wild sea and unvisited regions I am about to explore' (Shelley 2000: 33).

16. It is doubtful that Shelley would have known the revised 1817 version of *The Rime of the Ancient Mariner* at the time that she composed *Frankenstein* from the summer of 1816 until she completed a fair-copy draft in May 1817 (*Frankenstein* was submitted to publishers in the summer of 1817 and sent to print in December 1817) (Shelley 1996a: xciii, xciv–xcv). In July 1817 Coleridge published the revised version of the *Ancient Mariner* in *Sibylline Leaves* where he pruned the archaic spellings, and responded to criticisms that the poem was hard to follow (Coleridge 2004: 27). Shelley records hiding behind a couch as a child to hear Coleridge recite the 1798 *Ancient Mariner* to Godwin and friends (Shelley 2012: 2)

17. Crook raises the possibility of a fictive editor, whose presence is not felt in the novel, or of a surreal time frame within this otherwise historically accurate narrative (Shelley 1996a: note 14). Shelley painstakingly plots the novel's time frame around the date of her conception, birth and loss of her mother shortly afterwards, events which happened prior to the publication of the 1798 *Lyrical Ballads* (Shelley 2004: 49, note 1). Crook raises a third possible explanation that Walton may have met Coleridge in 1790s London (Shelley 1996a: note 14). But this is even less plausible, given Victor's

apparent knowledge of the poem as well. For a famous critique of such literalist attempts to establish historical coherence in the literary text, see L. C. Knights's 'How Many Children Had Lady Macbeth?' (Knights 1946).

18. Shelley's discussion of Rousseau is based largely on Victor-Donatien Musset-Pathay's survey of his major works (Shelley 2002b: xix). In his *Histoire de la vie et des ouvrages de J.-J. Rousseau*, Victor Musset-Pathay provides a synopsis of Rousseau's *Confessions*, of his narrative of the state of nature, and of the formation of a social contract (Musset-Pathay 1821: 365–72, 414–15).

19. Shelley's criticism of Rousseau in this encyclopaedia entry has been extensively analysed by O'Rourke (1989), Greg Kucich (Kucich 2000: 211) and Julian North (North 2009: 27–8).

20. For arguments about Shelley's work as an extension of Wollstonecraft's, see Mellor (Mellor 1988: 223). Barbara Johnson reads *Frankenstein* as a 'depiction of the ambivalence of motherhood', which begins with Shelley's own sense of her birth and writing as an act of matricide (Johnson 2014: 21, 24). Khalip argues that Shelley 'responds to Wollstonecraft's model of reason by conceiving melancholy as the condition of a deeply recalcitrant female subject', developing Wollstonecraft's melancholy into an existential condition (Khalip 2009: 160).

21. Despite Wollstonecraft's many divergences from Rousseau's social theory, Barbara Taylor notes 'that Wollstonecraft *was* a Rousseauist is indisputable' (Taylor 2003: 73). Wollstonecraft moved to revolutionary Paris to join a coterie with a 'Rousseauist and sentimental social and political philosophy' (Kelly 2000: 148). She espoused Rousseau's critique of aristocratic decadence and was influenced by his radical vision of equality (Taylor 2003: 159, 165).

22. In the *Vindication of the Rights of Woman*, Wollstonecraft presents Rousseau as a champion of progress dispirited by contingent circumstances:

> Impressed by . . . the misery and disorder which pervaded society, and fatigued with jostling against artificial fools, Rousseau became enamoured of solitude, and, being at the same time an optimist, he labours with uncommon eloquence to prove that man was naturally a solitary animal. (Wollstonecraft 2007b: 30)

Daniel O'Neill suggests that Wollstonecraft's criticism of Rousseau reflected the Scottish Enlightenment's view of social order as naturally generated (O'Neill 2008: 35).

23. On Shelley's melancholic representation of Wollstonecraft as an absence, see Mary Jacobus (1995) and Marie Mulvey-Roberts (Mulvey-Roberts 2000: 199).

24. Nanette C. Le Coat relates the traveller's melancholic reflections on society to Rousseau (Le Coat 1989: 369). In contrast to Rousseau, de Volney develops 'a resolutely optimistic perspective in which history is no longer seen as a litany of human misdeeds but rather as the collective memory of a nation' (ibid. 369–70).

25. Kareem suggests that the creature learns Smith's model of sympathy from his exposure to de Volney (Kareem 2014: 216). Instead of sympathy the creature meets disgust and rejection, undermining a model of admiration

that Kareem outlines in her reading of the *Theory of Moral Sentiments* (ibid. 217).

26. De Volney argues that European colonisers took advantage of their natural superiority of strength and subordinated indigenous societies: 'paternal despotism laid the foundations of despotism in government' (de Volney 1828: 49).

27. According to Crook the Shelleys originally feared that readers would have a hard time finding sympathy with the creature, but in fact readers have always sided with the creature against Victor (Crook 2000: 17).

28. Shelley asks 'how I, then a young girl, came to think of, and to dilate upon, so very hideous an idea' (Shelley 1996a: 175). She explains that *Frankenstein* was not her own doing, but rather a collaborative work formed by her upbringing and her parents' legacies, her friendship with Byron, and her marriage to Percy Shelley:

> invention, it must be humbly admitted, does not consist in creating out of void, but out of chaos; the materials must, in the first place, be afforded: it can give form to dark, shapeless substances, but cannot bring into being the substance itself. (Shelley 1996a: 178)

Conclusion:
The Ends of Romanticism

> After having shown that *perfectibility*, social virtues, and the other facul-
> ties that Natural man had received in potentiality could never develop by
> themselves, that in order to develop they needed the chance combination of
> several foreign causes which might never have arisen and without which he
> would have remained eternally in his primitive constitution, it remains for me
> to consider and bring together the different accidents that were able to perfect
> human reason while deteriorating the species, make a being evil while making
> him sociable, and from such a distant origin finally bring man and the world
> to the point where we see them. (Rousseau 1992a: 42)

This epigraph, taken from Jean-Jacques Rousseau's *Discourse on
the Origins of Inequality*, departs from characterisations of humankind as inherently social, and produces a contingent account of the
political. Society happened by accident. Uprooted from an antecedent
Aristotelian totality, humans lose their integrity, making them evil in
Rousseau's terms – consumed by aggressions which develop from social
interactions. Modern culture has remained fascinated with Rousseau's
arbitrary account of the social, and with his sceptical notion of nature
as an ideological fiction. This book has argued that Romantic literature is one of the first cultural movements to pursue the costs of this
change. Within Romantic texts, truncated elements of the body politic
subvert Aristotelian ideals of holism. This reading of Romanticism
through a model of internal conflict provides an alternative understanding of the Romantic movement to current distinctions which are
organised by genre and by revolutionary and counterrevolutionary
political orientation. Readings by genre overlook Coleridge's engagements with Rousseau in his essays, letters and poetry, and the significant
overlap of philosophy and fiction in Godwin's writings. The breaking down of standard political distinctions provides a keener sense of
Romanticism's ideological diversity. Hence, Wordsworth's shift from a
concern with friction between individual and general wills towards his

later utopianism emerges with greater clarity in this reading, as well as the different cultural contexts of the 1818 and 1831 *Frankenstein*s. The coherence of Romanticism is to be found in the critical disruption of the relation between individuals and the social body, played out in the tension between literary and philosophical texts.

Sartor Resartus and Post-Romanticism

Thomas Carlyle's essays circa the 1830s and *Sartor Resartus* (1834) part ways with social contract theory, expressing the sense that Romanticism has ended.[1] Carlyle turns towards a millennial Idealism and Christian mysticism. He regards his times as 'the decay of old ways of believing, the preparation afar off for new and better and wider ways' (Carlyle 2001: 198). Carlyle assesses that the secularism of the last three hundred years, catalysed by the Enlightenment, has ended a former time of stability in European society. In an imagined past, societies had united individuals within a broader body politic. The social body around 1830 is at a crucial point of death and rebirth, positions which coexist uneasily within one another, characterising the present as a dark time of flux and confusion. Carlyle recasts recent Romantic history as a particularly low ebb in a cycle towards renewed totality, which redefines the disruption between the individual and the social collective through metaphors of temporary physical upheaval instead of the irreversible chemical change of Rousseau's *Social Contract*.

In *Sartor Resartus* Carlyle pronounces society as 'a Phœnix': 'a new heavenborn young one will rise out of her ashes!' (Carlyle 2000: 175). He imagines the social body through imagery that evokes Frankenstein's monster:

> if Government is, so to speak, the outward SKIN of the Body Politic, holding the whole together and protecting it; and all your Craft-Guilds, and Associations for Industry, of hand or of head, are the Fleshly Clothes, the muscular and osseous Tissues (lying *under* such SKIN), whereby Society stands and works; - then is Religion the inmost Pericardial and Nervous Tissue, which ministers Life and warm Circulation to the whole. Without which Pericardial Tissue the Bones and Muscles (of Industry) were inert, or animated only by a Galvanic vitality; the SKIN would become a shrivelled pelt, or fast-rotting raw-hide; and Society itself a dead carcass. (Carlyle 2000: 159)

Religion is the animating spark that galvanises this composite body politic, which is in a corpse-like state awaiting rebirth.[2] Without faith, Carlyle suggests, the social body threatens to heave apart and become a living corpse, a secular monstrosity that fractures into pelts, hides and parts. Carlyle repeats the imagery of *Frankenstein*, relating monstrosity to the ills of empiricism (here called utilitarianism). In invoking destruction and rebirth, Carlyle portrays utilitarianism as an apocalyptic creature: 'the monster UTILITARIA, held back, indeed, and moderated by nose-rings, halters, foot-shackles, and every conceivable modification of rope, should go forth to do her work' (Carlyle 2000: 174). Much as Shelley bids her 'hideous progeny go forth' into the world in her introduction to the 1831 edition of *Frankenstein*, so Carlyle's monster catalyses a fortunate fall that is necessary if future social reform is to happen. Carlyle's use of the common type of chains invokes the broader context of humans as shackled into one social body. The female gendering of his monster diverges from empiricist orthodoxy, but conforms to its misogynistic prejudices against women as violators of social order in their ambiguous status as potential harbingers of patriarchal downfall, a position that echoes Shelley's critique of empiricism in *Frankenstein*.

Sartor Resartus's governing metaphor of clothes mounts a critique of the Scottish Enlightenment as excessively pragmatic and anti-theoretical in its focus on habit, which has eroded religion. Carlyle presents Diogenes Teufelsdröckh and his clothes philosophy as an alternative to Humean habits and social contracts:

> Why mention our disquisitions on the Social Contract, on the Standard of Taste, on the Migrations of the Herring? ... Man's whole life and environment have been laid open and elucidated; scarcely a fragment or fibre of his Soul, Body, and Possessions, but has been probed, dissected, distilled, desiccated, and scientifically decomposed. (Carlyle 2000: 3–4)

Echoing Wordsworth's assertion that we murder to dissect, Carlyle dismisses empiricist taxonomies that include social contracts, Hume's dissertation on aesthetics, 'Of the Standard of Taste', and natural histories, suggested by the reference to herring migrations. These theories open up a spiritual wasteland in Carlyle's view as they place value within the human, rather than the abstract or metaphysical.[3] Narratives of a state of nature giving birth to a state of society ossify the myth of 'the grand mother-idea, *Society in a state of Nakedness*' which Carlyle ridicules as 'Adamitism' – a wilful affectation of primitivism (Carlyle 2000: 49). Parodying the state of nature, Carlyle imagines that clothes, like individuals, do not have humble social origins that begin with 'the Aboriginal Savage, glaring fiercely from under his fleece of hair, which with the beard reached down to his loins' (ibid. 29). He traces Hume's focus on secular materialism to the school of Thomas Reid:

the singular conclusions at which Hume, setting out from their admitted premises, was arriving, brought this school into being; they let loose Instinct, as an undiscriminating bandog ... they tugged lustily at the logical chain by which Hume was so coldly towing them and the world into bottomless abysses of Atheism and Fatalism. (Carlyle 1984b: 38–9)

Repeating the well-hashed topos of chains, Carlyle interprets Scottish common sense philosophy as enforcing determinism, unleashing apocalyptic forces of godlessness and mechanism upon the world such as the industrial revolution, which further precipitates social decline: 'men are grown mechanical in head and in heart, as well as in hand. They have lost faith in individual endeavour, and in natural force of any kind' (Carlyle 1984b: 37). Enlightenment materialism penetrates all aspects of human existence until it replaces religion: modern culture's 'true Deity is Mechanism' (ibid. 46). The French Revolution, the topic of Carlyle's famous history, is only a symptom of this larger snowballing effect, rather than its cause (ibid. 53). Carlyle analyses the French Revolution as a direct response to mechanism: 'faith is gone out; Scepticism is come in. Evil abounds and accumulates; no man has Faith to withstand it' (Carlyle 1934: 13). In this dereliction of all principles, nature must take its purgative course and re-establish the lost order, following Carlyle's cyclical model of historiography:

> nature is true and not a lie. No lie can you speak or act but it will come, after longer or shorter circulation, like a Bill drawn on Nature's Reality, and be presented there for payment – with the answer *No effects*. (Carlyle 1934: 54)

Carlyle undermines the Enlightenment by emphasising that for all its purported value of reason, its concerns are actually with the supernatural. He suggests that Samuel Johnson's pursuit of the Cock Lane ghost was motivated by an underlying sense that he, like all mortals, was essentially only a ghost himself: 'again, could anything be more miraculous than an actual authentic Ghost? The English Johnson longed, all his life, to see one; but could not, though he went to Cock Lane, and thence to the church-vaults, and tapped on coffins' (Carlyle 2000: 194). Johnson's Frankensteinian shadow-hunting retraces the path of Victor's ill-fated foray into books on alchemy and the occult that lead to vaults and coffins in *Frankenstein*. E. J. Clery interprets this craving for the supernatural as Johnson's desire to believe in religious and social unity in the face of secularism and religious collapse (Clery 1999: 21). Johnson uses empiricist tools to court the non-empirical; Carlyle turned to Idealism for the same reasons. Ghostliness represents a modern predicament of dissociation from an ideal of social totality that is no longer attainable, and a concomitant longing for it – like Smith's

Aristotelian phantom limb, which Carlyle projects into an imagined millennial future rebirth.

The future is presented in ghostly terms, too distant to be tangible or really achievable, and riddled with hermeneutical pitfalls. Teufelsdröckh's visionary *Clothes, their Origin and Influence* arrives in England in six paper bags of Idealist fragments sent by Herr Hofrath Heuschrecke, who hopes it will be collated, translated, published and marketed in England and America.[4] The Editor reports contacting Oliver Yorke, pseudonym of William Maginn, editor of *Fraser's Magazine*, where Teufelsdröckh's edited and translated doctrine plus the Editor's commentary are finally published (Carlyle 2000: 248, note 10.18).[5] The novel's quasi-realistic setting, which reiterates its own logistics of magazine publication, is undermined by the parodic fictionality of its characters. The Editor repeatedly puzzles over how to read Teufelsdröckh, and suspects him of lying:

> Could it be expected, indeed, that a man so known for impenetrable reticence as Teufelsdröckh, would all at once frankly unlock his private citadel to an English Editor and a German Hofrath; and not rather deceptively *in*lock both Editor and Hofrath, in the labyrinthic tortuosities and covered ways of said citadel (having enticed them thither), to see, in his half-devilish way, how the fools would look? (Carlyle 2000: 150)

Carlyle's Editor harbours 'a suspicion, in one word, that these Autobiographical Documents are partly a Mystification! What if many a so-called Fact were little better than a Fiction' (Carlyle 2000: 150). Through the Editor's reflections Carlyle challenges the reader to avoid idealist acts of poetic faith and remember that, like the Editor, what you are perusing is only a fiction, following Rousseau's metafictional scepticism in *Julie* or in *Rousseau, Judge of Jean-Jacques*. The Editor worries about the ill effects of 'this piebald, entangled, hyper-metaphorical style of writing, not to say of thinking, become general among our Literary men!' (ibid. 215). He complains that Teufelsdröckh's ideas profoundly want structure and conjunction:

> each Part overlaps, and indents, and indeed runs quite through the other ... like some mad banquet, wherein all courses had been confounded, and fish and flesh, soup and solid, oyster-sauce, lettuces, Rhine-wine and French mustard, were hurled into one huge tureen or trough, and the hungry Public invited to help itself. To bring what order we can out of this chaos will be part of our endeavour. (Carlyle 2000: 26)

These reflections parody Henry Fielding's introductory chapter to *Tom Jones*, which cites the 'bill of fare' as a metafictional vehicle for reflections on style and readerly expectations.[6] With anti-Levitical gusto, the reading public consumes a hodgepodge of dishes which may be palatable in isolation but are heinous in conjunction. The collapse of national cuisines typifies a breakdown of local European cultural traditions, so that the Rhineland and France are served up together with British staples (oyster-sauces, lettuces), in a great melting pot of languages and cultures. Carlyle adds British Romanticism to this stylistic medley. Teufelsdröckh's childhood is profoundly Wordsworthian, in contrast with the Editor's own arid focus on reason. Although he mocks Teufelsdröckh's early life as a foundling and then as an inept schoolboy, the implied reader of *Fraser's* – trained by Wordsworth and Coleridge – is apt to identify Teufelsdröckh's now familiar narrative of an exceptional being who becomes nature's chosen prophet and must find his vocation in the cultural mayhem of modernity.

From within this cultural anarchy Rousseau emerges as a distinctive voice, privileged with an approach to language that transcends print culture and empiricism. Rummaging through the Hofrath's paper bags, the Editor happens upon an overlooked slip, 'the ink being all but invisible' (Carlyle 2000: 150).[7] Teufelsdröckh's note is a tribute to Rousseau and a sneer at the empiricists:

> Facts are engraved Hierograms, for which the fewest have the key. And then how your Blockhead (*Dummkopf*) studies not their Meaning; but simply whether they are well or ill cut, what he calls Moral or Immortal! Still worse is with your Bungler (*Pfuscher*): such I have seen reading some Rousseau, with pretences of interpretation; and missing the ill-cut Serpent-of-Eternity for a common poisonous Reptile! (Carlyle 2000: 150)

Rousseau opposes empiricist determinism by being able to discern the serpent, with its complex symbolism, from the commonplace snake, with its connotations of Enlightenment taxonomies. Where the poisonous reptile signifies fallen mortality, the serpent represents spiritual and social rebirth, fusing individual desire with sociability as positions that coexist in tandem (Carlyle 2000: 180). By Carlyle's account, empiricism hoodwinks readers, who are unable to distinguish fiction from fact, matter from spirit and the snake from the serpent. He refers to the publishing industry as 'whole meat-devouring and man-devouring hosts of Boa-constrictors' – an industry that trivialises the spiritual (ibid. 149).

Teufelsdröckh, whose name means 'Devil's dung', is an abject and shady spreader of media muck, echoing Jonathan Swift's association of the media with excremental imagery in *Gulliver's Travels*, where the yahoos defecate on Gulliver in an allegory of filthy journalistic sensationalism (Swift 2005: 210). The allusion to devil's dung recalls

Reid's complaint that Hume's *Treatise of Human Nature* degraded human beings to Swiftian yahoos (Jessop 1997: 180). Journalism and literature form a solipsistic hermeneutic circle, a parody that degrades the serpent of eternity with its tail in its mouth: 'all literature has become one boundless, self-devouring Review; and, as in London routs, we have to *do* nothing, but only to *see* others do nothing. – Thus does Literature also, like a sick thing, superabundantly "listen to itself"' (Carlyle 1984a: 87).[8] This industry misinterprets Rousseau's philosophical works, deriving dry atheist principles from a richly agnostic and ambiguous text. Carlyle's *On Heroes, Hero Worship, and the Heroic in History* lionises Rousseau as 'a prophet of his Time' who understood 'that this Life of ours is true; not a scepticism, Theorem, or persiflage, but a Fact, an awful reality' (Carlyle 2001: 215). Rousseau's 'promulgat[ion of] his new Evangel of a *Contrat Social*; explaining the whole mystery of government and how it is *contracted* and bargained for – to universal satisfaction' is a catalyst in the process of revolution and cultural apocalypse leading to rebirth (Carlyle 1934: 44).

Teufelsdröckh's drafting of his critique of empiricism in invisible ink is an additional tribute to Rousseau. In book five of *The Confessions*, Rousseau attempts making an invisible 'sympathetic' ink that explodes in his face (Rousseau 1995: 183). He interprets the ensuing six weeks of blindness as punishment for his own recidivist pursuit of individual desire in his quasi-incestuous affair with Madame de Warens, alias *maman*: 'the sword outwears the scabbard, it is sometimes said. That is my story. My passions have made me live, and my passions have killed me' (ibid. 183). The phallic serpent – like the sword, a symbol of the individual will – inscribes its noxious slights on empiricism in invisible ink. But this critique underwrites the empiricist project of transparent epistemology and communication touted by the Editor. Teufelsdröckh's fictional doctrine and Rousseau's autobiographical *Confessions* are comparably unreliable sources. In 'White Mythology' Jacques Derrida criticises western metaphysics, which 'has erased within itself the fabulous scene that had produced it, the scene that nevertheless remains active and stirring, inscribed in white ink, an invisible design covered over in the palimpsest' (Derrida 1982: 213). Derrida destabilises the claim that philosophy is truer than poetry. Paul de Man observes that this primacy of the literary is consistent with Rousseau's attention to the figurative aspect of discourse (de Man 1983: 119). Like Rousseau, Carlyle weaves a web of paradoxes to reject Enlightenment models of immediacy, reason and certitude, and to collapse the boundaries between philosophy and fiction. His writing is less concerned with affirming its purported millennial aspirations for the future than with articulating the conflicts of its past and present.

Reflecting back on the legacy of the social contract, H. G. Wells understands the tie between the eighteenth and twentieth centuries in terms of a common effort to integrate individuals into a unified community. *The Shape of Things to Come* (1933) written a century after *Sartor Resartus*, reflects similarly on a change in epistemes; Wells argues that

> the history of mankind, as we unfold it to the contemporary student, is a story of ever increasing communication and ever increasing interdependence. Insensibly the material side of individual freedom was modified into unavoidable cooperation with the community. (Wells 2005: 442–3)

Sigmund Freud's *Civilization and Its Discontents* (1930) follows Rousseau in defining socialisation as a fundamentally unhappy development (Freud 2010: 141). Freud argues that society fails to acknowledge the central role played by aggression in human nature, essentially repeating Hobbes's argument that social interactions originate in a primordial state of violence, and Rousseau's warning that society will become violent if *amour propre* is not contained. Freud emphasises that society must recognise the hostilities that motivate human relations. Failing to do so is tantamount to 'behaving as though one were to equip people starting on a Polar exhibition with summer clothing and maps of the Italian Lakes' (ibid. 132, note 1). Freud's topos draws on imagery from the Romantic poems and novels considered in this book. European lakeside rambles, voyages to the Poles, shipwrecks at sea, being lost in the Alps, or isolated in a cottage – these serve as a shorthand for an impasse in recent political thought. The self finds sociability to be inherently at odds with a newly minted disposition of individualism; finally, neither individual nor society emerge as a viable concept, and the self is exiled to an alternative landscape beyond the limits of social totality.

Freud observes that advances in technology now mean that humans 'would have no difficulty in exterminating one another to the last man' (Freud 2010: 149). Would this extermination contain the possibility of re-galvanisation, as Carlyle suggests it might? James Strachey, the translator of *Civilization and Its Discontents* into English, draws attention to Freud's appendage of a rhetorical question to *Civilization and Its Discontents* in 1931, reflecting his growing awareness of the Nazi menace. Freud qualifies any possible triumph over the human tendency to violence with the caveat, 'but who can foresee with what success and with what result?' (ibid. 149, note A) This book has focused on literary responses to post-Enlightenment theories of society's origins. In thinking about society's ends, understood through the model of contract, agreements among individuals are not permanently able to stave off conflict, but at best to offer ad hoc, temporary solutions. Post-Romantic sociability always contains the possibility of relapse to this state of isolation, which is inherent both to its origins and also to its foreseeable end.

Notes

1. Ian Duncan argues that *Sartor Resartus* pronounces the end of the Scottish Enlightenment, a movement closely related to Romanticism (Duncan 2007: 307).
2. Chris Baldick argues that Carlyle belongs to a tradition that begins with *Frankenstein*, 'a Galvanic World in which the inward sanctuary of organic human authenticity has been abandoned to the rule of the corpse' (Baldick 1990: 105).
3. Ralph Jessop suggests that Carlyle's analysis of Scottish common sense philosophy is based on a fundamental misunderstanding of this tradition as promoting Lockean mechanism, whereas the Scottish Enlightenment emphasised the role of cognition in socialisation (Jessop 1997: 127).
4. The Hofrath parodies Malthusian positions and writes a tract entitled *Institute for the Repression of Population*, suggesting that he himself is poorly equipped to understand Teufelsdröckh's Idealism (Carlyle 2000: 167).
5. *Sartor*'s own serial appearance within *Fraser's Magazine* repeats this narrative. Mark Parker observes that *Sartor* began as a two-part article, no longer in existence for *Fraser's Magazine*, which probably corresponded with its first book dealing with Teufelsdröckh's history of clothes (Parker 2000: 162). *Sartor* was then expanded into a book (also lost), for which Carlyle could not find a publisher. It was subsequently broken up and published anonymously in its sole existent form in *Fraser's*. Despite this complex history, which involves the plan of an independent novel, Parker finds strong lines of similarity between *Sartor* and the serialised format in terms of its critiques of laissez-faire economics and of the Reform Bill in the later chapters, ideologies shared by *Fraser's*, as well as the portioning of the argument into discrete episodes suitable for serialisation (ibid. 168).
6. In their introduction to the Oxford University Press edition of Sartor *Resartus*, Kerry McSweeney and Peter Sabor note Carlyle's close affinity to the eighteenth-century novel and to Swift, Fielding and Sterne (Carlyle 2008: x).
7. J. Hillis Miller reads this passage as an invitation to the reader 'to read the whole as a hieroglyphical rather than as literal truth' (Miller 1989: 4).
8. The distancing of authority created by this self-criticism has led Janice Haney to foreground Carlyle's focus on irony, indebted to Schlegel, whereby process is apotheosised and absolute truths forestalled (Haney 1978: 314).

Ralph Jessop similarly argues that Carlyle's metafictional palimpsestic style fosters an anti-mechanical method of reading that opposes Scottish Enlightenment determinism and forces the reader to formulate independent positions (Jessop 1997: 157).

Works Cited

Abbott, Andrew (2007), 'Against Narrative: A Preface to Lyrical Sociology', *Sociological Theory*, 25:1, 67–99.

Abrams, M. H. (1965), 'Structure and Style in the Greater Romantic Lyric', in *From Sensibility to Romanticism: Essays Presented to Frederick A. Pottle*, ed. Frederick W. Hilles and Harold Bloom, Oxford: Oxford University Press, pp. 527–61.

Abrams, M. H. [1953] (1971), *The Mirror and the Lamp: Romantic Theory and the Critical Tradition*, Oxford: Oxford University Press.

Abrams, M. H. [1971] (1973), *Natural Supernaturalism: Tradition and Revolution in Romantic Literature*, New York: Norton.

Adelman, Richard (2011), *Idleness, Contemplation and the Aesthetic, 1750–1830*, Cambridge: Cambridge University Press.

Affeldt, Steven G. (1999), 'The Force of Freedom: Rousseau on Forcing to Be Free', *Political-Theory*, 27:2, 299–333.

Affeldt, Steven G. (2000), 'Society as a Way of Life: Perfectibility, Self-Transformation, and the Origination of Society in Rousseau', *Monist*, 83:4, 552–606.

Ahnert, Thomas and Susan Manning (eds) (2011), *Character, Self and Sociability in the Scottish Enlightenment*, Houndmills: Palgrave Macmillan.

Allen, Richard C. (1996), 'Charles Lloyd, Coleridge, and *Edmund Oliver*', *Studies in Romanticism*, 35:3, 245–94.

Allsop, Thomas [1836] (1864), *Letters, Conversations, and Recollections of S. T. Coleridge*, London: Farrah.

Althusser, Louis [1972] (1982), 'Rousseau: *The Social Contract* (The Discrepancies)', in *Montesquieu, Rousseau, Marx: Politics and History*, trans. Ben Brewster, London: Verso, pp. 111–60.

Appiah, Kwame Anthony (2005), *The Ethics of Identity*, Princeton: Princeton University Press.

Aravamudan, Srinivas (2011), *Enlightenment Orientalism: Resisting the Rise of the Novel*, Chicago: University of Chicago Press.

Aristotle [c. 350 BC] (1995), *The Politics*, trans. Ernest Barker, ed. R. F. Stalley, Oxford: Oxford University Press.

Ashton, Rosemary [1980] (1994), *The German Idea: Four English Writers and the Reception of German Thought, 1800–1860*, 2nd edn, London: Libris.

Babbitt, Irving [1919] (1966), *Rousseau and Romanticism*, New York: Meridian Press.

Bakhtin, Mikhail [1975] (1981), *The Dialogical Imagination: Four Essays*, trans. Caryl Emerson and Michael Holquist, Austin: University of Texas Press.

Baldick, Chris (1990), *In Frankenstein's Shadow: Myth, Monstrosity, and Nineteenth-Century Writing*, Oxford: Oxford University Press.

Bannet, Eve Tavor (2005), '"Secret History": Or, Talebearing Inside and Outside the Secretorie', *The Huntington Library Quarterly*, 68, 375–96.

Barrell, John (2000), *Imagining the King's Death: Figurative Treason, Fantasies of Regicide 1793–1796*, Oxford: Oxford University Press.

Bates, David William (2012), *States of War: Enlightenment Origins of the Political*, New York: Columbia University Press.

Bender, John (1994), 'Impersonal Violence: The Penetrating Gaze and the Field of Narration in *Caleb Williams*', in *Critical Reconstructions: The Relationship of Fiction and Life*, ed. Roger B. Menkle and Robert M. Polhemus, Stanford: Stanford University Press, pp. 111–26.

Bernasconi, Robert (1997), 'Opening the Future: The Paradox of Promising in the Hobbesian Social Contract', *Philosophy Today* 4:1, 77–86.

Bewell, Alan (1989), *Wordsworth and the Enlightenment: Nature, Man and Society in the Experimental Poetry*, New Haven: Yale University Press.

Boltanski, Luc (1999), *Distant Suffering: Morality, Media and Politics*, trans. Graham Burchell, Cambridge: Cambridge University Press.

Boulton, James T. (1963), *The Language of Politics in the Age of Wilkes and Burke*, London: Routledge.

Boyson, Rowan (2012), *Wordsworth and the Enlightenment Idea of Pleasure*, Cambridge: Cambridge University Press.

Brewer, John (1986), *The Common People and Politics, 1750–1790s*, Cambridge: Chadwyck.

Brewer, William D. (2000), 'Male Rivalry and Friendship in the Novels of William Godwin', in *Mapping Male Sexuality: Nineteenth-Century England*, ed. William D. Brewer and Jay Losey, Madison, NJ: Fairleigh Dickson University Press, pp. 49–68.

Bromwich, David (1998), *Disowned by Memory: Wordsworth's Poetry of the 1790s*, Chicago: University of Chicago Press.

Brown, Huntington (1945), 'The Gloss to *The Rime of the Ancient Mariner*', *Modern Language Quarterly*, 6, 319–24.

Brown, Marshall (1991), *Preromanticism*, Stanford: Stanford University Press.

Brown, Marshall (2004), 'Negative Poetics: On Skepticism and the Lyric Voice', *Representations*, 86:1, 120–40.

Budge, Gavin (ed.) (2007), *Romantic Empiricism: Poetics and the Philosophy of Common Sense 1780–1830*, Lewisburg: Bucknell University Press.

Budick, Sanford (2010), *Kant and Milton*, Cambridge, MA: Harvard University Press.

Bugg, John (2013), *Five Long Winters: The Trials of British Romanticism*, Stanford: Stanford University Press, <http://site.ebrary.com.proxy3.library.mcgill.ca/lib> (last accessed 1 July 2015).

Burke, Edmund [1756] (1982), *A Vindication of Natural Society Or, A View of the Miseries and Evils Arising to Mankind from Every Species of Artificial Society*, ed. Frank N. Pagano, Indianapolis: Liberty.

Burke, Edmund [1790] (1987), *Reflections on the Revolution in France*, ed. J. G. A Pocock, Indianapolis: Hackett.

Burt, Ellen (2005), 'Jean-Jacques Rousseau', in *Johns Hopkins Guide to Literary*

Theory and Criticism, 2nd edn, ed. Michael Groden, Martin Kreisworth, and Imre Szeman, Baltimore: Johns Hopkins University Press, pp. 809–12.

Bushell, Sally (2003), 'Reading below the Surface: Wordsworth and a Compositional Method', *The Wordsworth Circle*, 34:1, 9–13.

Butler, Judith [1990] (1999), *Gender Trouble: Feminism and the Subversion of Identity*, New York: Routledge.

Butler, Marilyn (1981), *Romantic Rebels and Reactionaries: English Literature and Its Backgrounds, 1760–1830*, Oxford: Oxford University Press.

Caldwell, Janis McLarren (1999), 'Sympathy and Science in *Frankenstein*', in *The Ethics in Literature*, ed. Andrew Hadfield, Dominic Rainsford and Tim Woods, Basingstoke: Macmillan, pp. 262–73.

Campbell, T. D. (1971), *Adam Smith's Science of Morals*, London: George Allen.

Canning, George and George Ellis [1798] (1799), 'New Morality', in *The Beauties of the Anti-Jacobin; or, Weekly Examiner*, London: 293–311

Carlson, Julie A. (2007), *England's First Family of Writers: Mary Wollstonecraft, William Godwin, Mary Shelley*, Baltimore: Johns Hopkins University Press.

Carlson, Julie A. (2011), 'On Literary Fractures', *Wordsworth Circle*, 42:2, 129–38.

Carlyle, Thomas [1837] (1934), *The French Revolution: A History*, New York: Modern Library.

Carlyle, Thomas [1831] (1984a), 'Characteristics', in *A Carlyle Reader*, ed. G. B. Tennyson, Cambridge: Cambridge University Press, pp. 67–103.

Carlyle, Thomas [1829] (1984b), 'Sign of the Times', in *A Carlyle Reader*, ed. G. B. Tennyson, Cambridge: Cambridge University Press, pp. 31–54.

Carlyle, Thomas [1833–4] (2000), *Sartor Resartus: The Life and Opinions of Herr Teufelsdröckh in Three Books*, ed. Mark Engel and Rodger L. Tarr, Berkeley: University of California Press.

Carlyle, Thomas [1840] (2001), *On Heroes, Hero Worship, and the Heroic in History*, London: Electric Book, <http://site.ebrary.com/id/2001657> (last accessed 6 February 2015).

Carlyle, Thomas [1833–4] (2008), *Sartor Resartus*, ed. Kerry McSweeney and Peter Sabor, Oxford: Oxford University Press.

Carroll, Siobhan (2015), *An Empire of Air and Water: Uncolonizable Space in the British Imagination, 1750–1850*, Philadelphia: University of Pennsylvania Press.

Caruth, Cathy (1991), *Empirical Truths and Critical Fictions: Locke, Wordsworth, Kant, Freud*, Baltimore: Johns Hopkins University Press.

Cavell, Stanley (1988), *In Quest of the Ordinary: Lines of Skepticism and Romanticism*, Chicago: University of Chicago Press.

Chandler, James K. (1984), *Wordsworth's Second Nature: A Study of the Poetry and Politics*, Chicago: University of Chicago Press.

Chandler, James K. (1998), *England in 1819: The Politics of Literary Culture and the Case of Romantic Historicism*, Chicago: University of Chicago Press.

Chandler, James K. (2013), *An Archaeology of Sympathy: The Sentimental Mode in Literature and Cinema*, Chicago: University of Chicago Press.

Chattarjee, Ranita (2007), 'Filial Ties: Godwin's *Deloraine* and Mary Shelley's Writings', *European Romantic Review*, 18:1, 29–41.

Clark, Anna E. (2014), '*Frankenstein*; or, the Modern Protagonist', *English Literary History*, 81:1, 245–68.

Class, Monika (2012), *Coleridge and Kantian Ideas in England, 1796–1817*, London: Bloomsbury.

Clemit, Pamela (2005), 'Self-Analysis as Social Critique: The Autobiographical Writings of Godwin and Rousseau', *Romanticism*, 11:2, 161–80.

Clery, E. J. [1995] (1999), *The Rise of Supernatural Fiction, 1762–1800*, Cambridge: Cambridge University Press.

Cohen, Margaret (2010), *The Novel and the Sea*, Princeton: Princeton University Press.

Coleridge, Samuel Taylor (1968), *Coleridge on the Seventeenth Century*, ed. Roberta Florence Brinkley, New York: Greenwood.

Coleridge, Samuel Taylor [1809–10] (1969a), *The Friend*, ed. Barbara E. Rooke, vol. 4. I of *The Collected Works of Samuel Taylor Coleridge*, Princeton: Princeton University Press.

Coleridge, Samuel Taylor [1795] (1969b), *Lectures 1795 on Politics and Religion*, ed. Lewis Patton and Peter Mann, vol. 1 of *The Collected Works of Samuel Taylor Coleridge*, Princeton: Princeton University Press.

Coleridge, Samuel Taylor [1816] (1972), *The Statesman's Manual*, in *Lay Sermons*, ed. R. J. White, vol. 6 of *The Collected Works of Samuel Taylor Coleridge*, Princeton: Princeton University Press, pp. 1–114.

Coleridge, Samuel Taylor [1829] (1976), *On the Constitution of the Church and State*, ed. John Colmer, vol. 16 of *The Collected Works of Samuel Taylor Coleridge*, Princeton: Princeton University Press.

Coleridge, Samuel Taylor [1818] (1983), *Biographia Literaria: Or, Biographical Sketches of My Literary Life and Opinions*, ed. James Engell and W. Jackson Bate, 2 vols, vol. 7 of *The Collected Works of Samuel Taylor Coleridge*, Princeton: Princeton University Press.

Coleridge, Samuel Taylor [1835] (1990), *Table Talk*, ed. Carl Woodring, vols 14.1–2 of *The Collected Works of Samuel Taylor Coleridge*, Princeton: Princeton University Press.

Coleridge, Samuel Taylor [1825] (1993), *Aids to Reflection*, ed. John Beer, vol. 9 of *The Collected Writings of Samuel Taylor Coleridge*, Princeton: Princeton University Press.

Coleridge, Samuel Taylor [1789–99] (2001), *Poetical Works, Poems (Reading Text): Part 1*, ed. J. C. C. Mays, vol. 16. I. I of *The Collected Works of Samuel Taylor Coleridge*, Princeton: Princeton University Press.

Coleridge, Samuel Taylor [1956–71] (2002), *The Collected Letters of Samuel Taylor Coleridge*, ed. Earl Lesley Griggs, 6 vols, Charlottesville: Past Masters, <http://library.nlx.com.proxy1.library.mcgill.ca/xtf/view?docId=coleridge_c/coleridge_c.00.xml;chunk.id=div.coleridge.pmpreface.1;toc.depth=2;toc.id=div.coleridge.pmpreface.1;hit.rank=0;brand=default> (last accessed 12 February 2015).

Coleridge, Samuel Taylor (2004), *Coleridge's Poetry and Prose: Authoritative Texts and Criticism*, ed. Nicholas Halmi, Paul Magnuson and Raimonda Modiano, New York: Norton.

Connell, Philip (2001), *Romanticism, Economics and the Question of 'Culture'*, Oxford: Oxford University Press.

Cope, Kevin L. (1989), 'Defoe, Berkeley, and Mackenzie and the Social Contract of Genre', *Studies on Voltaire and the Eighteenth Century*, 264, 937–40.

Corber, Robert J. (1990), '"Representing the Unspeakable": William Godwin and the Politics of Homophobia', *Journal of the History of Sexuality*, 1, 85–101.

Courtemanche, Eleanor (2011), *The 'Invisible Hand' and British Fiction 1818–1860: Adam Smith, Political Economy and the Genre of Realism*, Houndmills: Palgrave MacMillan.
Craig, Cairns (2004), 'Coleridge, Hume, and the Chains of the Romantic Imagination', in *Scotland and the Borders of Romanticism*, ed. Leith Davis, Ian Duncan and Janet Sorensen, Cambridge: Cambridge University Press, pp. 20–37.
Crook, Nora (2000), 'In Defence of the 1831 *Frankenstein*', in *Mary Shelley's Fictions: From Frankenstein to Falkner*, ed. Michael Eberle-Sinatra, New York: St. Martin's Press, pp. 3–21.
Damrosch, Leo (2005), *Jean Jacques Rousseau, Restless Genius*, New York: Houghton Mifflin.
Dart, Gregory (1999), *Rousseau, Robespierre and English Romanticism*, Cambridge: Cambridge University Press.
Davis, Leith, Ian Duncan and Janet Sorensen (eds) (2004), *Scotland and the Borders of Romanticism*, Cambridge: Cambridge University Press.
De Man, Paul (1979), *Allegories of Reading: Figural Language in Rousseau, Nietzsche, Rilke, and Proust*, New Haven: Yale University Press.
De Man, Paul [1971] (1983), *Blindness and Insight: Essays in the Rhetoric of Contemporary Criticism*, 2nd edn, Minneapolis: University of Minnesota Press.
De Man, Paul (1984), 'Shelley Disfigured', in *The Rhetoric of Romanticism*, New York: Columbia University Press, pp. 93–123.
De Volney, Constantin François Chasseboeuf [1802] (1828), *Volney's Ruins; or, Meditation on the Revolutions of Empires*, trans. Joel Barlow, New York, <http://www.gutenberg.org/files/1397/1397-h/1397-h.htm> (last accessed 12 February 2015).
Derrida, Jacques (1974), *Of Grammatology*, trans. Gayatri Chakravorty Spivak, Baltimore: Johns Hopkins University Press.
Derrida, Jacques (1982), *Margins of Philosophy*, trans. Allan Bass, Chicago: University of Chicago Press.
Dick, Alexander (2013), *Romanticism and the Gold Standard: Money, Literature and Economic Debate in Britain 1790–1830*, Houndmills: Palgrave.
Di Giovanni, George (2005), *Freedom and Religion in Kant and His Immediate Successors: The Vocation of Humankind, 1774–1800*, Cambridge: Cambridge University Press.
Disch, Lisa (1994), 'Claire Loves Julie: Reading the Story of Women's Friendship in *La Nouvelle Héloïse*', *Hypatia*, 9:3, 19–45.
Donald, Diana (1996), *The Age of Caricature: Satirical Prints in the Reign of George III*, New Haven: Yale University Press.
Dubrow, Heather (2008), *The Challenges of Orpheus: Lyric Poetry and Early Modern England*, Baltimore: Johns Hopkins University Press.
Duffy, Edward (1979), *Rousseau in England: The Context for Shelley's Critique of the Enlightenment*, Berkeley: University of California Press.
Duncan, Ian (2007), *Scott's Shadow: The Novel in Romantic Edinburgh*, Princeton: Princeton University Press.
Eldridge, Richard (2001), *The Persistence of Romanticism: Essays in Philosophy and Literature*, Cambridge: Cambridge University Press.
Eliot, T. S. [1919] (2000), 'Tradition and the Individual Talent', in *The Norton Anthology of English Literature*, vol. 2, ed. M. H. Abrams, New York: Norton, pp. 2395–401.

Ellison, Julie (1989), 'Rousseau in the Text of Coleridge: The Ghost-Dance of History', *Studies in Romanticism*, 28:3, 417–36.

Engell, James (1981), *The Creative Imagination: Enlightenment to Romanticism*, Cambridge, MA: Harvard University Press.

Esterhammer, Angela (2000), *The Romantic Performative: Language and Action in British and German Romanticism*, Stanford: Stanford University Press.

Evans, Frank B. III (1940), 'Shelley, Godwin, Hume, and the Doctrine of Necessity', *Studies in Philology*, 37:4, 632–40.

Felman, Shoshana [1983] (2003), *The Scandal of the Speaking Body: Don Juan with J. L. Austin, or Seduction in Two Languages*, trans. Catherine Porter, Stanford: Stanford University Press.

Ferguson, Adam [1792] (1978), *Principles of Moral and Political Science*, ed. René Wellek, 2 vols, New York: Garland Press.

Ferguson, Adam [1768] (1995), *An Essay on the History of Civil Society*, ed. Fania Oz-Salzburger, Cambridge: Cambridge University Press.

Fielding, Henry [1742] (1987), *Joseph Andrews*, in *Joseph Andrews with Shamela and Related Writings*, ed. Homer Goldberg, New York: Norton, pp. 1–269.

Fielding Henry [1749] (1995), *Tom Jones*, ed. Sheridan Baker, New York: Norton.

Fielding, Penny (2009), '"No Such Thing as Action": Godwin, the Decision and the Secret', *Novel*, 42:3, 380–6.

Flitter, Derek (1992), *Spanish Romantic Literary Theory and Criticism*, Cambridge: Cambridge University Press.

Foucault, Michel [1984] (1991), *The Foucault Reader: An Introduction to Foucault's Thought*, ed. Paul Rabinow, London: Penguin.

Foucault, Michel [1966] (2002), *The Order of Things: An Archeology of the Human Sciences*, trans. Alan Sheridan, London: Routledge.

Franta, Andrew (2007), *Romanticism and the Rise of the Mass Public*, Cambridge: Cambridge University Press.

Freud, Sigmund [1930] (2010), *Civilization and Its Discontents*, trans. James Strachey, New York: Norton.

Friedman, Albert B. (1961), *The Ballad Revival: Studies in the Influence of Popular on Sophisticated Poetry*, Chicago: University of Chicago Press.

Gallagher, Catherine (2006), *The Body Economic: Life, Death, and Sensation in Political Economy and the Victorian Novel*, Princeton: Princeton University Press.

Gallagher, Catherine (2010), 'A Factual History of Counterfactual History: From Leibniz to Clausewitz', unpublished article.

Gauthier, David (1977), 'The Social Contract as Ideology', *Philosophy and Public Affairs*, 6:2, 130–64.

Gill, Stephen (1989), *William Wordsworth: A Life*, Oxford: Clarendon.

Gilmartin, Kevin (2007), *Writing against Revolution: Literary Conservatism in Britain, 1790–1832*, Cambridge: Cambridge University Press.

Göçmen, Doğan (2007), *Adam Smith Problem: Reconciling Human Nature and Society in the 'Theory of Moral Sentiments' and 'Wealth of Nations'*, London: Tauris.

Godwin, William (1797), *The Enquirer: Reflections on Education, Manners, and Literature, in a Series of Essays*, Philadelphia: Campbell.

Godwin, William [1833] (1992a), *Deloraine*, ed. Maurice Hindle, vol. 8 of *The*

Collected Novels and Memoirs of William Godwin, London: Pickering and Chatto.

Godwin, William [1817] (1992b), *Mandeville, A Tale of Seventeenth Century England*, ed. Pamela Clemit, vol. 6 of *The Collected Novels and Memoirs of William Godwin*, London: Pickering and Chatto.

Godwin, William [1793] (1993a), *An Enquiry Concerning Political Justice*, ed. Mark Philp, vol. 3 of *Political and Philosophical Writings of William Godwin*, London: Pickering and Chatto.

Godwin, William [1798] (1993b), *An Enquiry Concerning Political Justice Variants*, ed. Mark Philp, vol. 4 of *Political and Philosophical Writings of William Godwin*, London: Pickering and Chatto.

Godwin, William [1794] (2000), *Things as They Are; or, The Adventures of Caleb Williams*, ed. Gary Handwerk and A. A. Markley, Peterborough: Broadview.

Godwin, William [1805] (2001a), *Fleetwood: Or, the New Man of Feeling*, ed. Gary Handwerk and A. A. Markley, Peterborough: Broadview.

Godwin, William [1798] (2001b), *Memoirs of the Author of A Vindication of the Rights of Woman*, ed. Pamela Clemit and Gina Luria Walker, Peterborough: Broadview.

Godwin, William [1799] (2006), *St. Leon: A Tale of the Sixteenth Century*, ed. William Brewer, Peterborough: Broadview.

Godwin, William [1798] (2007a), 'Analysis of Own Character', in *Collected Novels and Memoirs of William Godwin*, ed. Mark Philp, vol 1, London: Pickering and Chatto, pp. 55–60.

Godwin, William (2007b), 'Autobiography', in *Collected Novels and Memoirs of William Godwin*, ed. Mark Philp, vol. 1, London: Pickering and Chatto, pp. 1–54.

Gold, Alex Jr. (1977), 'It's Only Love: The Politics of Passion in Godwin's *Caleb Williams*', *Texas Studies in Language and Literature*, 19, 135–60.

Greiner, Rae (2011), *Sympathetic Realism in Nineteenth-Century British Fiction*, Baltimore: Johns Hopkins University Press.

Grenby, M. O. (2001), *The Anti Jacobin Novel. British Conservatism and the French Revolution*, Cambridge: Cambridge University Press.

Griswold, Charles L. (2010), 'Smith and Rousseau in Dialogue: Sympathy, Pitié, Spectatorship and Narrative', in *The Philosophy of Adam Smith: Essays Commemorating the 250th Anniversary of The Theory of Moral Sentiments*, ed. Vivienne Brown and Samuel Fleischacker, London: Routledge, pp. 59–84.

Habermas, Jürgen [1962] (2002), *The Structural Transformation of the Public Sphere: An Inquiry into a Category of Bourgeois Society*, trans. Thomas Burger, Cambridge, MA: MIT University Press.

Hamilton, Elizabeth [1800] (2000), *Memoirs of Modern Philosophers*, ed. Claire Grogan, Peterborough: Broadview Press.

Hamilton, Paul (1990), 'Coleridge and Godwin in the 1790s', in *The Coleridge Connection: Essays for Thomas McFarland*, ed. Richard Gravil and Molly Lefebure, Basingstoke: Macmillan, pp. 41–59.

Haney, Janice L. (1978), '"Shadow-Hunting": Romantic Irony, *Sartor Resartus*, and Victorian Romanticism', *Studies in Romanticism*, 17:3, 307–33.

Harrison, Peter (2011), 'Adam Smith and the History of the Invisible Hand', *Journal of the History of Ideas*, 27:1, 29–49.

Hazlitt, William (1830), *The Life of Napoleon Buonaparte*, 4 vols, London: Effingham Wilson.

Hegel, G. W. F. [1807] (1977), *Phenomenology of Spirit*, trans. A. V. Miller, Oxford: Oxford University Press.

Hénaff, Marcel (1992), 'Cannibalistic City', *SubStance*, 67:1, 3–23.

Hewitt, Regina (1990), *Wordsworth and the Empirical Dilemma*, New York: Peter Lang.

Hewitt, Regina (1997), *The Possibilities of Society: Wordsworth, Coleridge, and the Sociological Viewpoint of English Romanticism*, Albany, NY: State University of New York Press.

Heydt-Stevenson, Jillian and Charlotte Sussman (eds) (2008), *Recognizing the Romantic Novel: New Histories of British Fiction, 1780–1830*, Liverpool: Liverpool University Press.

Hill, Christopher [1965] (1997), *The Intellectual Origins of the English Revolution, Revised*, Oxford: Clarendon Press.

Hinnant, Charles H. (1980), *Thomas Hobbes: A Reference Guide*, Boston: G. K. Hall.

Hirschman, Albert O. (1997), *Passions and the Interests: Political Arguments for Capitalism before its Triumph*, Princeton: Princeton University Press.

Hobbes, Thomas [1641] (1998), *On the Citizen*, ed. and trans. Richard Tuck and Michael Silverthorne, Cambridge: Cambridge University Press.

Hobbes, Thomas [1651] (2003), *Leviathan*, ed. C. A. J. Rogers and Karl Schuhmann, vol. 2, Bristol: Thoemmes.

Howell, Peter (2004), 'Godwin, Contractarianism, and the Political Dead End of Empiricism', *Eighteenth-Century Life*, 28:2, 61–86.

Hume, David [1752] (1800), *Essays and Treatises on Several Topics*, 2 vols, Edinburgh: George Cow.

Hume, David [1748] (1958), 'Of the Original Contract', in *Social Contract Essays by Locke, Hume and Rousseau*, ed. Earnest Barker, London: Oxford University Press, pp. 209–36.

Hume, David [1739] (1978), *A Treatise of Human Nature*, ed. P. H. Nidditch, Oxford: Clarendon Press.

Hume, David [1748] (2000), *Enquiry Concerning Human Understanding*, in *The Complete Works and Correspondence of David Hume*, Charlottesville, VA: InteLex Corp, <http://library.nlx.com.proxy3.library.mcgill.ca/xtf/view?docId=hume/hume.05.xml;chunk.id=div.britphil.v37.5;toc.depth=1;toc.id=div.britphil.v37.5;brand=default> (last accessed 5 August 2015).

Hutcheson, Francis [1725] (1971), *An Inquiry into the Original of our Ideas of Beauty and Virtue*, vol. 1 of *The Collected Works of Francis Hutcheson*, Hildesheim: Georg Olms Verlagsbuchhandlung.

Jacob, Margaret C. (2002), 'Sociability and the International Republican Conversation', in *Romantic Sociability: Social Networks and Literary Culture in Britain 1770–1840*, ed. Gillian Russell and Clara Tuite, Cambridge: Cambridge University Press, pp. 24–42.

Jacobus, Mary (1995), *First Things: The Maternal Imaginary in Literature, Art, and Psychoanalysis*, New York: Routledge, pp. 63–82.

Jarrells, Anthony (2009), 'Provincializing Enlightenment: "Edinburgh" Historicism and the Blackwoodian Regional Tale', *Studies in Romanticism*, 48:2, 257–77.

Jauss, Hans Robert (1970), 'Literary History as a Challenge to Literary Theory', *New Literary History*, 2:1, 7–37.

Jeffrey, Francis (October 1802), '"Thalaba the Destroyer": Robert Southey', *The Edinburgh Review*, 1: 1, 63–83.

Jeffrey, Francis [1814] (1860), 'Wordsworth's Excursion', *Contributions to The Edinburgh Review*, New York: D. Appleton, pp. 457–69, <http://catalog.hathitrust.org/Record/001910267> (last accessed 12 February 2015).

Jenson, Deborah (2001), *Trauma and Its Representations: The Social Life of Mimesis in Post-Revolutionary France*, Baltimore and London: Johns Hopkins University Press.

Jessop, Ralph (1997), *Carlyle and Scottish Thought*, Houndmills: Palgrave Macmillan.

Johnson, Barbara (1998), 'Anthropomorphism in Lyric and the Law', *Yale Journal of Law in the Humanities*, 10, 549–74.

Johnson, Barbara (2014), *A Life with Mary Shelley*, ed. Cathy Caruth and Mary Wilson Carpenter, Stanford: Stanford University Press.

Johnston, Kenneth R. (1984), *Wordsworth and The Recluse*, New Haven: Yale University Press.

Jones, Ewan James (2014), *Coleridge and the Philosophy of Poetic Form*, Cambridge: Cambridge University Press.

Joseph, Gerhard (1993), 'Virginal Sex, Vaginal Text: The "Folds" of *Frankenstein*', in *Virginal Sexuality and Textuality in Victorian Literature*, ed. Lloyd Davis, Albany, NY: State University of New York Press, pp. 25–32.

Kahn, Victoria (2004), *Wayward Contracts: The Crisis of Political Obligation in England, 1640–1671*, Princeton: Princeton University Press.

Kant, Immanuel [1785] (1997), *Groundwork of the Metaphysics of Morals*, trans. Mary Gregor, Cambridge: Cambridge University Press.

Kant, Immanuel [1790] (2000), *The Critique of Judgment*, trans. J. H. Bernard, New York: Prometheus Press.

Kant, Immanuel [1784] (2009), *Idea for a Universal History with a Cosmopolitan Aim: A Critical Guide*, trans. Allan Wood, ed. Amélie Oksenberg Rorty and James Schmidt, Cambridge: Cambridge University Press.

Kantorowicz, Ernest H. (1957), *The King's Two Bodies: A Study in Medieval Political Theory*, Princeton: Princeton University Press.

Kareem, Sarah Tindal (2014), *Eighteenth-Century Fiction and the Reinvention of Wonder*, Oxford: Oxford University Press.

Keats, John [1818] (2009), 'Letter to Richard Woodhouse, October 27, 1818', in *Keats's Poetry and Prose*, ed. Jeffrey N. Cox, New York: Norton, pp. 294–5.

Kelley, Paul (1976) 'Rousseau's "Discourse on the Origins of Inequality" and Wordsworth's "Salisbury Plain"', *Notes and Queries*, 222, 329.

Kelly, Christopher (1987), *Rousseau's Exemplary Life: The Confessions as Political Philosophy*, Ithaca: Cornell University Press.

Kelly, Gary (1976), *The English Jacobin Novel 1780–1805*, Oxford: Clarendon.

Kelly, Gary (1982), '"The Romance of Real Life": Autobiography in Rousseau and William Godwin', *Man and Nature: Proceedings of the Canadian Society for Eighteenth-Century Studies*, 1, 93–101.

Kelly, Gary (2000), 'Politicizing the Personal: Mary Wollstonecraft, Mary Shelley, and the Coterie Novel', in *Mary Shelley in her Times*, ed. Betty T. Bennett and Stuart Curran, Baltimore: Johns Hopkins University Press, pp. 147–59.

Khalip, Jacques (2009), *Anonymous Life: Romanticism and Dispossession*, Stanford: Stanford University Press.

Kipperman, Mark (1986), *Beyond Enchantment: German Idealism and English Romantic Poetry*, Philadelphia: University of Pennsylvania Press.

Knights, C. L. [1933] (1946), 'How Many Children Had Lady Macbeth?', in *Explorations: Essays on Criticism Mainly on the Literature of the Seventeenth Century*, New York: George W. Stuart, pp. 15–54.

Kucich, Greg (2000), 'Mary Shelley's Lives and the Reengendering of History', in *Mary Shelley in her Times*, ed. Betty T. Bennett and Stuart Curran, Baltimore: Johns Hopkins University Press, pp. 198–213.

Lamb, Robert (2006), 'The Foundations of Godwinian Impartiality', *Utilitas*, 18, 134–56.

Lamb, Robert (2009), 'Was William Godwin a Utilitarian?' *Journal of the History of Ideas*, 70:1, 119–41.

Lanser, Susan S. (2005), 'The Novel Body Politic', in *A Companion to the Eighteenth-Century Novel*, ed. Paula Backscheider and Catherine Ingrassia, Liphook: Blackwell, pp. 481–503.

Lau, Beth (2009), 'Romantic Ambivalence in *Frankenstein* and *The Rime of the Ancient Mariner*', in *Fellow Romantics: Male and Female Writers, 1790–1835*, Burlington, VT: Ashgate, pp. 71–98.

Le Coat, Nanette C. (1989), 'Ironies of Representation: The Legislator in Rousseau, Robespierre and Volney', *Neophilologus*, 73:3, 358–72.

Levinson, Marjorie (1986), *Wordsworth's Great Period Poems: Four Essays*, Cambridge: Cambridge University Press.

Levy, Michelle (2004), 'Discovery and the Domestic Affections in Coleridge and Shelley', *SEL: Studies in English Literature, 1500–1900*, 44:4, 693–713.

Liu, Alan (1989), *Wordsworth: The Sense of History*, Stanford: Stanford University Press.

Lloyd, Charles (1799), *A Letter to the Anti-Jacobin Reviewers*, Birmingham: James Belcher.

Lloyd, Charles [1798] (2005), *Edmund Oliver*, ed. Philip Cox, vol. 2 of *Anti-Jacobin Novels*, London: Pickering and Chatto.

Locke, John [1690] (1993a), *An Essay Concerning Human Understanding*, ed. John W. Yolton, London: Everyman.

Locke, John [1689] (1993b), *The Second Treatise of Government*, in *John Locke: Political Writings*, ed. David Wootton, London: Penguin, pp. 261–386.

London, April (2000), 'Novel and History in Anti-Jacobin Satire', *Yearbook of English Studies*, 30, 71–81.

Lynch, Deidre Shauna (1998), *The Economy of Character: Novels, Market Culture, and the Business of Inner Meaning*, Chicago: University of Chicago Press.

Macpherson, C. B. (1962), *The Political Theory of Possessive Individualism: Hobbes to Locke*, Oxford: Oxford University Press.

Macpherson, Sandra (2010), *Harm's Way: Tragic Responsibility and the Novel Form*, Baltimore: Johns Hopkins University Press.

Magnusen, Paul (2002), 'The "Conversation" Poems', in *The Cambridge Companion to Coleridge*, ed. Lucy Newlyn, Cambridge: Cambridge University Press, pp. 32–44.

Mandeville, Bernard [1723] (1997), *The Fable of the Bees: or, Private Vices, Public Benefits*, in *The Fable of the Bees and Other Writings*, ed. E. J. Hundert, Indianapolis: Hackett Press, pp. 19–194.

Markley, A. A. (2004), '"The Success of Gentleness": Homosocial Desire and the Homosocial Personality in the Novels of William Godwin', *Romanticism on the Net*, 36: 39 paragraphs <http://www.erudit.org/revue/ron/2005/v/n36–37/011139ar.html?vue=resume> (last accessed 14 March 2010).

Marshall, David (1988), *The Surprising Effects of Sympathy: Marivaux, Diderot, Rousseau and Mary Shelley*, Chicago: University of Chicago Press.

Masters, Roger D. (1968), *The Political Philosophy of Rousseau*, Princeton: Princeton University Press.

McCracken, David (1970), 'Godwin's *Caleb Williams*: A Fictional Rebuttal of Burke', *Studies in Burke and his Times*, 11, 1442–52.

McDonald, Christie (1973), 'The Extravagant Shepherd: A Study of the Pastoral Vision in Rousseau's *Nouvelle Heloïse*', ed. Theodore Besterman, *Studies on Voltaire and the Eighteenth Century*, 105, 1–184.

McFarland, Thomas (1995), *Romanticism and the Heritage of Rousseau*, Oxford: Clarendon Press.

McGann, Jerome (1981), 'The Meaning of the *Ancient Mariner*', *Critical Inquiry*, 8:1, 35–67.

McGann, Jerome (1983), *The Romantic Ideology: A Critical Investigation*, Chicago: University of Chicago Press.

McHale, Brian (2009), 'Beginning to Think about Narrative in Poetry', *Narrative*, 17:1, 11–27.

McKeon, Michael (2005), *The Secret History of Domesticity: Public, Private, and the Division of Knowledge*, Baltimore: Johns Hopkins University Press.

McLane, Maureen N. (2008), *Balladeering, Minstrelsy, and the Making of British Romantic Poetry*, Cambridge: Cambridge University Press.

Mee, Jon (2002), '"Reciprocal Expressions of Kindness": Robert Merry, Della Cruscanism and the Limits of Sociability', in *Romantic Sociability: Social Networks and Literary Culture in Britain 1770–1840*, ed. Gillian Russell and Clara Tuite, Cambridge: Cambridge University Press, pp. 104–22.

Mee, Jon (2011), *Conversable Worlds: Literature, Contention, and Community: 1762–1830*, Oxford: Oxford University Press.

Mellor, Anne K. (1988), 'Possessing Nature: The Female in *Frankenstein*', in *Romanticism and Feminism*, ed. Anne K. Mellor, Bloomington: Indiana University Press, pp. 221–32.

Mellor, Anne K. (1989), *Mary Shelley: Her Life, Her Fiction, Her Monsters*, New York: Routledge.

Melzer, Arthur M. (1990), *The Natural Goodness of Man: On the System of Rousseau's Thought*, Chicago: University of Chicago Press.

Miller, J. Hillis (1989), '"Hieroglyphical Truth" in *Sartor Resartus*: Carlyle and the Language of Parable', in *Victorian Perspectives: Six Essays*, ed. John Clubbe and Jerome Meckier, Houndmills: Macmillan, pp. 1–20.

Mitchell, Robert (2005), 'Adam Smith and Coleridge on the Love of Systems', *The Coleridge Bulletin*, 25, 54–60.

Mitchell, Robert (2007), *Sympathy and the State in the Romantic Era: Systems, State Finance and the Shadows of Futurity*, New York: Routledge.

Morgan, Monique (2006), '*Frankenstein's* Singular Events: Inductive Reasoning, Narrative Technique and Generic Classification', *Romanticism on the Net*, 44:4, 25 paragraphs <https://www.erudit.org/revue/ron/2006/v/n44/013998ar.html> (last accessed 16 February 2015).

Morgan, Monique (2009), *Narrative Means to Lyric Ends: Temporality in the Nineteenth-Century British Long Poem*, Columbus: Ohio State University Press.

Mulvey-Roberts, Marie (2000), 'The Corpse in the Corpus: *Frankenstein*,

Rewriting Wollstonecraft and the Abject', in *Mary Shelley's Fictions: From Frankenstein to Falkner*, ed. Michael Eberle-Sinatra, Basingstoke: Macmillan, pp. 197–210.

Musset-Pathay, Victor-Donatien (1821), *Histoire de la vie et des ouvrages de J.-J. Rousseau*, Paris: Pélicier.

Myers, Mitzi (1983), 'Godwin's Memoirs of Wollstonecraft: The Shaping of Self and Subject', *Studies in Romanticism*, 20:3, 299–316.

Nablow, Ralph A. (1989), 'Shelley's "Ozymandias" and Volney's *Les Ruines*', *Notes and Queries*, 36:1, 172–3.

Nancy, Jean-Luc (1991), *The Inoperative Community*, trans. Peter Connor, Lisa Garbus, Michael Holland and Simona Sawhney, ed. Peter Connor, Minneapolis: University of Minnesota Press.

Nazar, Hina (2012), *Enlightened Sentiments: Judgment and Autonomy in the Age of Sensibility*, New York: Fordham University Press.

Nercessian, Anahid (2012), 'Radical Love and the Political Romance: Shelley after the Jacobin Novel', *English Literary History*, 79:1, 111–34.

Nicholson, Eirwen E. C. (1999), 'English Political Prints ca. 1640 – ca. 1830: The Potential for Emblematic Research and the Failure of Prints Scholarship', in *Deviceful Settings: The English Renaissance Emblem and Its Contexts*, ed. Michael Bath and Daniel Russell, New York: AMS Press, pp. 139–65.

Nietzsche, Friedrich [1886] (2002), *Beyond Good and Evil*, trans. Judith Norman, Cambridge: Cambridge University Press.

North, Julian (2009), *The Domestication of Genius: Biography and the Romantic Poet*, Oxford: Oxford University Press.

O'Neill, Daniel (2008), *The Burke-Wollstonecraft Debate: Savagery, Civilization, and Democracy*, University Park: Pennsylvania State University Press.

Onorato, Richard J. (1971), *The Character of the Poet: Wordsworth in The Prelude*, Princeton: Princeton University Press.

O'Rourke, James (1989), '"Nothing More Unnatural": Mary Shelley's Revision of Rousseau', *English Literary History*, 56:3, 543–69.

O'Rourke, James (1999), 'The 1831 Introductions and Revisions to *Frankenstein*: Mary Shelley Dictates her Legacy', *Studies in Romanticism*, 38:3, 365–85.

Paley, Morton D. (1999), *Apocalypse and Millennium in English Romantic Poetry*, Oxford: Oxford University Press.

Parker, Mark (2000), *Literary Magazines and British Romanticism*, Cambridge: Cambridge University Press.

Pateman, Carole (1988), *The Sexual Contract*, Stanford: Stanford University Press.

Paulson, Ronald (1983), *Representations of Revolution (1789–1820)*, New Haven: Yale University Press.

Perkins, David (1996), 'The "Ancient Mariner" and Its Interpreters: Some Versions of Coleridge', *Modern Language Quarterly*, 57:3, 425–48.

Perry, Seamus (2001), 'Coleridge and the End of Autonomy', in *Samuel Taylor Coleridge and the Secrets of Life*, ed. Nicholas Roe, Oxford: Oxford University Press, pp. 246–68.

Pettit, Philip (2008), *Made with Words: Hobbes on Language, Mind, and Politics*, Princeton: Princeton University Press.

Philp, Mark (1986), *Godwin's Political Justice*, Ithaca: Cornell University Press.

Poole, Margaret E. Sandford (1888), *Thomas Poole and his Friends*, vol. 1 of 2 vols, New York: Macmillan.

Poovey, Mary (1995), *Making a Social Body: British Cultural Formation, 1830–1864*, Chicago: University of Chicago Press.

Poovey, Mary (1998), *A History of the Modern Fact: Problems of Knowledge in the Sciences of Wealth and Society*, Chicago: University of Chicago Press.

Poovey, Mary (2008), *Genres of the Credit Economy: Mediating Value in the Enlightenment and in Eighteenth- and Nineteenth-Century Britain*, Chicago: University of Chicago Press.

Radcliffe, Evan (2000), 'Godwin from "Metaphysician" to Novelist: *Political Justice, Caleb Williams*, and the Tension between Philosophical Argument and Narrative', *Modern Philology*, 97:4, 528–53.

Rasmussen, Dennis C. (2013), 'Adam Smith and Rousseau: Enlightenment and Counter-Enlightenment', in *The Handbook of Adam Smith*, ed. Christopher J. Berry, Maria Pia Paganelli and Craig Smith, Oxford: Oxford University Press, pp. 54–76.

Reese, Diana (2006), 'A Troubled Legacy: Mary Shelley's *Frankenstein* and the Inheritance of Human Rights', *Representations*, 96, 48–72.

Reid, Ian (2004), *Wordsworth and the Formation of English Studies*, Aldershot: Ashgate.

Rheingold, Howard (1993), *The Virtual Community: Homesteading on the Electric Frontier*, Reading: William Patrick.

Richardson, Allan (1991), 'From *Emile* to *Frankenstein*: The Education of Monsters', *European Romantic Review* 1:2, 147–62.

Richardson, Samuel [1740] (2008), *Pamela; or, Virtue Rewarded*, ed. Thomas Keymer and Alice Wakely, Oxford: Oxford University Press.

Roe, Nicholas (1988), *Wordsworth and Coleridge: The Radical Years*, Oxford: Clarendon.

Roe, Nicholas (2002), *The Politics of Nature: William Wordsworth and Some Contemporaries*, Basingstoke: Palgrave.

Rousseau, Jean-Jacques [1761] (1970), *Julie ou la Nouvelle Héloïse*, présentation de Jean Starobinski, Lausanne: Éditions Rencontre.

Rousseau, Jean-Jacques [1776] (1990), *Rousseau, Judge of Jean-Jacques: Dialogues*, trans. Judith R. Bush, Christopher Kelly and Roger G. Masters, vol. 1 of *The Collected Writings of Rousseau*, Hanover: University Press of New England.

Rousseau, Jean-Jacques [1755] (1992a), *Discourse on the Origins of Inequality (Second Discourse)*, in *Discourse on the Origins of Inequality (Second Discourse), Polemics and Political Economy*, trans. Judith R. Bush, Roger D. Masters and Christopher Kelly, vol. 3 of *The Collected Writings of Rousseau*, Hanover: University Press of New England, pp. 1–95, 176–88.

Rousseau, Jean-Jacques [1755] (1992b), *Discourse on Political Economy*, in *Discourse on the Origins of Inequality (Second Discourse), Polemics and Political Economy*, trans. Judith R. Bush, Roger D. Masters and Christopher Kelly, vol. 3 of *The Collected Writings of Rousseau*, Hanover: University Press of New England, pp. 140–71.

Rousseau, Jean-Jacques [1861] (1992c) 'Preface to a Second Letter to Bordes', in *Discourse on the Sciences and Arts (First Discourse) and Polemics*, trans. Judith R. Bush, Roger D. Masters and Christopher Kelly, vol. 2 of *The Collected Writings of Rousseau*, Hanover: University Press of New England, pp. 182–5.

Rousseau, Jean-Jacques [1913] (1994a), 'Geneva Manuscript (First Version of *The Social Contract*)', in *Social Contract, Discourse on the Virtue Most Necessary for a Hero, Political Fragments and Geneva Manuscript*, trans. Judith R. Bush, Roger D. Masters and Christopher Kelly, vol. 4 of *The Collected Writings of Rousseau*, Hanover: University Press of New England, pp. 76–124.

Rousseau, Jean-Jacques [1915] (1994b), 'Political Fragments', in *Social Contract, Discourse on the Virtue Most Necessary for a Hero, Political Fragments and Geneva Manuscript*, trans. Judith R. Bush, Roger D. Masters and Christopher Kelly, vol. 4 of *The Collected Writings of Rousseau*, Hanover: University Press of New England, pp. 16–75.

Rousseau, Jean-Jacques [1762] (1994c), *The Social Contract*, in *Social Contract, Discourse on the Virtue Most Necessary for a Hero, Political Fragments and Geneva Manuscript*, trans. Judith R. Bush, Roger D. Masters and Christopher Kelly, vol. 4 of *The Collected Writings of Rousseau*, Hanover: University Press of New England, pp. 127–224.

Rousseau, Jean-Jacques (1994d), 'Introduction: Rousseau's *Social Contract*', in *Social Contract, Discourse on the Virtue Most Necessary for a Hero, Political Fragments and Geneva Manuscript*, trans. Judith R. Bush, Roger D. Masters and Christopher Kelly, vol. 4 of *The Collected Writings of Rousseau*, Hanover: University Press of New England.

Rousseau, Jean-Jacques [1770] (1995), *The Confessions*, in *The Confessions and Correspondence, Including the Letters to Malesherbes*, trans. Christopher Kelly, vol. 5 of *The Collected Writings of Rousseau*, Hanover: University Press of New England, pp. 1–550.

Rousseau, Jean-Jacques [1761] (1997), *Julie, or the New Heloise. Letters of Two Lovers who Live in a Small Town at the Foot of the Alps*, trans. Philip Stuart and Jean Vaché, vol. 6 of *The Collected Writings of Rousseau*, Hanover: University Press of New England.

Rousseau, Jean-Jacques [1782] (2000), *The Reveries of the Solitary Walker*, in *The Reveries of the Solitary Walker, Botanical Writings, and Letter to Franquières*, trans. Charles E. Butterworth, vol. 8 of *The Collected Writings of Rousseau*, Hanover: University Press of New England, pp. 1–90.

Rousseau, Jean-Jacques [1758] (2004), *Letter to d'Alembert*, in *Letter to d'Alembert and Writings for the Theater*, trans. Allan Bloom, vol. 10 of *The Collected Writings of Rousseau*, Hanover: University Press of New England, pp. 237–53.

Rousseau, Jean-Jacques [1762] (2010), *Emile, Or on Education: Includes Emile and Sophie, or the Solitaries*, trans. Christopher Kelly and Allan Bloom, vol. 13 of *The Collected Writings of Rousseau*, Hanover: University Press of New England.

Rowe, Katherine (1999), *Dead Hands: Fictions of Agency, Renaissance to Modern*, Stanford: Stanford University Press.

Rowland, Anna Wierda (2008), 'Romantic Poetry and the Romantic Novel', in *The Cambridge Companion to British Romantic Poetry*, ed. James K. Chandler and Maureen McLane, Cambridge: Cambridge University Press, pp. 117–33.

Rowlinson, Matthew (2010), *Real Money and Romanticism*, Cambridge: Cambridge University Press.

Rubinstein, Chris (2004), 'Coleridge and Jews', *The Coleridge Bulletin*, 24, 91–6.

Russell, Gillian and Clara Tuite (eds) (2002), *Romantic Sociability: Social*

Networks and Literary Culture in Britain, 1770–1840, Cambridge: Cambridge University Press.

Rzepka, Charles (1986), *The Self as Mind: Vision and Identity in Wordsworth, Coleridge, and Keats*, Cambridge, MA: Harvard University Press.

Sabin, Margery (1970), 'Imagination in Rousseau and Wordsworth', *Comparative Literature* 22, 328–45.

Sabin, Margery (1976), *English Romanticism and the French Tradition*, Cambridge, MA: Harvard University Press.

Saccamano, Neil (1992), 'Rhetoric, Consensus and the Law in Rousseau's *Contrat social*', *Modern Language Notes*, 107:4, 730–51.

St. Clair, William (1989), *The Godwins and the Shelleys: The Biography of a Family*, London: Faber.

Scheuermann, Mona (1983), 'The Study of the Mind: The Later Novels of William Godwin', *Forum for Modern Language Studies*, 19:1, 16–30.

Schiller, Friedrich [1795] (2001a) *Letters on the Aesthetic Education of Man*, in *Essays*, trans. Elizabeth M. Wilkinson and L. A. Willoughby, ed. Walter Hinderer and Daniel O. Dahlstrom, New York: Continuum, pp. 86–178.

Schiller, Friedrich [1800] (2001b) 'On Naive and Sentimental Poetry', in *Essays*, trans. Daniel O. Dahlstrom, ed. Walter Hinderer and Daniel O. Dahlstrom, New York: Continuum, pp. 179–260.

Schneewind, J. B. (1998), *The Invention of Autonomy: A History of Modern Moral Philosophy*, Cambridge: Cambridge University Press.

Schutjer, Karin (2001), *Narrating Community after Kant: Schiller, Goethe, and Hölderlin*, Detroit: Wayne State Press.

Sedgwick, Eve Kosofsky (1985), *Between Men: English Literature and Male Homosocial Desire*, New York: Columbia University Press.

Shaftesbury, Anthony Ashley Cooper [1709] (1900), 'November 7', in *The Life, Unpublished Letters, and Philosophical Regimen of Anthony, Earl of Shaftesbury*, ed. Benjamin Rand, London: Swan Sonnenschein, pp. 413–17.

Shakespeare, William [1603] (2003), *Hamlet*, ed. Burton Raffel and Harold Bloom, New Haven: Yale University Press.

Shanley, Mary Lyndon (1979), 'Marriage Contract and Social Contract in Seventeenth-Century English Political Thought', *The Western Political Quarterly*, 32:1, 79–91.

Shelley, Mary Wollstonecraft (1823), 'Madame D'Houtetot', in *The Liberal: Verse and Prose from the South*, ed. Leigh Hunt, vol. 2, London: John Hunt, pp. 67–83.

Shelley, Mary Wollstonecraft (1980), *The Letters of Mary Wollstonecraft Shelley*, ed. Betty T. Bennet, Baltimore: Johns Hopkins University Press.

Shelley Mary Wollstonecraft (1987), *The Journals of Mary Shelley, 1814–1844*, ed. Paula R. Feldman and Diana Scott-Kilvert, 2 vols, Oxford: Clarendon Press.

Shelley, Mary Wollstonecraft [1818] (1996a), *Frankenstein, Or, The Modern Prometheus*, ed. Nora Crook, vol. 1 of *The Novels and Selected Works of Mary Shelley*, London: Pickering and Chatto.

Shelley, Mary Wollstonecraft [1820] (1996b), *Matilda*, in *Matilda, Dramas, Reviews and Essays, Prefaces and Notes*, ed. Pamela Clemit, vol. 2 of *The Novels and Selected Works of Mary Shelley*, London: Pickering and Chatto, pp. 5–68.

Shelley, Mary [1831] (2000), *Frankenstein, Second Edition*, ed. Johanna M. Smith, Boston: Bedford Press.

Shelley, Mary Wollstonecraft [1839] (2002a), 'Rousseau', in *Mary Shelley's Literary Lives and Other Writings*, ed. Clarissa Campbell Orr, vol. 3 of *French Lives (Molière to Madame de Staël)*, London: Pickering and Chatto, pp. 320–66.

Shelley, Mary Wollstonecraft (2002b), 'Notes on *French Lives II*', in *Mary Shelley's Literary Lives and Other Writings*, ed. Clarissa Campbell Orr, vol. 3 *French Lives (Molière to Madame de Staël)*, London: Pickering and Chatto.

Shelley, Mary Wollstonecraft [1818] (2004), *Frankenstein; Or, the Modern Prometheus: The 1818 Version*, 2nd edn, ed. D. L. Macdonald and Kathleen Scherf, Peterborough: Broadview.

Shelley, Mary Wollstonecraft [1818] (2012), *The Annotated Frankenstein*, ed. Susan J. Wolfson and Ronaldo Levao, Cambridge, MA: Harvard University Press.

Shelley, Percy Bysshe (1964), *The Letters of Percy Bysshe Shelley*, ed. Frederick L. Jones, vol. 2 of 2 vols, Oxford: Clarendon.

Shelley, Percy Bysshe (2002), *Shelley's Poetry and Prose*, 2nd edn, ed. Donald H. Reiman and Neil Fraistat, New York: Norton.

Simpson, David (1993), *Romanticism, Nationalism, and the Revolt against Theory*, Chicago: University of Chicago Press.

Simpson, David (2009), *Wordsworth, Commodification and Social Concern: The Poetics of Modernity*, Cambridge: Cambridge University Press.

Smith, Adam [1755] (1980a), *History of Astronomy*, in *Essays on Philosophical Subjects with Dugald Stewart's Account of Adam Smith*, ed. W. P. D. Wightman and J. C. Bryce, vol. 3 of *The Glasgow Edition of the Works and Correspondences of Adam Smith*, Oxford: Clarendon, pp. 33–105.

Smith, Adam [1755] (1980b), 'Letter to the *Edinburgh Review*', in *Essays on Philosophical Subjects with Dugald Stewart's Account of Adam Smith*, ed. W. P. D. Wightman and J. C. Bryce, vol. 3 of *The Glasgow Edition of the Works and Correspondences of Adam Smith*, Oxford: Clarendon, pp. 242–59.

Smith, Adam [1776] (1993), *An Inquiry into the Nature and Causes of the Wealth of Nations*, ed. Kathryn Sutherland, Oxford: Oxford University Press.

Smith, Adam [1759–90] (2002), *The Theory of Moral Sentiments*, ed. Knud Haakonssen, Cambridge: Cambridge University Press.

Spivak, Gayatri Chakravorty (1985), 'Three Women's Texts and a Critique of Imperialism', *Critical Inquiry*, 12:1, 243–61.

Spivak, Gayatri Chakravorty [1988] (1995), 'Can the Subaltern Speak?', in *Colonial Discourse and Postcolonial Theory: A Reader*, ed. Patrick Williams and Laura Chrisman, New York: Columbia University Press, pp. 66–111.

Starobinski, Jean (1977), 'Eloquence and Liberty', *Journal of the History of Ideas*, 38:2, 195–210.

Starr, G. A. (1994), 'Sentimental Novels of the Later Eighteenth Century', in *The Columbia History of the British Novel*, ed. John Richetti et al., New York: Columbia University Press, pp. 181–98.

Stelzig, Eugene (2000), *The Romantic Subject in Autobiography: Rousseau and Goethe*, Charlottesville: University Press of Virginia.

Stelzig, Eugene (2010), *Henry Crabb Robinson in Germany: A Study in Nineteenth-Century Life Writing*, Lewisburg: Bucknell University Press.

Strong, Tracy B. [1994] (2002), *Jean-Jacques Rousseau: The Politics of the Ordinary*, Oxford: Rowman.

Swift, Jonathan [1726] (2005), *Gulliver's Travels*, ed. Ian Higgins and Claude Rawson, Oxford: Oxford University Press.

Taylor, Barbara (2003), *Mary Wollstonecraft and the Feminist Imagination*, Cambridge: Cambridge University Press.

Taylor, Charles (2004), *Modern Social Imaginaries*, Durham, NC: Duke University Press.

Terada, Rei (2009), *Looking Away: Phenomenology and Dissatisfaction, Kant to Adorno*, Cambridge, MA: Harvard University Press.

Timár, Andrea (2007), 'Re-Contextualizing "Kubla Khan" (c. 1798) and the "Preface" (1816): Hallucinatory Readings, Drugs, and Performatives in the Context of Coleridge's Essay on Luther and Rousseau (1812)', *Hungarian Journal of English and American Studies*, 13: 1–2, 165–80.

Todorov, Tzvetan (1975), *The Fantastic: A Structural Approach to Literary Genre*, Ithaca: Cornell University Press.

Toremans, Tom (2015), 'Killing what is Already Dead: "Original Materialism", Translation, and Romanticism after de Man (With a Coda on Coleridge and Carlyle)', in *Romantic Circles*, 17 paragraphs <http://www.rc.umd.edu/praxis/materialities/index.html> (last accessed 10 February 2015).

Tuite, Clara (1998), 'Frankenstein's Monster and Malthus's "Jaundiced Eye": Population, Body Politics and the Monstrous Sublime', *Eighteenth-Century Life*, 22:1, 141–55.

Turner, James Grantham (1994), 'Novel Panic: Picture and Performance in the Reception of Richardson's Pamela', *Representations*, 48, 70–96.

Valenza, Robin (2009), *Literature, Language, and the Rise of the Intellectual Disciplines in Britain, 1680–1820*, Cambridge: Cambridge University Press.

Virgil [29 BCE] (2002), *Georgics IV*, trans. Kristina Chew, Indianapolis: Hackett.

Voltaire [1759] (2005), *Candide, or Optimism*, trans. Burton Raffel, New Haven: Yale University Press.

Wall, Wendy (1987), 'Interpreting Poetic Shadows: The Gloss of "The Rime of the Ancient Mariner"', *Criticism*, 29:2, 179–95.

Wallace, Miriam (ed.) (2009a), *Enlightening Romanticism, Romancing the Enlightenment: British Novels from 1750 to 1832*, Farnham: Ashgate Press.

Wallace, Miriam (2009b), *Revolutionary Subjects in the English 'Jacobin' Novel, 1790–1805*, Cranbury, NJ: Bucknell University Press.

Warning, Rainer (1992), 'Philosophers as Story-Tellers. Difficulty of the Enlightenment with Morality', in *Telling Stories: Studies in Honour of Ulrich Broich on the Occasion of His 60th Birthday*, ed. Elmar Lehmann and Bernd Lenz, Amsterdam: Grüner, pp. 126–46.

Wells, H. G. (1939), *The Fate of Homo Sapiens: An Unemotional Statement of the Things that are Happening to Him Now, and of the Immediate Possibilities Confronting Him*, London: Secker.

Wells, H. G. [1933] (2005), *The Shape of Things to Come*, ed. Patrick Parrinder, London: Penguin.

Wolfson, Susan (1997), *Formal Charges: The Shaping of Poetry in British Romanticism*, Stanford: Stanford University Press.

Wolin, Sheldon S. (1970), *Hobbes and the Epic Tradition of Political Theory*, Los Angeles: University of California Press.

Wollstonecraft, Mary [1796] (1989), *Letters Written During a Short Residence in Sweden, Norway and Denmark*, ed. Janet Todd and Marilyn Butler, vol. 6 of *The Works of Mary Wollstonecraft*, London: Pickering and Chatto.

Wollstonecraft, Mary [1787] (1994), *Thoughts on the Education of Daughters*, Oxford: Woodstock.
Wollstonecraft, Mary [1798] (2007a), *The Wrongs of Woman, or Maria*, in *A Vindication of the Rights of Women and The Wrongs of Woman, or Maria*, ed. Anne K. Mellor and Noelle Chao, New York: Longman, pp. 245–357.
Wollstonecraft, Mary [1792] (2007b), *A Vindication of the Rights of Woman*, in *A Vindication of the Rights of Women and The Wrongs of Woman, or Maria*, ed. Anne K. Mellor and Noelle Chao, New York: Longman, pp. 15–232.
Womersley, David (1986), 'Hume and Mary Shelley', *Notes and Queries*, 33:2, 164–5.
Woodmansee, Martha and Mark Osteen (1999), *The New Economic Criticism: Studies at the Intersection of Literature and Economics*, London: Routledge.
Wordsworth, Jonathan (1992), 'Revision as Making: *The Prelude* and Its Peers,' in *Romantic Revisions*, ed. Rob Brinkley and Keith Hanley, Cambridge: Cambridge University Press, pp. 18–42.
Wordsworth, William [1808] (1915), *Tract on the Convention of Cintra*, London: Humphrey Milford.
Wordsworth, William [1815] (1974a), 'Essay, Supplementary to the Preface of *Lyrical Ballads* (1800)', in vol. 3 of *The Prose Works of William Wordsworth*, ed. W. J. B. Owen and Jane Worthington Smyser, Oxford: Clarendon, pp. 55–107.
Wordsworth, William [1876] (1974b) 'A Letter to the Bishop of Llandaff', in vol. 1 of *The Prose Works of William Wordsworth*, ed. W. J. B. Owen and Jane Worthington Smyser, Oxford: Clarendon, pp. 19–66.
Wordsworth, William [1850] (1985), *The Fourteen Book Prelude*, ed. W. J. B. Owen, vol. 1, Ithaca: Cornell University Press.
Wordsworth, William [1935] (1988), *The Letters of William and Dorothy Wordsworth: The Early Years, 1787–1805*, vol. 1, 2nd edn, ed. Ernest de Selincourt, Oxford: Clarendon.
Wordsworth, William [1926] (1991), *The Thirteen Book Prelude*, vol. 1, ed. Mark L. Reed, Ithaca: Cornell University Press.
Wordsworth, William [1939] (2000a), *The Letters of William and Dorothy Wordsworth: The Later Years, 1829–1834*, vol. 5, 2nd edn, ed. Ernest de Selincourt, Oxford: Clarendon.
Wordsworth, William [1802] (2000b), 'Preface to *Lyrical Ballads*, with Pastoral and Other Poems (1802)', in *William Wordsworth: The Major Works*, ed. Stephen Gill, Oxford: Oxford University Press, pp. 596–615.
Wordsworth, William [1814] (2007), *The Excursion*, ed. Sally Bushell, James A. Butler and Michael Jaye, with the assistance of David García, Ithaca: Cornell University Press.
Wordsworth, William and Samuel Taylor Coleridge [1798–1802] (2008), *Lyrical Ballads: 1798–1800*, ed. Michael Gamer and Daliah Porter, Peterborough: Broadview.
Wu, Duncan (1994), *Wordsworth's Reading 1770–1799*, Cambridge: Cambridge University Press.
Wyatt, John (1995), *Wordsworth and the Geologists*, Cambridge: Cambridge University Press.
Yousef, Nancy (2004), *Isolated Cases: The Anxiety of Autonomy in Enlightenment Philosophy and Romantic Literature*, Ithaca: Cornell University Press.

Yousef, Nancy (2013), *Romantic Intimacy*, Stanford: Stanford University Press, <http://site.ebrary.com.proxy2.library.mcgill.ca/lib/mcgill/reader.action?doc ID=10741747&ppg=1> (last accessed 18 December 2014).

Zarka, Yves Charles (2004), 'The Political Subject', in *Leviathan after 350 Years*, ed. Tom Sorell and Luc Foisneau, Oxford: Clarendon, pp. 167–82.

Zimmerman, Sarah (2000), *Reading, Writing and Romanticism: The Anxiety of Reception*, Oxford: Oxford University Press.

Index

EU Authorised Representative:

Easy Access System Europe Mustamäe tee 50, 10621 Tallinn, Estonia

gpsr.requests@easproject.com

Printed and bound by CPI Group (UK) Ltd, Croydon, CR0 4YY

03/06/2025

01891028-0001